Focus on GRAMMAR 2A

FOURTH EDITION

Irene E. Schoenberg

ALWAYS LEARNING

PEARSON

Focus on Grammar 2A: An Integrated Skills Approach, Fourth Edition

Pearson Education, 10 Bank Street, White Plains, NY 10606

Staff credits: The people who made up the *Focus on Grammar 2A, Fourth Edition*
team, representing editorial, production, design, and manufacturing, are Elizabeth Carlson,
Tracey Cataldo, Aerin Csigay, Dave Dickey, Christine Edmonds, Nancy Flagmann, Ann France,
Lise Minovitz, Barbara Perez, Robert Ruvo, Debbie Sistino, and Kim Steiner.

Cover image: Shutterstock.com
Text composition: ElectraGraphics, Inc.
Text font: New Aster

PEARSON LONGMAN ON THE **WEB**

Pearsonlongman.com offers online
resources for teachers and students. Access
our Companion Websites, our online catalog,
and our local offices around the world.

Visit us at **pearsonlongman.com**.

Printed in the United States of America

ISBN 10: 0-13-211444-5
ISBN 13: 978-0-13-211444-8

1 2 3 4 5 6 7 8 9 10—V082—16 15 14 13 12 11

ISBN 10: 0-13-211445-3 (with MyLab)
ISBN 13: 978-0-13-211445-5 (with MyLab)

1 2 3 4 5 6 7 8 9 10—V082—16 15 14 13 12 11

CONTENTS

WELCOME TO *FOCUS ON GRAMMAR*

Now in a new edition, the popular five-level *Focus on Grammar* course continues to provide an integrated-skills approach to help students understand and practice English grammar. Centered on thematic instruction, *Focus on Grammar* combines controlled and communicative practice with critical thinking skills and ongoing assessment. Students gain the confidence they need to speak and write English accurately and fluently.

NEW for the FOURTH EDITION

VOCABULARY

Key vocabulary is highlighted, practiced, and recycled throughout the unit.

PRONUNCIATION

Now, in every unit, pronunciation points and activities help students improve spoken accuracy and fluency.

LISTENING

Expanded listening tasks allow students to develop a range of listening skills.

UPDATED CHARTS and NOTES

Target structures are presented in a clear, easy-to-read format.

NEW READINGS

High-interest readings, updated or completely new, in a variety of genres integrate grammar and vocabulary in natural contexts.

NEW UNIT REVIEWS

Students can check their understanding and monitor their progress after completing each unit.

MyFocusOnGrammarLab

An easy-to-use online learning and assessment program offers online homework and individualized instruction anywhere, anytime.

Teacher's Resource Pack One compact resource includes:

THE TEACHER'S MANUAL: General Teaching Notes, Unit Teaching Notes, the Student Book Audioscript, and the Student Book Answer Key.

TEACHER'S RESOURCE DISC: Bound into the Resource Pack, this CD-ROM contains reproducible Placement, Part, and Unit Tests, as well as customizable Test-Generating Software. It also includes reproducible Internet Activities and PowerPoint® Grammar Presentations.

THE *FOCUS ON GRAMMAR* APPROACH

The new edition follows the same successful four-step approach of previous editions. The books provide an abundance of both controlled and communicative exercises so that students can bridge the gap between identifying grammatical structures and using them. The many communicative activities in each Student Book provide opportunities for critical thinking while enabling students to personalize what they have learned.

- **STEP 1: GRAMMAR IN CONTEXT** highlights the target structures in realistic contexts, such as conversations, magazine articles, and blog posts.

- **STEP 2: GRAMMAR PRESENTATION** presents the structures in clear and accessible grammar charts and notes with multiple examples of form and usage.

- **STEP 3: FOCUSED PRACTICE** provides numerous and varied controlled exercises for both the form and meaning of the new structures.

- **STEP 4: COMMUNICATION PRACTICE** includes listening and pronunciation and allows students to use the new structures freely and creatively in motivating, open-ended speaking and writing activities.

Recycling

Underpinning the scope and sequence of the *Focus on Grammar* series is the belief that students need to use target structures and vocabulary many times, in different contexts. New grammar and vocabulary are recycled throughout the book. Students have maximum exposure and become confident using the language in speech and in writing.

Assessment

Extensive testing informs instruction and allows teachers and students to measure progress.

- **Unit Reviews** at the end of every Student Book unit assess students' understanding of the grammar and allow students to monitor their own progress.

- Easy to administer and score, **Part and Unit Tests** provide teachers with a valid and reliable means to determine how well students know the material they are about to study and to assess students' mastery after they complete the material. These tests can be found on MyFocusOnGrammarLab, where they include immediate feedback and remediation, and as reproducible tests on the Teacher's Resource Disc.

- **Test-Generating Software** on the Teacher's Resource Disc includes a bank of *additional* test items teachers can use to create customized tests.

- A reproducible **Placement Test** on the Teacher's Resource Disc is designed to help teachers place students into one of the five levels of the *Focus on Grammar* course.

COMPONENTS

In addition to the Student Books, Teacher's Resource Packs, and MyLabs, the complete *Focus on Grammar* course includes:

Workbooks Contain additional contextualized exercises appropriate for self-study.

Audio Program Includes all of the listening and pronunciation exercises and opening passages from the Student Book. Some Student Books are packaged with the complete audio program (mp3 files). Alternatively, the audio program is available on a classroom set of CDs and on the MyLab.

THE *FOCUS ON GRAMMAR* UNIT

Focus on Grammar introduces grammar structures in the context of unified themes. All units follow a **four-step approach**, taking learners from grammar in context to communicative practice.

STEP 1 GRAMMAR IN CONTEXT

This section presents the target structure(s) in a natural context. As students read the **high-interest texts**, they encounter the form, meaning, and use of the grammar. **Before You Read** activities create interest and elicit students' knowledge about the topic. **After You Read** activities build students' reading vocabulary and comprehension.

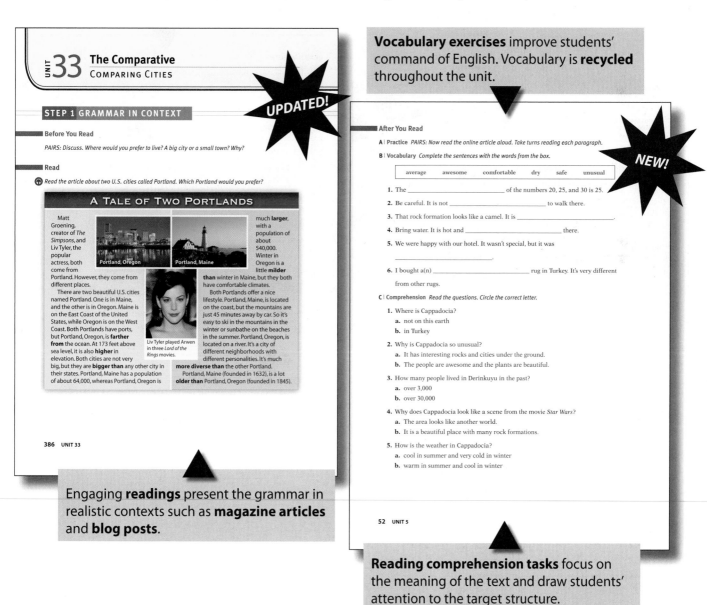

Vocabulary exercises improve students' command of English. Vocabulary is **recycled** throughout the unit.

Engaging **readings** present the grammar in realistic contexts such as **magazine articles** and **blog posts**.

Reading comprehension tasks focus on the meaning of the text and draw students' attention to the target structure.

STEP 2 GRAMMAR PRESENTATION

This section gives students a comprehensive and explicit overview of the grammar with detailed **Grammar Charts** and **Grammar Notes** that present the form, meaning, and use of the structure(s).

Grammar Charts present the structure in a clear, easy-to-read format.

Grammar Notes give concise, simple **explanations** and **examples** to ensure students' understanding.

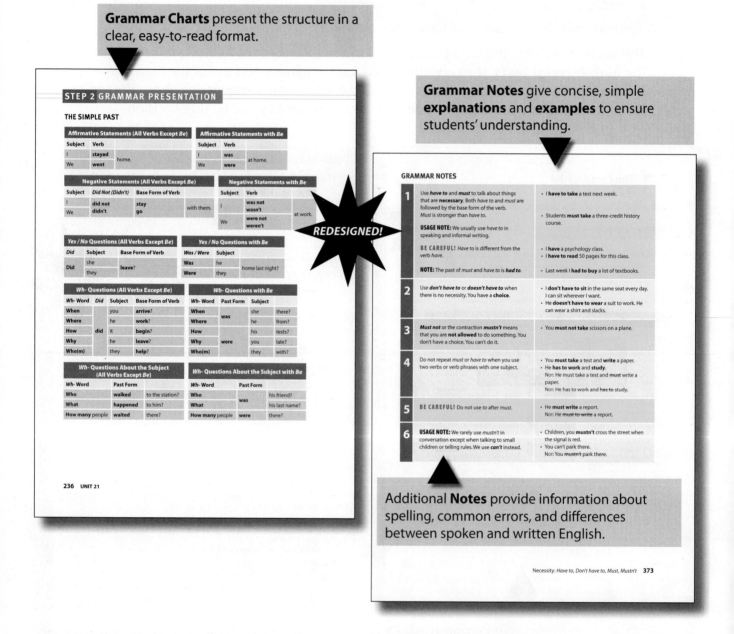

Additional **Notes** provide information about spelling, common errors, and differences between spoken and written English.

STEP 3 FOCUSED PRACTICE

Controlled practice activities in this section lead students to master form, meaning, and use of the target grammar.

STEP 3 FOCUSED PRACTICE

EXERCISE 1: Discover the Grammar

Underline the simple present. Circle the present progressive. Underline twice all non-action verbs.

Raisa has a new phone with a lot of great features. She likes her phone a lot. Her phone keeps her in touch with her friends wherever she is. Right now Raisa is texting friends. They are making plans for the evening. She and her friends often text. They don't talk much on the phone. They also connect through Facebook®. Raisa often adds new friends to her site. Sometimes she doesn't know them very well. Raisa's mother, Olga, worries about that. Olga doesn't use social networks. She prefers to talk on the phone or connect through email.

EXERCISE 2: Simple Present; Non-Action Verbs; Present Progressive *(Grammar Notes 1–5)*

Complete the conversation with the words in parentheses. Use the simple present or present progressive. Use contractions when possible.

A: What _____are_____ you _____doing_____?
  1.   2. (do)

B: I _____ my messages. Look. That's my friend from high school.
  3. (check)

She _____ three kids now. They _____ happy birthday to
  4. (have)   5. (sing)
their father.

A: Oh. That's nice.

B: _____ you _____ social networking sites?
  6.   7. (use)

A: No, I _____. I _____ to email my friends. I _____
  8.   9. (prefer)   10. (think)
it's more personal. Also, I _____ there are privacy features in social
  11. (know)
networking sites, but I _____ about my privacy.
  12. (worry)

Simple Present and Present Progressive; Non-Action Verbs **189**

Discover the Grammar activities develop students' recognition and understanding of the target structure before they are asked to produce it.

A **variety of exercise types** engage students and guide them from recognition and understanding to accurate production of the grammar structures.

EXERCISE 4: Comparison of Adjectives *(Grammar Notes 1–7)*

Complete the paragraph with the adjectives in parentheses. Use the comparative form.

You are choosing between two cities to live in, Los Angeles or Glendale. You aren't sure which is a _____better_____ choice. Los
  1. (good)
Angeles is a much _____ city than
  2. (big)
Glendale, and it has all the problems of big cities. Los Angeles is _____ than
  3. (polluted)
Glendale, and traffic is _____.
  4. (bad)
The streets of downtown Los Angeles are

_____ too. However, Los Angeles is much _____ than Glendale.
  5. (busy)   6. (exciting)
Los Angeles has a great night life. Glendale
is much _____ at night. Both
  7. (quiet)
cities have the same great climate. It's hard
to compare housing costs. Some parts of Los
Angeles are _____ than Glendale
  8. (more / expensive)
and other parts are _____. Both
  9. (less / expensive)
cities are close, so if you make a mistake, you
can always move.

Rodeo Drive, Los Angeles

Bicycle trail, Glendale, California

EXERCISE 5: Editing

Correct the sentences. There are seven mistakes. The first one is already corrected. Find and correct six more.

1. Our new apartment is ^more comfortable than our old one.
2. Florida is more hotter than Maine.
3. Oregon is far north than California.
4. A motorcycle is more fast than a bicycle.
5. Traffic at 8:00 A.M. is more heavy than traffic at 10:00 A.M.
6. The climate in Portland, Oregon, is mild than the climate in Anchorage, Alaska.
7. The location of Jake's apartment is more convenient than his sister.

394 UNIT 33

An **Editing** exercise ends every Focused Practice section and teaches students to find and correct typical mistakes.

This section provides practice with the structure in **listening** and **pronunciation** exercises as well as in communicative, open-ended **speaking** and **writing** activities that move students toward fluency.

Listening activities allow students to hear the grammar in natural contexts and to practice a range of listening skills.

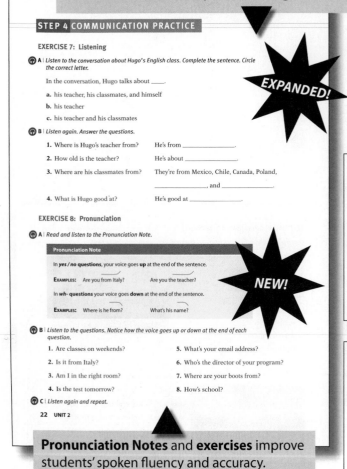

STEP 4 COMMUNICATION PRACTICE

EXERCISE 7: Listening

A | *Listen to the conversation about Hugo's English class. Complete the sentence. Circle the correct letter.*

In the conversation, Hugo talks about _____.

a. his teacher, his classmates, and himself

b. his teacher

c. his teacher and his classmates

B | *Listen again. Answer the questions.*

1. Where is Hugo's teacher from?   He's from _____.

2. How old is the teacher?   He's about _____.

3. Where are his classmates from?   They're from Mexico, Chile, Canada, Poland, _____, and _____.

4. What is Hugo good at?   He's good at _____.

EXERCISE 8: Pronunciation

A | *Read and listen to the Pronunciation Note.*

Pronunciation Note

In **yes / no questions**, your voice goes **up** at the end of the sentence.

EXAMPLES: Are you from Italy?   Are you the teacher?

In **wh- questions** your voice goes **down** at the end of the sentence.

EXAMPLES: Where is he from?   What's his name?

B | *Listen to the questions. Notice how the voice goes up or down at the end of each question.*

1. Are classes on weekends?

2. Is it from Italy?

3. Am I in the right room?

4. Is the test tomorrow?

5. What's your email address?

6. Who's the director of your program?

7. Where are your boots from?

8. How's school?

C | *Listen again and repeat.*

22 UNIT 2

EXPANDED!

NEW!

Pronunciation Notes and **exercises** improve students' spoken fluency and accuracy.

Speaking activities help students synthesize the grammar through discussions, debates, games, and problem-solving tasks, developing their fluency.

EXERCISE 8: Comparing Train Systems

PAIRS: Look at the information about the London Underground and the Moscow Metro. Together write as many comparative questions as you can. Ask other pairs your questions. Answer their questions. Then compare these subways to others you know.

EXAMPLE: **A:** Is the Underground faster than the Moscow Metro?
B: No, it isn't. It's slower.

	London Underground	Moscow Metro
Year opened	1863	1935
Length of tracks	250 miles (400 kilometers)	187.2 miles (301.2 kilometers)
Number of passengers each day	4 million	6.6 million
Hours of operation	5:30 A.M. to 1:15 A.M. (Fri. & Sat. closes at 2:00 A.M.)	5:30 A.M. to 1:00 A.M.
Cost of ride in euros	4 euros for shortest distance	26 rubles = .66 euro
Speed	20.5 mph (33 km / h)	25.82 mph (41.55 km / h)

EXERCISE 11: Writing

A | *Compare two ways of travel. Use at least three comparative adjectives.*

EXAMPLE: Most cities have busses and trains, but in San Francisco some people also travel by trolley, and in Venice people sometimes travel by gondola. Both the trolley and the gondola are more fun than the bus or the train. The gondola is more romantic than the trolley, but the trolley is more exciting, especially when you're traveling down one of San Francisco's steep streets.

B | *Check your work. Use the Editing Checklist.*

Editing Checklist

Did you . . . ?
☐ use comparative adjectives correctly
☐ check your spelling

NEW!

Writing activities encourage students to produce meaningful writing that integrates the grammar structure.

An **Editing Checklist** teaches students to correct their mistakes and revise their work.

The *Focus on Grammar* Unit

Unit Reviews give students the opportunity to check their understanding of the target structure. **Answers** at the back of the book allow students to monitor their own progress.

Check your answers on page UR-7.
Do you need to review anything?

UNIT 33 Review

NEW!

A | *Circle the correct words to complete the sentences.*

1. She is **more / much** younger than he is.

2. It is colder **then / than** it was yesterday.

3. This singing group is **more popular / popular more** than the other one.

4. The traffic is **more worse / worse** now than it was an hour ago.

5. Which city has a **high / higher** elevation, Bogota or Mexico City?

6. Which city has a **better / more good** transportation system, Quebec or Vancouver?

7. Is your car more comfortable than your **brother / brother's**?

B | *Look at the chart. Make comparisons. Use the words in parentheses.*

	New City	Sun City
Bus fare	$2.00	$3.00
Cup of coffee	$1.20	$1.50
Average home	$200,000	$300,000
Average income	$65,000	$90,000

1. _____
   (bus / expensive)

2. _____
   (cup of coffee / cheap)

3. _____
   (average home / less / expensive)

4. _____
   (average income / high)

C | *Correct the paragraph. There are nine mistakes.*

We moved to the countryside, and we're mu...
larger, and the air is cleaner and polluted less.
and vegetables are more cheap. The people ar...
is more bad; it's much more long, but we lister...
more good.

398 Unit 33 Review: The Comparative

Extended writing tasks help students integrate the grammar structure as they follow the steps of the **writing process.**

PART XI From Grammar to Writing
THE ORDER OF ADJECTIVES BEFORE NOUNS

1 | *Complete the sentences with the words in parentheses.*

1. I saw a _____ on Main Street.
   (funny / monkey / brown / little)

2. Maria wore a _____.
   (red / dress / beautiful / silk)

2 | *Study this information about the order of adjectives before nouns. When you use adjectives, write them in this order.*

1

1. opinion	2. size	3. shape	4. age	5. color	6. origin	7. material	8. noun
beautiful	big	square	new	red	French	silk	scarf

2

We use adjectives to describe nouns. Descriptions make writing more lively. They also help the reader form mental pictures. When **several adjectives** come before a noun, they follow a **special order**.
• I saw a **beautiful young** woman.
  Nor: I saw a ~~young beautiful~~ woman.

3

Use **and** to connect adjectives from the same category.
• The shirt was *cotton* **and** *polyester*.
• The blouse was *red* **and** *white*.

3 | *Complete the sentences with the words in parentheses. Use the correct order.*

1. He ate a(n) _____ pear.
   (brown / big / Asian)

2. His cashmere coat was not as expensive as her _____
   (Italian / new / leather / black)
   _____ jacket.

3. They bought three _____ bowls.
   (silver / beautiful / Mexican)

From Grammar to Writing **433**

SCOPE AND SEQUENCE

SPEAKING	PRONUNCIATION	VOCABULARY	
Pair Discussion: Occupations *Class Discussion*: Talented People	Tips for *he, she, he's,* and *she's*	athlete busy exciting	famous husband talented
Pair Activity: Asking and Answering Questions *Role Play*: Meeting at a Party	Rising intonation in *yes / no* questions Falling intonation in *wh-* questions	by the way excuse me on time	right room
Guided Conversation: Describing the Weather *Group Discussion*: The First Day of School	Extra pronounced syllable in negative forms of *be* Clipped /t/ sound in *wasn't, weren't*	a big deal boring busy	make money still
Game: Describing Things *Game*: Comparing Choices	Sound of plurals: /s/, /z/, /ɪz/	all over almost be born	holiday special striking
Group Discussion: Asking Questions about a Place	Syllable stress	average awesome comfortable	dry safe unusual
Game: Guessing Countries *Game*: Describing Locations	Stressed words for emphasis	appointment be free cafeteria	flight rest room sculpture
Pair Activity: Making Suggestions for You and Another Person *Pair Activity*: Giving Advice *Pair Activity*: Giving Directions	Linking sound in *don't + you*	advice dead island	nap pray secret

UNIT	READING	WRITING	LISTENING
8 page 81 **Grammar:** Simple Present: Affirmative and Negative Statements **Theme:** Shopping	An online article: *Teen Trends*	A paragraph about the way you and a relative dress	A conversation about shopping
9 page 91 **Grammar:** Simple Present: *Yes / No* Questions and Short Answers **Theme:** Roommates	A questionnaire: *Roommate Questionnaire*	An email of introduction to a new roommate	A conversation about finding a compatible roommate
10 page 102 **Grammar:** Simple Present: *Wh-* Questions **Theme:** Dreams	A radio talk show interview: *Dreams*	A paragraph about a dream or daydream	A conversation about a dream and its interpretation
PART III **From Grammar to Writing**, page 114 **Time Word Connectors: *First, Next, After that, Then, Finally***			
11 page 116 **Grammar:** *There is / There are* **Theme:** Shopping Malls	An advertisement: West Edmonton Mall, Canada	A paragraph about a place where you like to shop	A conversation about directions
12 page 130 **Grammar:** Possessives: Nouns, Adjectives, Pronouns; Object Pronouns; Questions with *Whose* **Theme:** Possessions	A conversation: Student compositions	A paragraph about yourself and your family for a school newsletter	A conversation about possessions
13 page 143 **Grammar:** Ability: *Can* or *Could* **Theme:** Abilities of Animals	An online article: *A Genius Parrot*	A paragraph about an interesting pet or other animal	A conversation about dolphins' abilities
14 page 153 **Grammar:** Permission: *Can* or *May* **Theme:** Health and Diet	An online article: *The Right Diet*	Sentences about the requirements of a diet	A telephone conversation between a patient and a doctor
PART IV **From Grammar to Writing**, page 163 **Punctuation I: The Apostrophe, The Comma, The Period, The Question Mark**			

SPEAKING	PRONUNCIATION	VOCABULARY	
Pair Discussion: Likes and Dislikes *Group Discussion*: Clothing Customs of the World	Third person singular ending /s/, /z/, or /ɪz/	alone companies cute	middle school senior teenager
Pair Discussion: Comparing Habits and Personality *Game*: Find Someone Who . . . *Game*: What's in Your Backpack?	Linking sound in *does it* and *does he*	bother easygoing messy neat	outgoing private stay up wake up
Pair Survey: Sleeping Habits *Group Survey*: Sleeping Habits *Pair Activity*: Information Gap	Consonant clusters with /r/ and /l/	author guest nightmares	remember unfortunately
Pair Activity: Comparing Pictures of a Street *Game*: Tic Tac Toe	Homophones: *there*, *their*, and *they're*	amusement park attraction get away include	indoor international market one of a kind
Class Activity: Asking about Family Photos *Game*: Find Someone Who . . .	Ending sounds with possessives: /z/, /s/, /ɪz/	back composition grade	handwriting recognize
Game: Find Someone Who . . . *Game*: What Can Your Group Do?	Reduced vowel in *can* when followed by base form verb Stressed vowel in *can't*	be surprised genius intelligent	invent professor
Information Gap: Asking Questions about a Website	Vowel sounds /eɪ/ and /ɛ/	especially gain lose	overweight pound

SPEAKING	PRONUNCIATION	VOCABULARY	
Game: Describing a Classroom Photo	Unstressed -*ing* ending in the present progressive	competition extracurricular give up	top tough wealthy
Role Play: Talking about Movies *Pair Activity*: Describing Pictures for a Partner to Draw	Stressed final syllable in abbreviations	catch a cold classic cough	favorite fever scene
Pair Discussion: Guessing About People *Group Activity*: Survey	Intonation to express emotions	connect constantly improving	minor waterproof

SPEAKING	PRONUNCIATION	VOCABULARY	
Pair Discussion: Talking About your Weekend *Game*: Truths or Lies	Final sound with simple past verbs: /d/, /t/, or /ɪd/	bumpy canceled freezing	landed picked up
Group Activity: A Memory Game *Group Discussion*: A Wonderful and Terrible Day	Vowel sounds /æ/ and /ɛ/	appeared border lucky	shout suddenly terrible
Pair Discussion: Describing a Performance or Event	/dʒ/ and /y/ sounds	author be out mystery	play poem

	SPEAKING	PRONUNCIATION	VOCABULARY	
	Group Activity: A Quiz Show *Pair Discussion*: What Were You Like as a Child? *Information Gap*: Guess the Musician	/ɜ˞/ and /ɔ/ and the consonant cluster /kt/		noticed statue
	Pair Discussion: Preferences *Game*: What Do I Do? *Pair Activity*: Problem Solving	Unstresse… Lin…		…s clothes …nality …ble
	Information Gap: Inventions	Stress on… compound…		
	Pair Discussion: Changes in Your Life	Reduced pronunciation of *going to* "gonna"	…inst announced be worth it	in my opinion increased tuition
	Group Activity: Survey *Class Survey*: In the Future *Class Activity*: Making Predictions	Linking between subject pronoun and *will*	common disappear meal	spend time vegetarian
	Pair Discussion: Describing Plans	Stress on numbers ending in *-ty* and *-teen*	commute entire flooding highways	mild predicted storm
	Class Activity: Cooking Class Presentation *Group Discussion*: Your Favorite Restaurant	Schwa sound /ə/ in the indefinite article	atmosphere delicious main course	menu reservation service

mess 杂乱 [mes] 困境
neat 整洁
generous
close 接近
behind 后面 ; 在…之后
in back of 后面
in front of 前面
road 路.
until 直到…以前
commet 注释 评论

UNIT	READING	WRITING	LISTENING
28 page 321 **Grammar:** *How much / How many*, Quantifiers, *Enough*, Adverbs of Frequency **Theme:** Desserts, Cooking, and Baking	A conversation: Desserts	A paragraph describing desserts	A conversation about a recipe
29 page 334 **Grammar:** *Too much / Too many, Too* + Adjective **Theme:** The Right Place to Live	An online article: Three U.S. cities	An email of complaint to a newspaper about an aspect of city life	A conversation about apartment rentals
PART IX **From Grammar to Writing**, page 344 **A Business Letter**			
30 page 348 **Grammar:** Advice: *Should, Ought to, Had better* **Theme:** Dos and Don'ts of the Business World	An online article: Global Business	A paragraph of advice to a businessperson about a culture that you know well	A conversation about travels to Japan
31 page 360 **Grammar:** Requests, Desires, and Offers: *Would you, Could you, Can you . . . ?, I'd like . . .* **Theme:** Neighbors	A message board: Problems with neighbors	Two email requests to neighbors	A telephone conversation between neighbors
32 page 370 **Grammar:** Necessity: *Have to, Don't Have to, Must, Mustn't* **Theme:** Rules at School	A conversation: Requirements for a history class	A paragraph about an elementary school where you grew up	Advice from a college counselor to a student
PART X **From Grammar to Writing**, page 382 **Expressing and Supporting an Opinion**			
33 page 386 **Grammar:** The Comparative **Theme:** Comparing Cities	An article: *A Tale of Two Portlands*	A paragraph comparing two ways to travel	A conversation about city improvements

SPEAKING	PRONUNCIATION	VOCABULARY	
Class Survey: Eating Habits *Information Gap*: Recipes *Group Presentation*: Desserts	/aʊ/ sound	in season ingredients neighborhood	prepare pretty good taste
Role Play: Living Situations *Group Discussion*: Describing Your City	/t/, /θ/, and /ð/ sounds	climate crime free time	housing pollution unemployment
Pair Discussion: Gift Giving *Group Discussion*: Body Language	Reduction of /t/ sound after *shouldn't* before a verb	business receptions confusion consider	customs insult
Group Survey: Making Requests *Role Play*: Making Polite Requests *Pair Activity*: Offering Invitations *Role Play*: Offering Invitations and Making Requests	Vowel sound /ʊ/ in *would*; Reduced forms of *would you* /wʊdʒə/ and *could you* /kʊdʒə/	be hurt go away lend me a hand	post a message selfish
Class Discussion: School Rules *Class Survey*: Preventing Cheating	Stress and unstress in *have to* or *has to*	average due final hard copy	midterm outline pass percent
Pair Activity: Comparing Train Systems *Pair Discussion*: Making Comparisons *Class Discussion*: Comparing Cities	Unstressed vowel in *than*	be located coast diverse mild	personality port sea level ski

UNIT	READING	WRITING	LISTENING
34 page 399 **Grammar:** Adverbs of Manner **Theme:** Public Speaking	A blog: *Public Speaking*	A paragraph describing a sports event	Tips for giving a speech
35 page 408 **Grammar:** *Enough, Too / Very, As* + Adjective + *As, Same / Different* **Theme:** Proms and Parties	A conversation: High school prom dates	A paragraph comparing two friends or two events	A discussion between two managers
36 page 421 **Grammar:** The Superlative **Theme:** Penguins	An online article: *The Penguin*	A paragraph about animals in the zoo, literature, or movies	A quiz show
PART XI **From Grammar to Writing,** page 433 **The Order of Adjectives Before Nouns**			

SPEAKING	PRONUNCIATION	VOCABULARY	
Group Game: A Chain Story *Pair Discussion*: A Sports Event	Intonation to express emotions	applause appreciated audience facts	jokes polite seriously
Pair Activity: Describing Yourself *Class Survey*: Comparing Similarities	Unstressed vowel in *as . . . as*	I'm a loser I'm not going to make a fool of myself I'm not his type Making excuses No one can get a word in edgewise	
Group Survey: Animals	Unstressed *-est* syllable in superlatives	centimeter explorer extinct feathers	inch kilogram pound species

ABOUT THE AUTHOR

Irene E. Schoenberg has taught ESL for more than two decades at Hunter College's International English Language Institute and at Columbia University's American Language Program. Ms. Schoenberg holds a master's degree in TESOL from Columbia University. She has trained ESL and EFL teachers at Columbia University's Teachers College and at the New School University. She has given workshops and academic presentations at conferences, English language schools, and universities in Brazil, Chile, Dubai, El Salvador, Guatemala, Japan, Mexico, Nicaragua, Peru, Taiwan, Thailand, Vietnam, and throughout the United States.

Ms. Schoenberg is the author of *Talk about Trivia*; *Talk about Values*; *Speaking of Values 1: Conversation and Listening*; *Topics from A to Z*, Books 1 and 2; and *Focus on Grammar 2: An Integrated Skills Approach*. She is the co-author with Jay Maurer of the *True Colors* series and *Focus on Grammar 1: An Integrated Skills Approach*. She is one of the authors of *Future 1: English for Results* and *Future 3: English for Results*.

ACKNOWLEDGMENTS

I gratefully acknowledge the many reviewers for their suggestions and comments. There are many people at Pearson who have contributed to the development and production of this edition. I would like to thank them all, in particular:

- The people in production who helped carry the project through: **Rhea Banker** and especially **Robert Ruvo** for his indefatigable efforts.
- **Lise Minovitz**, the supervising editor, for her expert guidance and unflagging energy in keeping a very complex project on target.
- **Debbie Sistino**, the series director, who, in addition to managing the entire series, was always available to answer any of my questions.
- **Joanne Dresner** for her original vision and guidance of the *Focus on Grammar* series.
- My editors of the first three editions for helping to bring the books to fruition.
- **Ann France**, for her attractive new design, and **Aerin Csigay** and **Kim Steiner** for great photos that make the pages come alive.
- Above all, I'm most grateful to my editor **Kim Steiner**. Her dedication to the project, her brilliant solutions to problems, her creativity, her availability and her eye for detail, have made working on the revised edition a joy.
- Finally, I thank my family for their love and understanding: **Harris**, **Dan**, **Dahlia**, **Jonathan**, and **Olivia**.

REVIEWERS

We are grateful to the following reviewers for their many helpful comments:

Aida Aganagic, Seneca College, Toronto, Canada; **Aftab Ahmed**, American University of Sharjah, Sharjah, United Arab Emirates; **Todd Allen**, English Language Institute, Gainesville, FL; **Anthony Anderson**, University of Texas, Austin, TX; **Anna K. Andrade**, ASA Institute, New York, NY; **Bayda Asbridge**, Worcester State College, Worcester, MA; **Raquel Ashkenasi**, American Language Institute, La Jolla, CA; **James Bakker**, Mt. San Antonio College, Walnut, CA; **Kate Baldrige-Hale**, Harper College, Palatine, IL; **Leticia S. Banks**, ALCI-SDUSM, San Marcos, CA; **Aegina Barnes**, York College CUNY, Forest Hills, NY; **Sarah Barnhardt**, Community College of Baltimore County, Reisterstown, MD; **Kimberly Becker**, Nashville State Community College, Nashville, TN; **Holly Bell**, California State University, San Marcos, CA; **Anne Bliss**, University of Colorado, Boulder, CO; **Diana Booth**, Elgin Community College, Elgin, IL; **Barbara Boyer**, South Plainfield High School, South Plainfield, NJ; **Janna Brink**, Mt. San Antonio College, Walnut, CA; **AJ Brown**, Portland State University, Portland, OR; **Amanda Burgoyne**, Worcester State College, Worcester, MA; **Brenda Burlingame**, Independence High School, Charlotte, NC; **Sandra Byrd**, Shelby County High School and Kentucky State University, Shelbyville, KY; **Edward Carlstedt**, American University of Sharjah, Sharjah, United Arab Emirates; **Sean Cochran**, American Language Institute, Fullerton, CA; **Yanely Cordero**, Miami Dade College, Miami, FL; **Lin Cui**, William Rainey Harper College, Palatine, IL; **Sheila Detweiler**, College Lake County, Libertyville, IL; **Ann Duncan**, University of Texas, Austin, TX; **Debra Edell**, Merrill Middle School, Denver, CO; **Virginia Edwards**, Chandler-Gilbert Community College, Chandler, AZ; **Kenneth Fackler**, University of Tennessee, Martin, TN; **Jennifer Farnell**, American Language Program, Stamford, CT; **Allen P. Feiste**, Suwon University, Hwaseong, South Korea; **Mina Fowler**, Mt. San Antonio Community College, Rancho Cucamonga, CA; **Rosemary Franklin**, University of Cincinnati, Cincinnati, OH; **Christiane Galvani**, Texas Southern University, Sugar Land, TX; **Chester Gates**, Community College of Baltimore County, Baltimore, MD; **Luka Gavrilovic**, Quest Language Studies, Toronto, Canada; **Sally Gearhart**, Santa Rosa Community College, Santa Rosa, CA; **Shannon Gerrity**, James Lick Middle School, San Francisco, CA; **Jeanette Gerrity Gomez**, Prince George's Community College, Largo, MD; **Carlos Gonzalez**, Miami Dade College, Miami, FL; **Therese Gormley Hirmer**, University of Guelph, Guelph, Canada; **Sudeepa Gulati**, Long Beach City College, Long Beach, CA; **Anthony Halderman**, Cuesta College, San Luis Obispo, CA; **Ann A. Hall**, University of Texas, Austin, TX; **Cora Higgins**, Boston Academy of English, Boston, MA; **Michelle Hilton**, South Lane School District, Cottage Grove, OR; **Nicole Hines**, Troy University, Atlanta, GA; **Rosemary Hiruma**, American Language Institute, Long Beach, CA; **Harriet Hoffman**, University of Texas, Austin, TX; **Leah Holck**, Michigan State University, East Lansing, MI; **Christy Hunt**, English for Internationals, Roswell, GA; **Osmany Hurtado**, Miami Dade College, Miami, FL; **Isabel Innocenti**, Miami Dade College, Miami, FL; **Donna Janian**, Oxford Intensive School of English, Medford, MA; **Scott Jenison**, Antelope Valley College, Lancaster, CA; **Grace Kim**, Mt. San Antonio College, Diamond Bar, CA; **Brian King**, ELS Language Center, Chicago, IL; **Pam Kopitzke**, Modesto Junior College, Modesto, CA; **Elena Lattarulo**, American Language Institute, San Diego, CA; **Karen Lavaty**, Mt. San Antonio College, Glendora, CA; **JJ Lee-Gilbert**, Menlo-Atherton High School, Foster City, CA; **Ruth Luman**, Modesto Junior College, Modesto, CA; **Yvette Lyons**, Tarrant County College, Fort Worth, TX; **Janet Magnoni**, Diablo Valley College, Pleasant Hill, CA; **Meg Maher**, YWCA Princeton, Princeton, NJ; **Carmen Marquez-Rivera**, Curie Metropolitan High School, Chicago, IL; **Meredith Massey**, Prince George's Community College, Hyattsville, MD; **Linda Maynard**, Coastline Community College, Westminster, CA; **Eve Mazereeuw**, University of Guelph, Guelph, Canada; **Susanne McLaughlin**, Roosevelt University, Chicago, IL; **Madeline Medeiros**, Cuesta College, San Luis Obispo, CA; **Gioconda Melendez**, Miami Dade College, Miami, FL; **Marcia Menaker**, Passaic County Community College, Morris Plains, NJ; **Seabrook Mendoza**, Cal State San Marcos University, Wildomar, CA; **Anadalia Mendoza**, Felix Varela Senior High School, Miami, FL; **Charmaine Mergulhao**, Quest Language Studies, Toronto, Canada; **Dana Miho**, Mt. San Antonio College, San Jacinto, CA; **Sonia Nelson**, Centennial Middle School, Portland, OR; **Manuel Niebla**, Miami Dade College, Miami, FL; **Alice Nitta**, Leeward Community College, Pearl City, HI; **Gabriela Oliva**, Quest Language Studies, Toronto, Canada; **Sara Packer**, Portland State University, Portland, OR; **Lesley Painter**, New School, New York, NY; **Carlos Paz-Perez**, Miami Dade College, Miami, FL; **Ileana Perez**, Miami Dade College, Miami, FL; **Barbara Pogue**, Essex County College, Newark, NJ; **Phillips Potash**, University of Texas, Austin, TX; **Jada Pothina**, University of Texas, Austin, TX; **Ewa Pratt**, Des Moines Area Community College, Des Moines, IA; **Pedro Prentt**, Hudson County Community College, Jersey City, NJ; **Maida Purdy**, Miami Dade College, Miami, FL; **Dolores Quiles**, SUNY Ulster, Stone Ridge, NY; **Mark Rau**, American River College, Sacramento, CA; **Lynne Raxlen**, Seneca College, Toronto, Canada; **Lauren Rein**, English for Internationals, Sandy Springs, GA; **Diana Rivers**, NOCCCD, Cypress, CA; **Silvia Rodriguez**, Santa Ana College, Mission Viejo, CA; **Rolando Romero**, Miami Dade College, Miami, FL; **Pedro Rosabal**, Miami Dade College, Miami, FL; **Natalie Rublik**, University of Quebec, Chicoutimi, Quebec, Canada; **Matilde Sanchez**, Oxnard College, Oxnard, CA; **Therese Sarkis-Kruse**, Wilson Commencement, Rochester, NY; **Mike Sfiropoulos**, Palm Beach Community College, Boynton Beach, FL; **Amy Shearon**, Rice University, Houston, TX; **Sara Shore**, Modesto Junior College, Modesto, CA; **Patricia Silva**, Richard Daley College, Chicago, IL; **Stephanie Solomon**, Seattle Central Community College, Vashon, WA; **Roberta Steinberg**, Mount Ida College, Newton, MA; **Teresa Szymula**, Curie Metropolitan High School, Chicago, IL; **Hui-Lien Tang**, Jasper High School, Plano, TX; **Christine Tierney**, Houston Community College, Sugar Land, TX; **Ileana Torres**, Miami Dade College, Miami, FL; **Michelle Van Slyke**, Western Washington University, Bellingham, WA; **Melissa Villamil**, Houston Community College, Sugar Land, TX; **Elizabeth Wagenheim**, Prince George's Community College, Lago, MD; **Mark Wagner**, Worcester State College, Worcester, MA; **Angela Waigand**, American University of Sharjah, Sharjah, United Arab Emirates; **Merari Weber**, Metropolitan Skills Center, Los Angeles, CA; **Sonia Wei**, Seneca College, Toronto, Canada; and **Vicki Woodward**, Indiana University, Bloomington, IN.

Be: PRESENT AND PAST

1

Present of *Be*: Statements
FAMOUS PEOPLE

STEP 1 GRAMMAR IN CONTEXT

Before You Read

GROUPS: Name a young and famous person. Tell your group one thing about this person.

> **EXAMPLE:** Lionel Messi. He is a great soccer player.

Read

🎧 *Read the article about the people in the photos.*

couple
ˈkʌplʲ
- 对
配偶

pianist
[ˈpiənɪst]

Famous Couples

POP Culture News

They're young. They're rich. They're talented and famous. Who **are** they? Where **are** they from? What do they do?

The woman on the left **is** Carrie Underwood. She **is** from the United States. She's from the state of Oklahoma. Carrie **is** an American country singer. She **isn't** just a singer. She's also a pianist and a songwriter.

Carrie is married to Mike Fisher. He **is** also talented and famous. He **isn't** from the United States, and he **isn't** a singer. He's an athlete from Ottawa, Canada. Now he's an ice hockey player for the Nashville Predators. Carrie Underwood and Mike Fisher have homes in the United States and Canada.

Who **are** the people in the second photo? They're Gisele Bündchen and Tom Brady. Gisele **is** a supermodel. She's from Brazil, but she **is** famous all over the world. Her husband **is** Tom Brady. He **is** an American football player. He's from California. He plays quarterback for the New England Patriots.

The lives of these famous people **are** exciting. Their lives **aren't** easy. They **are** always very busy.

It's wonderful to be young and famous. Many young people want to be rich and famous. It takes talent, hard work, and good luck.

After You Read

A | Practice PAIRS: Now read the article aloud. Take turns reading each paragraph.

B | Vocabulary Complete the sentences with the words from the box.

| athlete | busy | exciting | famous | husband | talented |

1. Mike Fisher is Carrie Underwood's ___husband___.

2. Carrie Underwood plays piano, sings, and writes music. She is very ___talented___.

3. People know Gisele Bündchen all over the world. She is very ___famous___.

4. Tom Brady is a great ___athlete___. He's a football player for the New England Patriots.

5. Brady works hard. He is ___busy___ all the time.

6. Bündchen goes to many parties and travels to many interesting places. She has a(n) ___exciting___ life.

C | Comprehension Complete the sentences. Circle the correct letter.

1. Carrie Underwood is married to _____.
   a. Tom Brady   **b.** Mike Fisher

2. Underwood is a singer and _____.
   a. an athlete   **b.** a pianist

3. Underwood's husband is an _____.
   a. ice hockey player   **b.** actor

4. The New England Patriots are a _____.
   a. football team   **b.** talented player

5. Gisele Bündchen is a _____.
   a. supermodel   **b.** pianist

6. Bündchen is from _____.
   a. Canada   **b.** Brazil

7. Tom Brady is from _____.
   a. New England   **b.** California

8. To be rich and famous takes _____.
   a. time and money   **b.** hard work and good luck

PRESENT OF *BE*: STATEMENTS

Affirmative Statements

Singular			Plural		
Subject	*Be*		**Subject**	*Be*	
I	**am**		Masami and I / We		
You	**are**		You and Josh / You		students.
Mike / He		talented.	Ivona and Juan / They	**are**	
Carrie / She	**is**		Seoul and London / They		cities.
Hockey / It		a sport			

Contractions				
I am	→	**I'm**	we are	→ **we're**
you are	→	**you're**	you are	→ **you're**
he is	→	**he's**	they are	→ **they're**
she is	→	**she's**		
it is	→	**it's**		

Negative Statements

Singular		Plural	
Subject + *Be* / *Not*		**Subject + *Be* / *Not***	
I **am not** / I'**m not**		We **are not** / We'**re not** / We **aren't**	
You **are not** / You'**re not** / You **aren't**		You **are not** / You'**re not** / You **aren't**	in Brazil.
He **is not** / He'**s not** / He **isn't**	from California.	They **are not** / They'**re not** / They **aren't**	
She **is not** / She'**s not** / She **isn't**			
It **is not** / It'**s not** / It **isn't**	new.		

GRAMMAR NOTES

1	The **present of *be*** has three forms: ***am, is, are***.	• I **am** a student. • He **is** from Brazil. • They **are** famous.
2	Use the correct form of ***be*** + ***not*** to make a **negative statement**.	• I **am not** from Turkey. • It **is not** from Canada. • We **are not** famous.
3	Use **contractions** (short forms) in speaking and informal writing. There are two **negative contractions** for *is not* and *are not*.	• I**'m** from Mexico. • I**'m not** from Ecuador. • Mr. Crane**'s** from Los Angeles. • It**'s not** difficult. OR It **isn't** difficult. • We**'re not** single. OR We **aren't** single.
4	All **sentences** have a **subject** and a **verb**. **BE CAREFUL!** You cannot make a sentence without a subject. You cannot make a sentence without a verb.	SUBJECT VERB • **Gisele is** from Brazil. Not: ~~Is from Brazil.~~ Not: ~~Gisele from Brazil.~~
5	The **subject** is a noun or a pronoun. Subject pronouns (*I, you, he, she, it we, you, they*) replace subject nouns. **BE CAREFUL!** You cannot put a subject pronoun right after a subject noun.	SUBJECT NOUN • **Mike Fisher** is from Canada. SUBJECT PRONOUN • **He** is from Canada. Not: ~~Fisher he~~ is from England.

STEP 3 FOCUSED PRACTICE

EXERCISE 1: Discover the Grammar

A | *Check (✓) the negative statements.*

   ✓ **1.** Carrie Underwood isn't single.

_____ **2.** Underwood is married to Mike Fisher.

_____ **3.** Fisher and Tom Brady are athletes.

_____ **4.** They aren't actors.

_____ **5.** I'm from Canada.

_____ **6.** I'm not from the United States.

B | *Look back at Part A. Underline the contractions.*

C | *Look back at sentences 1–3 in Part A. Change the subject nouns to subject pronouns.*

EXERCISE 2: Affirmative Statements

(Grammar Note 1)

Complete the sentences with **am, is,** *or* **are.**

1. Soccer _____*is*_____ popular all over the world.

2. Football _____*is*_____ popular in the United States.

3. Football and soccer _____*are*_____ different sports.

4. Tom Brady _____*is*_____ a great football player.

5. Lionel Messi _____*is*_____ a great soccer player.

6. I _____*am*_____ a football fan. I love football.

7. My cousins _____*are*_____ soccer fans. They love soccer.

EXERCISE 3: Affirmative and Negative Statements

(Grammar Notes 1–2)

Complete the sentences with **am, is,** *or* **are,** *and the word in parentheses.*

Parminder Nagra _____*is*_____
                        1.
a talented actor. She and Keira Knightley

_____ the stars of the movie *Bend*
        2.
It Like Beckham. It _____ a comedy.
                            3.
In the movie, Nagra _____ a young
                            4.
Indian girl in England. She _____
                                    5.
a good soccer player, and she loves soccer.

But her parents _____ traditional. They _____ happy. They
                        6.   7. (not)
do not want her to play soccer. They say, "Soccer _____ for girls. Marriage
                                                            8. (not)
_____ for girls. Look at your sister. Your sister _____ a soccer
        9.   10. (not)
player, and she _____ about to marry." Parminder says, "I _____
                        11.   12. (not)
my sister."

6 UNIT 1

EXERCISE 4: Subject Pronouns and Contractions

(Grammar Notes 3, 5)

Change the underlined words. Change nouns to pronouns and write contractions of **be.**

1. Lionel Messi is from Argentina. <u>Messi is</u> a great soccer player.
   He's

2. Mr. Smith is a soccer fan. <u>Mr. Smith is</u> a football fan too.

3. My partner and I are on a soccer team. <u>My partner and I are</u> not on a football team.

4. Soccer is a great sport. <u>Soccer is</u> popular all over the world.

5. Parminder Nagra and Halle Berry are actors. <u>Nagra and Berry are</u> talented.

6. Ms. Brown is an English teacher. <u>Ms. Brown is</u> a supervisor too.

7. Tennis and ping-pong are great sports. <u>Tennis and ping-pong are</u> exciting games.

EXERCISE 5: Affirmative and Negative Contractions

(Grammar Notes 1–4)

Write true sentences with the words in parentheses. Use the affirmative or negative. Use contractions when possible.

1. Lionel Messi is a soccer player. (He / popular all over the world)

   He's popular all over the world.

2. Soccer is a great game. (It / popular in my country)

   _____

3. Rafael Nadal is a tennis player. (He / from Spain)

   _____

4. Cristiano Ronaldo and David Beckham are famous. (They / talented soccer players)

   _____

5. (I / a student)

   _____

6. (I / from London)

   _____

7. (My friends and I / soccer fans)

   _____

8. (Soccer / my favorite sport)

   _____

EXERCISE 6: Editing

Correct the paragraph. There are nine mistakes. The first mistake is already corrected. Find and correct eight more.

> My family *is* in Mexico. I in Los Angeles. My father is a businessman, and my mother a math teacher. Alessandra is my sister. She an engineer. Marco is my brother. Is in the family business with my father. We all soccer fans. Our favorite team is the Club de Fútbol Monterrey. Our team on TV very often. I call my family, and we talk about the game on TV. They far away, but thanks to email and cell phones, we close.

STEP 4 COMMUNICATION PRACTICE

EXERCISE 7: Pronunciation

A | *Read and listen to the Pronunciation Note.*

Pronunciation Note
Some students confuse **he** and **she**. To pronounce **he** and **she** correctly, follow these tips: • **Smile** when you say **he** or **he's**. • **Relax** your lips to say **she** or **she's**.

B | *Listen to the sentences. Check (✓) the correct box.*

	He's	She's
1.		✓
2.		
3.		
4.		
5.		
6.		

C | *Listen again and repeat.*

EXERCISE 8: Listening

A | *PAIRS: Look at the pictures. Do you know these talented people? Try to complete the chart with the words from the box. Follow the example answer.*

| actor [ˈæktə] | Argentina | ~~baseball player~~ | England | ice skater | Korea | soccer player | Ukraine |
| actress [ˈæktrɪs] | Barbados | Brazil 巴西 | film director [diˈrektə] | ~~Japan~~ | singer [ˈsɪŋə] | Taiwan | writer |

Name	Hideki Matsui	Lionel Messi	Rihanna	Kim Yu-na
Occupation	baseball player			
Country of Origin	Japan			

Name	Rob Pattinson	Olga Kurylenko	Paulo Coehlo	Ang Lee
Occupation				
Country of Origin				

B | *Listen and write the correct occupation and country of origin for each person. Discuss your answers with your partner.*

EXAMPLE: **A:** Who is Hideki Matsui?
B: He's a soccer player from Japan.
A: He's from Japan, but he's not a soccer player. He's a baseball player.

C | *Listen again and check your answers.*

EXERCISE 9: Talking about Occupations

A | *PAIRS: Look at the occupations. Make a list of other occupations. Check (✓) your occupation and the occupations of your relatives and friends.*

_____   _____
_____   _____
_____   _____

❑ a nurse   ❑ a stay-at-home mom or dad   ❑ a doctor   ❑ an athlete

❑ a plumber   ❑ a writer   ❑ an electrician   ❑ a detective

❑ a lawyer   ❑ a carpenter

B | *Talk about the occupations of your relatives and friends. Use the words from the box.*

boring	dangerous	difficult	exciting	interesting

EXAMPLE: **A:** My cousin is a detective. His job is dangerous, but it's interesting.
B: My uncle is a businessman. His job is difficult.

EXERCISE 10: Talking about Talented People

A | *PAIRS: Look at the list of qualities. Add four more qualities to the list.*

时灾

成功的
successful   funny   smart   hardworking

_____   _____   _____   _____

B | *Fill in the circles with information about a talented person you know. Then tell your partner.*

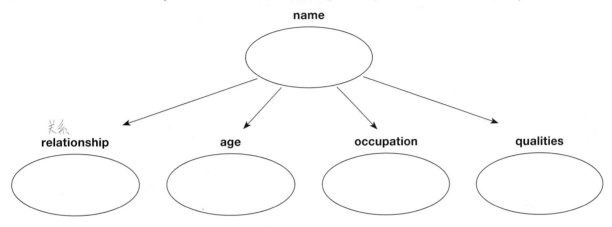

关系

relationship   age   occupation   qualities

> **EXAMPLE:**   Noah is my brother. He's 19 years old. He's a baseball player and a musician. He's talented and hardworking. His dream is to be a great musician. Noah is not famous now. But one day everyone will know him.

EXERCISE 11: Writing

A | *Write four sentences about a famous person from Exercise 8 or a talented friend or relative. Give the person's name, country, and qualities. Add any information you know about the person. Use the present form of* **be**.

> **EXAMPLE:**   Hideki Matsui is a baseball player. He's from Japan. His nickname is "Godzilla." He's big and strong and talented.

B | *Check your work. Use the Editing Checklist.*

Editing Checklist

Did you . . . ?
☐ use the present form of *be* correctly
☐ use a subject and verb in each sentence
☐ check your spelling

A | *Complete the sentences. Use* **am, is,** *or* **are.**

1. My brother and I _____is_____ baseball fans.

2. Our favorite sport _____is_____ baseball.

3. I _____am_____ a good baseball player.

4. My brother _____is_____ a good baseball player too.

5. We _____are_____ athletes.

B | *Complete the sentences. Use* **'m, 's,** *or* **'re.**

1. I'am from Korea.

2. She's from Brazil.

3. We're in school in New York.

4. It's a good school.

5. We're happy to be here.

C | *Change the underlined words. Change nouns to pronouns and use contractions.*

1. <u>Lionel Messi is not</u> in Argentina now. *He isn't*

2. <u>Soccer and baseball are</u> exciting sports. *They're*

3. <u>My partner and I are not</u> baseball fans. *We're not*

4. <u>Ms. Nagra is</u> the star of the movie *Bend It Like Beckham*. *She's*

D | *Correct the paragraph. There are six mistakes.*

My father and mother are from India, but they're in Canada now. My parents are doctors. My father a sports doctor, and my mother she is a foot doctor. My parents and I love sports. My father are a soccer fan, and my mother a baseball fan. I'm a soccer fan. My father and I am fans of Lionel Messi and Nuno Gomes. My sister no is good at sports. She's not a sports fan. She loves movies.

UNIT 2 Present of *Be*: *Yes / No* Questions and *Wh-* Questions

FIRST DAY OF SCHOOL

Before You Read

A | *Talk to four students. Write their names in the chart. Ask them the question, "Are you always on time for _____?" Write **Yes** or **No** for each response.*

Are you always on time for these things?				
Student's name	**School**	**Work**	**Dates**	**Parties**

EXAMPLE: **MARIA:** Juan, are you always on time for school?
JUAN: Yes, I am.

B | *Report to the class.*

EXAMPLE: **MARIA:** Juan is always on time for school. Sekura is always on time for dates.

🎧 *It's the first day of an English class. Read the conversation.*

ARRIVING IN CLASS

LIDA KOZLOV: Excuse me. **Where's room 2?**

ALEX BROWN: It's right here, next to the office.

LIDA: Thanks. Uh . . . **are we late for class?**

ALEX: No, we're right on time.

LIDA: Whew! That's good. I hate to be late on the first day. **Is the teacher here?**

ALEX: Yes, he is.

LIDA: **How is he? Is he a good teacher?**

ALEX: I think he's very good. My name is Alex, by the way. **What's your name?**

LIDA: Lida.

ALEX: Nice to meet you. **Are you new here?**

LIDA: Yes, I am.

ALEX: Nice jacket.

LIDA: Thanks. It's from Italy.

ALEX: Oh, **are you from Italy?**

LIDA: No, I'm from Moscow. Hey, your English is so good! . . . **Where are you from?**

ALEX: I'm from Michigan.

LIDA: Michigan? But that's in the United States. **Are you in the right class?**

ALEX: Yes, I am.

LIDA: **Why are you here? Who are you?**

ALEX: I'm not a new student. I'm a new teacher. I'm your new teacher.

LIDA: Oh . . . !

A | Practice *PAIRS: Read the conversation again aloud.*

B | Vocabulary *Complete the sentences with the words from the box. Remember to start sentences with a capital letter.*

by the way	excuse me	on time	right	room

1. _excuse me_, where's the elevator?

2. Your class is in _room_ 102 next to the stairs. 楼梯

3. Room 202 is _right_ over there, near the elevator.

4. We're _on time_. We're not late or early.

5. Thanks for the coffee. _by the way_, is the computer lab nearby?
实验室

C | Comprehension *Read the questions. Circle the correct letter.*

1. Are Lida and Alex on time for class?

   a. Yes, they are.   **b.** No, they're late.   **c.** They're early for class.

2. Where is Lida from?

   a. Italy   **b.** Michigan   **c.** Russia

3. Where is Michigan?

   a. in the United States   **b.** in Mexico   **c.** in Italy

4. Are Lida and Alex students?

   a. He is, but she isn't.   **b.** She is, but he isn't.   **c.** Yes, they are.

5. What's the teacher's name?

   a. Lida Kozlov   **b.** Alex Brown   **c.** Alex Kozlov

6. What do you know is true? Alex is ___.

   a. not in the right class   **b.** a good teacher   **c.** Lida's teacher

PRESENT OF *BE*: *YES* / *NO* QUESTIONS AND *WH-* QUESTIONS

Yes / *No* Questions

Singular		
Be	Subject	
Am	I	
Are	you	
	he	in room 2?
Is	she	
	it	

Plural		
Be	Subject	
	we	
Are	you	on time?
	they	

Short Answers

Singular			
Yes		No	
	you **are**.		you**'re not**. you **aren't**.
	I **am**.		I**'m not**.
Yes,	he **is**.	No,	he**'s not**. he **isn't**.
	she **is**.		she**'s not**. she **isn't**.
	it **is**.		it**'s not**. it **isn't**.

Plural			
Yes		No	
	you **are**.		you**'re not**. you **aren't**.
Yes,	we **are**.	No,	we**'re not**. we **aren't**.
	they **are**.		they**'re not**. they **aren't**.

Wh- Questions

Wh- Word	*Be*	Subject		Short Answers	Long Answers
Where		you	from?	Michigan.	I'm from Michigan.
Why	are	you	here?	I'm the teacher.	I'm here because I'm the teacher.
What		your	name?	Alex.	My name is Alex.
How	is	he?		Good.	He's a good teacher.
Who		she?		A student.	She's a student.

GRAMMAR NOTES

1	*Yes / no* **questions** usually have a *yes* or *no* answer.	**A:** Is he a student? **B: Yes**, he is. OR **No**, he isn't.
Wh- **questions** ask for information.	**A: Who** is he? **B:** He's the teacher.

2 | Use *am*, *is*, or *are* before a subject in *yes / no* **questions**. | BE   SUBJECT
• **Am** I in English 2?
• **Is** she a student?
• **Are** we late?

3 | We usually **answer** *yes / no* **questions** with short answers, but we can also give long answers.

BE CAREFUL! Do not use contractions in short answers with *yes*. | **A:** Are you a new student?
B: Yes. OR **Yes, I am.** OR **Yes, I am new.**

NOT: Yes, I'm.

4 | *Wh-* **questions** ask about the following:
Who ➞ people
What ➞ things
Where ➞ places
When ➞ time
How ➞ in what way

Why asks for a reason. We can give short or long answers. In long answers, use *because* before the reason. | • **Who** are they?
• **What** is in your bag?
• **Where** is our classroom?
• **When** is lunch?
• **How** is school?

A: Why are you late?
B: My bus was late. OR I'm late **because** my bus was late.

5 | Use a *wh-* **word** before *is* or *are* in *wh-* questions. | WH- WORD   BE
• **What** **is** your name?
• **Where** **are** the books?

6 | You can use **contractions** (short forms) with *wh-* words in speaking and informal writing.

We usually don't write the contraction with *are*. | • **Where's** the library?
• **When's** the class trip?

SPOKEN ONLY: Where're the kids?

7 | We usually give short answers to *wh-* questions. We can also give long answers. | **A:** Where are you from?
B: Mexico. OR **I'm from Mexico.**

8 | When we do not know the answer to a question, we say, "I don't know."

When someone asks a *yes / no* question that we think is true, we say, "Yes, I think so." If we think it is not true, we can say, "No, I don't think so." | **A:** Is the men's room nearby?
B: I don't know.

A: Is she in the library?
B: Yes, I think so. OR **No, I don't think so.**

EXERCISE 1: Discover the Grammar

Look at the picture. Match the questions and answers.

__e__ **1.** Is the door open?

__c__ **2.** What time is it?

__a__ **3.** Is the teacher a man?

__b__ **4.** Are the students hungry?

__h__ **5.** Is the woman at the door early?

__f__ **6.** Is the woman at the door unhappy?

__d__ **7.** Where is the teacher?

__g__ **8.** What month is it?

a. Yes, he is.

b. I don't know.

c. It's ten o'clock.

d. Near the blackboard.

e. No, it's not.

f. No, she's late.

g. September.

h. Yes, I think so.

EXERCISE 2: *Yes / No* Questions

(Grammar Note 2)

*Write **yes / no** questions about the statements in parentheses.*

1. (Today is Friday.) *Is today Friday?*

2. (We are in the right building.) Are we in the right building?

3. (You are a new student.) Are you a new student?

4. (The teacher is from Canada.) Is teacher from Canada

5. (It's ten o'clock.) Is it ten o'clock

6. (They are new computers.) _Are they new computers?_

7. (Two students are absent today.) _Are they absent today?_

8. (I'm in the right room.) _Am I in the right room?_

EXERCISE 3: Word Order of *Yes / No* Questions

(Grammar Notes 1–3)

*Write **yes / no** questions with the words in parentheses. Then write true short answers.*
*Use contractions when possible. Use **yes / no, I don't know,** or **I think so / I don't think so.***

1. (you / Are / usually early)

  A: _Are you usually early?_

  B: _Yes, I am. OR No, I'm not._

2. (your watch / fast / Is)

  A: _Is your watch fast?_

  B: _No, I don't know._

3. (from Italy / your jacket / Is)

  A: _Is your jacket form Italy?_

  B: _Yes. It is._

4. (your birthday / in the spring / Is)

  A: _Is your birthday in the spring?_

  B: _No It isn't_

5. (your name / Is / easy to pronounce)

  A: _Is your name easy to pronounce?_

  B: _Yes. it is_

6. (different cities / Are / from / you and your classmates)

  A: _Are you and your classmates from different cities?_

  B: _Yes, we are_

7. (busy / Are / your classmates / now)

  A: _Are your classmates busy now?_

  B: _No, We're not._

EXERCISE 4: _Wh-_ Questions (Grammar Notes 1–4)

Read the answers. Then write **wh-** questions with the words in parentheses.

1. **A:** (Who) _Who's Alex Brown?_

   B: Alex Brown is the teacher.

2. **A:** (Where) _Where are the computers_

   B: The computers are in room 304.

3. **A:** (What) _What is date today's?_

   B: Today's date is September 3.

4. **A:** (Why) _Why are your late?_

   B: We're late because we were in the wrong classroom.

5. **A:** (Why) _Why're you late?_

   B: She's the teacher because Alex isn't here today.

6. **A:** (How) _How is your computer class?_

   B: My computer class is great.

EXERCISE 5: _Yes / No_ Questions and _Wh-_ Questions (Grammar Notes 1–8)

A | _Read Alejandra's question on SmartGirl's blog. Write questions with the words in parentheses. Then write short answers._

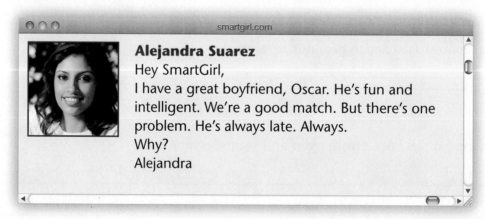

smartgirl.com

Alejandra Suarez
Hey SmartGirl,
I have a great boyfriend, Oscar. He's fun and intelligent. We're a good match. But there's one problem. He's always late. Always.
Why?
Alejandra

1. (Oscar / fun)

   A: _Is Oscar fun?_

   B: _Yes, he is._

2. (Oscar / smart)

   A: _Is Oscar smart?_

   B: _No, he isn't_

3. (Alejandra and Oscar / a good pair)

   A: _Are Alejandra and Oscar a good pair?_

   B: _No they aren't._

4. (Who / always late)

   A: _Who is always late_

   B: _Oscar_

B | *Now read SmartGirl's answer. Write **yes** / **no** questions. Use the words in parentheses. Then answer the questions with **Yes, I think so, No, I don't think so,** or **I don't know.***

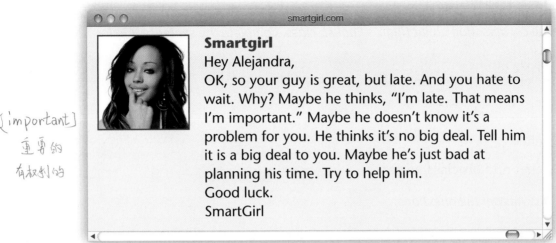

[important]
重要的
有权利的

Smartgirl
Hey Alejandra,
OK, so your guy is great, but late. And you hate to wait. Why? Maybe he thinks, "I'm late. That means I'm important." Maybe he doesn't know it's a problem for you. He thinks it's no big deal. Tell him it is a big deal to you. Maybe he's just bad at planning his time. Try to help him.
Good luck.
SmartGirl

1. (Oscar / great)

   A: Is Oscar great?

   B: _I don't know._

2. (Oscar / a bad boyfriend)

   A: _Is Oscar a bad boyfried?_

   B: _No. I don't think So._

计划 [plan]

3. (Oscar / bad at planning time)

   A: _Is Oscan bad at planning time?_

   B: _Yes. I think so._

4. (Smartgirl's answer / good)

   A: _Are Smartgirl's answer good?_

   B: _____

EXERCISE 6: Editing

Correct the conversations. There are nine mistakes. The first mistake is already corrected. Find and correct eight more.

1. A: Are you in the office?

         I am
   B: Yes, ~~I'm.~~

2. A: Is easy?

   B: No, it's hard.

3. A: He Korean?

   B: No, he's isn't.

4. A: Excuse me. Where's the office?

   B: Yes, it's here.

5. A: Is this English 3?

   B: Yes, I think.

6. A: Is they in room 102?

   B: I don't know.

7. A: Where you from?

   B: I'm from Peru.

8. A: How your class is?

   B: It's very good.

9. A: What your nickname?

   B: Susie.

EXERCISE 7: Listening

A | *Listen to the conversation about Hugo's English class. Complete the sentence. Circle the correct letter.*

In the conversation, Hugo talks about _____.

a. his teacher, his classmates, and himself

b. his teacher

c. his teacher and his classmates

B | *Listen again. Answer the questions.*

1. Where is Hugo's teacher from?   He's from _____.

2. How old is the teacher?   He's about _____.

3. Where are his classmates from?   They're from Mexico, Chile, Canada, Poland,

_____, and _____.

4. What is Hugo good at?   He's good at _____.

EXERCISE 8: Pronunciation

A | *Read and listen to the Pronunciation Note.*

Pronunciation Note

In *yes / no questions*, your voice goes **up** at the end of the sentence.

EXAMPLES: Are you from Italy?   Are you the teacher?

In *wh- questions*, your voice goes **down** at the end of the sentence.

EXAMPLES: Where is he from?   What's his name?

B | *Listen to the questions. Notice how the voice goes up or down at the end of each question.*

1. Are classes on weekends?   **5.** What's your email address?

2. Is it from Italy?   **6.** Who's the director of your program?

3. Am I in the right room?   **7.** Where are your boots from?

4. Is the test tomorrow?   **8.** How's school?

C | *Listen again and repeat.*

EXERCISE 9: Asking and Answering Questions

PAIRS: Look at Exercise 2 on page 18. Take turns. Ask your partner the questions. Use **yes / no** *short answers or* **I don't know, I think so,** *or* **I don't think so.**

EXERCISE 10: Role Play: Meeting at a Party

PAIRS: Imagine you and your partner are at a party. Give yourself a new name, a new country, and a new occupation. Introduce yourself to your partner.

> EXAMPLE: **A:** Hi, I'm Eun Young.
> **B:** Nice to meet you. I'm Ana. Are you from around here?
> **A:** No, I'm from Korea. I'm here on business. What about you?

EXERCISE 11: Writing

A *PAIRS: Read the ad for University Language School. Together write five* **wh-** *questions and five* **yes / no** *questions. Read your questions to other pairs. They close their books and answer your questions.*

LEARN ENGLISH AT ULS!

Register now for English classes at University Language School

Placement Test: Sept. 1 in Room 203

Classes begin September 8

Director: Jim Reilly

phone: 989-870-3456
email : ULS@GreatSchools.com
University Language School   650 Elm Street, Long Beach, New York

> EXAMPLES: **A:** Where is ULS?
> **B:** Who's the director?
> **A:** Is ULS in Canada?

B *Check your work. Use the Editing Checklist.*

Editing Checklist
Did you . . . ? ☐ use the correct word order for *yes / no* and *wh-* questions ☐ check your spelling

2 Review

Check your answers on page UR-1.

Do you need to review anything?

A | Complete the questions. Circle the correct word or words.

1. A: (Where's) / What's the library? **B:** In room 3.

2. A: Who's / (How's) your class? **B:** It's great.

3. A: (What's) / How's your name? **B:** Jin-Hee Lee.

4. A: Is / (Are) you from Seoul? **B:** Yes, I am.

5. A: (Is) / Are it cold in Seoul now? **B:** No, it isn't.

B | Complete the short answers.

1. A: Are you home? **B:** Yes, _____.

2. A: Is your nickname JD? **B:** No, _____.

3. A: Are they late? **B:** No, _____.

4. A: Are we in the right room? **B:** Yes, _____.

5. A: Am I late? **B:** No, _____.

C | Write questions. Use the words in parentheses.

1. ___What is today's date?_____ ?
   (What / today's date)

2. ___Where is the men's room?_____ ?
   (Where / the men's room)

3. ___Why he absent_____ ?
   (Why / he / absent)   使氏文體.

4. _____ ?
   (When / your first class)

5. _____ ?
   (Who / your teacher)

D | Correct the questions. There are five mistakes.

1. She your teacher?

2. What your name?

3. Where your class?

4. Is Bob and Molly good friends?

5. Why you late?

Past of *Be*: Statements, *Yes / No* Questions, *Wh-* Questions

FIRST JOBS

STEP 1 GRAMMAR IN CONTEXT

Before You Read

A | *Look at the pictures on this page and page 26. Guess the story.*

B | *PAIRS: Discuss the questions.*
  1. What was your first job?
  2. Was it easy? Was it hard?

Read

Read the story about Hugo Rubio's first job.

I **was** 16 years old. It **was** my first job. I **was** a lifeguard at a swimming pool for the summer. I **was** happy to have a job.

But I really wanted to be a hero. The weather **wasn't** hot, and the pool **wasn't** busy. Only five or six people **were** there every day. My days **were** long and boring. They **weren't** fun.

One day a woman slipped in the pool. I wanted to jump in to save her, but two guys **were** there before me.

They helped the woman, and they **were** the heroes.

(continued on next page)

[ˈfainəli] 最终

Finally it **was** the last day of the season. The pool **was** crowded. More than 50 people **were** there.

[kraud] 挤满

总监

A little boy fell in the pool. I jumped in and saved him.

[ˈmeiə] 市长

It **wasn't** a big deal, but the little boy **was** the son of the mayor. The next day my picture **was** in the paper. I **was** a hero. It **was** exciting and fun.

Lifeguard Saves Mayor's Son

After You Read

A | Practice *PAIRS: Now read the story aloud. Take turns reading each paragraph.*

B | Vocabulary *Complete the sentences with the words from the box.*

a big deal	boring	busy	make money	still

[stil]
平静的

1. I'm sorry. I don't have the report. I was very ___busy___ last week.

2. I can't study full time. I need to work and ___make money___.

3. I can work late today. It's not ___a big deal___.

4. It's 11:00 P.M. Is he ___still___ at work?

5. Every day I do the same thing. My job is ___boring___.

C | Comprehension *Answer the questions.*

1. What was Hugo's first job?   Hugo was a lifeguard.

2. How old was he?   He was 16 years old

3. Was he a hero?   Yes, he was

4. Was the job fun? Why or why not?   Yes, because he can bo heno.

5. Was Hugo happy to be in the news?   Hugo was saves mayor's son.

PAST OF *BE*: AFFIRMATIVE STATEMENTS

Singular					Plural			
Subject	*Be*		Time Marker		Subject	*Be*		Time Marker
I	was				We			
You	were	a student	last year.		You	were	in New York	two weeks ago.
He She	was				They			
It		busy						

PAST OF *BE*: NEGATIVE STATEMENTS

Singular					Plural			
Subject	*Be / Not*		Time Marker		Subject	*Be / Not*		Time Marker
I	was not wasn't				We			
You	were not weren't	at school	last night.		You	were not weren't	at work	last week.
He She It	was not wasn't				They			

PAST OF *BE*: *YES / NO* QUESTIONS

Singular				
Be	Subject		Time Marker	
Was	I			
Were	you	in the wrong room	yesterday?	
Was	he she it			

Plural				
Be	Subject		Time Marker	
Were	we you they	in the wrong building	last week?	

SHORT ANSWERS

Singular					
Yes	Subject	*Be*	*No*	Subject	*Be*
	you	were.		you	weren't.
Yes,	I he she it	was.	No,	I he she it	wasn't.

Plural					
Yes	Subject	*Be*	*No*	Subject	*Be*
	you			you	
Yes,	we	were.	No,	we	weren't.
	they			they	

PAST OF *BE*: *WH*- QUESTIONS

Wh- word	*Be*		LONG ANSWERS
What		your first job?	I was a ticket taker at a movie theater.
Where		the movie theater?	In Jacksonville, Florida.
When	**was**	the last movie over last night?	The last movie was over at 1:00 A.M.
How		the movie?	It was pretty bad.
Why		it bad?	The acting was bad.
Who	**were**	the actors?	I'm not sure.

GRAMMAR NOTES

1	The **past of *be*** has two forms: ***was*** and ***were***.	• She **was** at the airport. • They **were** late.
2	Use ***was*** or ***were*** + ***not*** to make **negative statements**.	• He **was not** at work. • They **were not** in class.
3	In informal writing and speaking, use the **contractions *wasn't*** and ***weren't*** in negative statements and negative short answers.	• He **wasn't** at an interview. • They **weren't** in class. • No, he **wasn't**. • No, they **weren't**.
4	To ask a ***yes / no* question**, put *was* or *were* before the subject. Use a ***wh*- word** before *was* or *were* in ***wh*- questions**.	BE SUBJECT • **Was** she at work? • **Were** you a server? • **How** was your day?
5	**Time markers** (*yesterday, last week, two days ago,* etc.) are usually at the end of statements. Time markers are sometimes at the beginning of statements. Time markers go at the end of a question.	• We **were** in Toronto **yesterday**. • **Yesterday** we **were** in Toronto. • **Was** he in Toronto **yesterday**?

EXERCISE 1: Discover the Grammar

Read about the first jobs of famous people. Then underline **was, wasn't, were,** *and* **weren't.**

A new job is exciting. A first job is very exciting. A first boss and a first paycheck are hard to forget. But a first job is not always the job of your dreams. Here are the first jobs of some famous people: Mick Jagger <u>wasn't</u> always a singer. As a teen he was an ice cream salesman. Ray Romano, the comedian, was a bank teller. Jennifer Aniston and Madonna weren't always stars. Before they were famous, they were servers in restaurants.

And Warren Beatty, the actor, was a rat catcher in a Virginia movie theater. So maybe you're not happy with your job today. Maybe it isn't the job you really want. Don't feel bad. Just keep looking.

EXERCISE 2: Questions and Answers

(Grammar Notes 1–4)

Complete the conversation. Use **was, wasn't, were,** *or* **weren't.**

A: _____ <u>Were</u> _____ you at work yesterday?

B: No, I _____. I _____ at a job interview.
                1.   **2.**

A: Oh? How _____ the interview?
                   3.

B: Good, I think.

A: _____ the questions hard?
          4.

B: Well, some _____ hard, but I _____ prepared.
                  5.   **6.**

A: Well, that sounds good. Good luck.

B: Thanks. It sounds like a good job. How _____ school?
                                    7.

A: It _____ fun. I really like my classmates.
          8.

B: _____ you on time?
          9.

A: Yes, but my teacher _____ there. She was away. We had a substitute.
                     10.

EXERCISE 3: Affirmative and Negative Statements

(Grammar Notes 1–3)

Complete the sentences. Change the statements from the present to the past.

1. They are busy now. Last month _____ they were busy _____ too.

2. It's not sunny today. _____ It wasn't sunny _____ yesterday either.

3. My uncle, Jun, is in Seoul now. _____ He was there _____ last year too.

4. Today it's cold. Yesterday _____ it was cold _____ too.

5. She's not in class this week. _____ she wasn't in class _____ last week.

6. He's at a job interview this morning. _____ He was at a job interview _____ yesterday morning too.

7. She's in the swimming pool now. She _____ she was in the swimming _____ last Wednesday too.

8. His phone is busy. It _____ was busy _____ yesterday evening too.

EXERCISE 4: Questions and Answers

(Grammar Notes 1–5)

Complete the conversation with the words in parentheses. Use the correct form of the past of **be**.

A: _____ Was David at the party Friday night _____ ?
   (David / be / at the party / Friday night)

B: _____ No. he wasn't. _____ .
   (No, he / not)

A: _____ Where was he _____ ?
   (Where / he)

B: _____ He was in Vancouver _____ .
   (He / in Vancouver)

A: _____ Why was hes in Vancouver _____ ?
   (Why / he / in Vancouver)

B: _____ He was there for work _____ .
   was **(He / there for work)**

A: _____ How the weather was in Vancouver _____ ?
   (How / the weather / in Vancouver)

B: _____ It was terrible _____ .
   (It / terrible)

A: _____ Was the airport closed _____ ?
   (the airport / closed)

B: _____ No, but all the planes were late _____ .
   (No, but all the planes / late)
   wasn't

EXERCISE 5: Editing

Correct the email. There are five mistakes. The first mistake is already corrected. Find and correct four more.

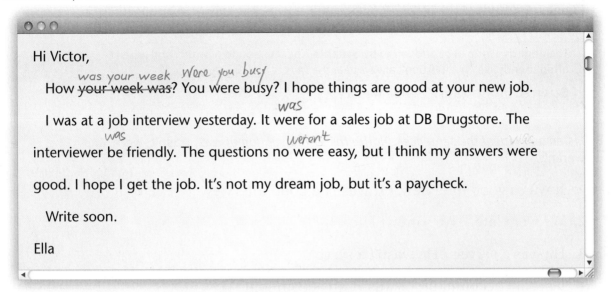

Hi Victor,

How ~~your week was~~ *was your week* *Were you busy*? ~~You were busy?~~ I hope things are good at your new job.

I was at a job interview yesterday. It ~~were~~ *was* for a sales job at DB Drugstore. The interviewer ~~be~~ *was* friendly. The questions ~~no were~~ *weren't* easy, but I think my answers were *was*

good. I hope I get the job. It's not my dream job, but it's a paycheck.

Write soon.

Ella

STEP 4 COMMUNICATION PRACTICE

EXERCISE 6: Listening

A | *Listen to the phone messages. Who is each message from? Check (✓) the correct column.*

	Friend	Family	Business
Message 1	✓		
Message 2			
Message 3			
Message 4			
Message 5			

B | *Listen again. Complete the quotes. Write the correct words or numbers.*

Message 1. "How was the ____*interview?*____"

Message 2. "The _____ was great. We _____ so happy to _____ Jay."

Message 3. "The _____ in Ottawa _____."

Message 4. "Please call me at _____."

Message 5. "We were _____ with Mona."

EXERCISE 7: Pronunciation

A | *Read and listen to the Pronunciation Note.*

> **Pronunciation Note**
>
> The **negative** form of *be* adds an **extra syllable**. The final sound of *wasn't* and *weren't* often sounds like **/ n /**. We don't always hear the **/ t /**.
>
> **EXAMPLES:**   was – **wasn't**   were – **weren't**

B | *Listen and repeat the sentences. Notice the pronunciation of* **was, wasn't, were,** *and* **weren't.**

1. It was a good interview. / It wasn't a good interview.

2. We were late. / We weren't late.

3. He was a server. / He wasn't a server.

4. I was an accountant. / I wasn't an accountant.

C | *Listen to the sentences. Which negative form do you hear? Check (✓) the correct box.*

	Was	Wasn't	Were	Weren't
1.		✓		
2.				
3.				
4.				
5.				

EXERCISE 8: Describing the Weather

A | *Study the words for weather.*

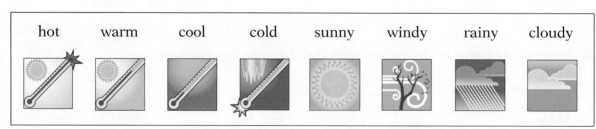

hot   warm   cool   cold   sunny   windy   rainy   cloudy

B | *PAIRS: Look at the chart below and choose a country. You are an airline flight attendant. A friend calls. Have a conversation about the weather in the country you are in. Take turns.*

A: Hello.

B: Maria? This is Bob. Where are you?

A: In _____.

B: How's the weather?

A: Well, today it's _____, but yesterday it was _____.

City	Yesterday	Today
Bangkok Asia 亚洲 Thailand		
Beijing Asia		
Budapest Europe 欧洲 Hungary		
Istanbul 伊斯坦布尔 土耳其		
Rio de Janeiro South America 南美 Brazil 巴西		
Seoul south korea		
Vancouver North America Canda		

EXERCISE 9: Talking about the First Day of School

GROUPS: Each student says one true thing about the first day in school. Use **was,** **wasn't, were,** *or* **weren't** *in each sentence. Continue as long as you can.*

> EXAMPLES: **A:** It was warm and sunny on the first day of class.
> **B:** I wasn't nervous.
> **C:** Our class was exciting.

EXERCISE 10: Writing

A | *Write an email message to a friend. Tell about last weekend. Use contractions and the past and present of* **be.**

> EXAMPLE:

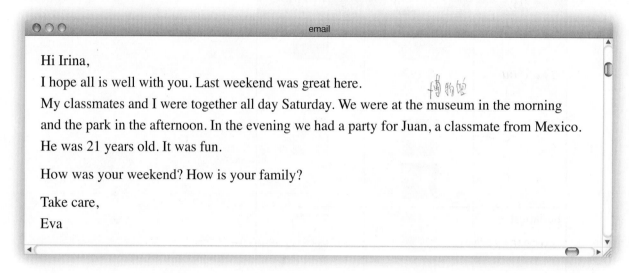

Hi Irina,

I hope all is well with you. Last weekend was great here.

My classmates and I were together all day Saturday. We were at the museum in the morning and the park in the afternoon. In the evening we had a party for Juan, a classmate from Mexico. He was 21 years old. It was fun.

How was your weekend? How is your family?

Take care,

Eva

B | *Check your work. Use the Editing Checklist.*

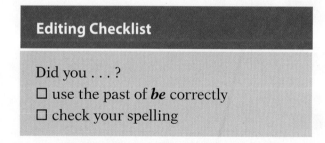

Editing Checklist

Did you . . . ?
- ☐ use the past of **be** correctly
- ☐ check your spelling

Check your answers on page UR-1.
Do you need to review anything?

A | *Complete the questions. Use* **was** *or* **were.**

1. When _____ *was* _____ your interview? 面诫

2. Where _____ *was* _____ your interview?

3. _____ *were* _____ you nervous? 焦虑.

4. How _____ *was* _____ the questions?

5. _____ *was* _____ she at a job interview too?

B | *Match the questions and answers.*

_*c*_ 1. How was the weather?   **a.** No, I wasn't.

_*b*_ 2. Who was there?   **b.** Jon and Sri.

_*d*_ 3. Were they home all evening?   **c.** Warm and sunny.

_*a*_ 4. Were you late last week?   **d.** No, they weren't.

C | *Complete the conversation. Use the affirmative or negative form of* **was** *or* **were.**

A: How _____ *was* _____ your weekend?
                    1.

B: Great. I _____ *was* _____ at the park all day Saturday.
                 2.

A: _____ *Were* _____ you with Ali?
          3.

B: Yes, I _____ *was* _____. We _____ *were* _____ together all day Saturday and
              4.   **5.**
Sunday.

A: Ali _____ *wasn't* _____ in class this morning. Where _____ *was* _____ he?
            6.   **7.**

B: I don't know.

D | *Correct the paragraph. There are four mistakes.*

     was   *was*

    John is at a job interview yesterday. It were for a job at a bank. The questions no

were easy, but John's answers were good. He was happy. It a good day for John.

weren't   *was*

From Grammar to Writing

CAPITALIZATION

1 | *Look at A and B. What's wrong with A?*

A	B
mr. john smith	Mr. John Smith
342 dryden road	342 Dryden Road
ithaca, new york	Ithaca, New York 14850

2 | *Study the information about capitalization.*

1	Use a **capital letter** for the first word in every sentence.	• **We** are new students.
2	Use capital letters for **titles**.	• This is **Mr.** Winston. • She is **Dr.** Jones.
3	Use capital letters for the names of **people** and **places** (proper nouns).	• **Lila Roberts** is from **Vancouver**, **Canada**.
4	Use capital letters for the names of **streets**, **cities**, **states**, **countries**, and **continents**.	• 5 **Elm Street** • **West Redding, Connecticut** • **USA** • **Africa**
5	Use a capital letter for the word *I*.	• **I** am happy to be here.

3 | *Add capital letters.*

1. this is ms. herrera.   *This is Ms. Herrera.*

2. her address is 4 riverdale avenue.   *Her addres is 4 Rivendale Avenue.*

3. i'm her good friend.   *I'm her good friend.*

4. she was in bangkok and taiwan last year.   *She was in Bangkok and Taiwan Last year.*

4 | *Correct the postcard from Ellen to Ruth. Add capital letters.*

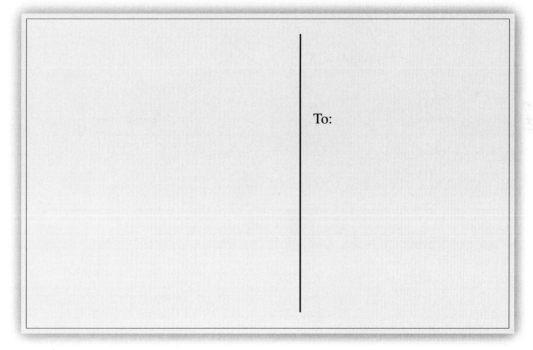

Hi ruth,

john and i are in acapulco this week. it's beautiful here. the people are friendly, and the weather is great. it's sunny and warm.

last week we were in mexico city for two days. i was there on business. my meetings were long and difficult, but our evenings were fun. hope all is well with you.

Regards,

ellen

To:

ms. ruth holland

10 oldwick st.

ringwood, new jersey 07456

usa

5 | *Write a postcard to a friend. Remember to use capital letters.*

To:

6 | *Exchange papers with a partner. Did your partner follow the directions? Correct any mistakes in grammar and spelling.*

7 | *Talk to your partner. Discuss the mistakes you made. Then rewrite your own paper and make any necessary changes.*

NOUNS, ADJECTIVES, PREPOSITIONS

名词　　　　　形容词　　　　　前置词，介词，放在前面

UNIT 4

Count Nouns and Proper Nouns

PHOTOGRAPHS AND PHOTOGRAPHERS

STEP 1 GRAMMAR IN CONTEXT

Before You Read

PAIRS: Where do you keep your photos? Talk about a photo you have.

> **EXAMPLE:** This is a photo of my sister. She's a nurse. She's 23 years old.

Read

Read the article about Henri Cartier-Bresson and one of his photographs.

A PHOTOGRAPHER AND A PHOTO

Henri Cartier-Bresson was **a photographer** and **an artist**. He was born in **France** in 1908. He died in 2004. At that time he was almost 96 **years** old. **Cartier-Bresson** traveled the **world**. He was in **West Africa**, the **United States**, **India**, **China**, **Egypt**, and **Russia**. His **photos** are from all over the **world**.

Cartier-Bresson is famous for "street" **photography**. Street **photographs** are about **people** in the **street** or other public **places** such as **parks** and **beaches**. They are sometimes about a special **moment** in **time**.

Look at this **photo** by **Cartier-Bresson**. Do you like it? It's **a photo** of **a woman** and **a man** on the **holiday** of **Easter**. They are both wearing fine **clothes**. The **woman** is wearing a big **hat** with many **flowers**. The man is wearing **a suit**. The **man** is looking at the **woman**. They are in **Harlem**, in **New York City**. It's 1947. **People** say **Cartier-Bresson's photos** are striking and beautiful. What do you think? Is it true for this **photo**?

Handwritten notes in margins:

artist
[ɑ:tɪst]
艺术家
[ˈtrævl]

Africa
[ˈæfrɪkə]
非洲

旅行

public 公共的
such 如此的
photographer
[fəˈtɒɡrəfə]
摄影师

striking 惊人的
true 真实的
photography
[fəˈtɒɡrəfi]
照相艺术

striking
惊人的
引足目的.

After You Read

A | Practice *PAIRS: Now read the article aloud. Take turns reading each paragraph.*

B | Vocabulary *Circle the best meaning for the words in blue.*

1. Henri Cartier-Bresson **was born** in France.

   ⓐ came into the world   **b.** lived

2. He was **almost** 96 years old.

   ⓐ less than   **b.** more than

3. His photos are from **all over** the world.

   a. in some parts of   ⓑ everywhere in

4. It's a **holiday**.

   ⓐ a day when you do not work   **b.** a birthday or anniversary

5. His photos are **striking** and beautiful.

   a. very dangerous 危险的   ⓑ unusual and attractive 周年纪念.
   不平常的

6. A holiday is a **special** time. It is exciting and different.

   ⓐ not ordinary   **b.** bad
   普通的

C | Comprehension *Write **T** (**True**) or **F** (**False**) for each statement.*

_F_ **1.** The place of Henri Cartier-Bresson's birth was Russia.

_F_ **2.** Almost all of Cartier-Bresson's photos were of Europe.

_T_ **3.** Cartier-Bresson was in many countries during his life.

_F_ **4.** Cartier-Bresson is famous for "street" photography.

_T_ **5.** Street photography shows people in places like parks or beaches.

_F_ **6.** Harlem, New York, is not in the United States.

during
[ˈdjuəriŋ]
在一期间
当……时候

Cartier-Bresson,
Automobile Show, Paris. 1968

SINGULAR AND PLURAL COUNT NOUNS; PROPER NOUNS

Singular Nouns	Plural Nouns
He is **a photographer**.	They are **photographers**.
He is **an artist**.	They are **artists**.

Irregular Plural Nouns

Singular	Plural
man	men
woman	women
child	children
foot	feet
tooth	teeth
person	people

Proper Nouns

Harlem is in **New York City**.

The poet **Maya Angelou** has a home in **Harlem**.

['Pauit]
诗人. 富有想象的艺术家

GRAMMAR NOTES

1	**Nouns** are names of people, places, and things.	• a **student**, **Jung Eun** • a **country**, **Korea** • a **camera**, a **photograph**
2	**Count nouns** are easy to count. They have a singular and plural form. 复数	• **one** photo, **two** photos, **three** photos
3	Use **a** before **singular count nouns** that begin with a **consonant sound** like / n / , / b / , / h / .	• She's **a n**urse. • He's **a b**aker. • It's **a h**ouse.
	BE CAREFUL! Use **a** before a **u** that sounds like "*yew*."	• This is **a u**nit about nouns. 单位 名词
	Use **an** before singular count nouns that begin with a **vowel sound**.	• She's **an a**rtist. • He's **an e**ngineer. 工程师 • It's **an u**mbrella.
	BE CAREFUL! Use **an** before an **h** that is silent.	• It's **an h**our too early. (*Hour* sounds like *our*.)

4	To form the **plural** of most **count nouns**, add -*s* or -*es*.	叠数	• one **friend** three **friends**
			• one **class** three **classes**
	Some nouns have irregular plural endings.		• one **man** two **men**
			• one **tooth** two **teeth**
	Some nouns such as *clothes*, *glasses*, *jeans*, *scissors* are always plural.	加上(的)	• My **jeans are** blue.
	Do not put *a* or *an* before plural nouns.		• They are **photos** of **friends**. NOT: They are a photos of a friends.
5	Names of specific people and places are **proper nouns**. Write these with a capital letter.	适当的	• **Paris** is in **France**. • **Harlem** is in **New York City**.
	Do not put *a* or *an* before proper nouns.		NOT: A Paris is in a France.

REFERENCE NOTE

For the **spelling and pronunciation** rules for **plural nouns**, see Appendix 5 on pages A-5–A-6.

STEP 3 FOCUSED PRACTICE

EXERCISE 1: Discover the Grammar 语法

A | *Read the conversation.*

MIKE: Is that you in the photo?

DOUG: Yes, it is. It's a photo of me with friends from college.

MIKE: Where are they now?

DOUG: Well, the woman on the left, Jasmine, is in Brazil.

MIKE: Really?

DOUG: Uh-huh. She's a teacher there. And the guy on the right, Bob, is here in New York. He's an accountant. 会计

MIKE: Who's the woman in the center? [ˈsɛntə] 中央. 中心

DOUG: That's Amy. She's a street photographer. Her camera is always with her. What a life! She travels all over the world. Last month she was in India. Before that she was in Central America. Now her photos are in a show at the library here.

MIKE: I'd love to see them.

DOUG: Them? Or her?

B | *Look back at the conversation in Part A. Find these nouns and write them:*

1. One noun that begins with a vowel: _____artist_____
元音

2. Two singular nouns that begin with a consonant (not proper nouns):
辅音

_____, _____

3. Two proper nouns: _____, _____

4. Two plural nouns: _____, _____
复数

EXERCISE 2: *A or An*   *(Grammar Note 3)*

A | *Write **a** or **an** before each word.*

1. _a_ man   **6.** _a_ suit

2. _a_ hand   **7.** _an_ eye

3. _a_ hat   **8.** _an_ ear

4. _an_ earring   **9.** _a_ lip

5. _a_ flower   **10.** _a_ woman

B | *Look at the photo,* Harlem, 1947. *Label the parts of the photo with the words from Part A. Number them **1–10**.*

EXERCISE 3: *A* or *An*

(Grammar Notes 3–5)

*Complete the sentences with **a** or **an**. Write Ø if you don't need **a** or **an**.*

1. Henri Cartier-Bresson was __a__ photographer. 摄影师

2. Cartier-Bresson and Ansel Adams were __Ø__ photographers.

3. Cartier-Bresson was __an__ artist too.

4. All good photographers are __Ø__ artists.

5. Adams was __a__ pianist before he was __a__ photographer.

6. Adams was born in __Ø__ San Francisco, California.

7. For Adams, photography began with __a__ trip to Yosemite National Park.

8. __Ø__ Cartier-Bresson was born in __Ø__ Normandy.

9. __Ø__ Normandy is in __Ø__ France.

10. Cartier-Bresson has __Ø__ photos in the Louvre Museum.

EXERCISE 4: Regular and Irregular Plural Nouns

(Grammar Note 4)

Complete the sentences with the nouns from the box. Use the correct form. Look at the spelling rules for plural nouns in Appendix 5 on page A-5 for help.

artist	class	country	fish	life	person
city	clothes	earrings	flower	museum	watch

1. San Francisco and Los Angeles are ____cities____ in California.

2. Brazil and France are ____country____.

3. The Louvre and the Prado are ____museum____.

4. Seiko and Rolex are kinds of ____watch____.

5. Your photos of ____fish____ in the water are striking. 醒目的

6. There are two ____person____, a man and a woman, in the photo *Harlem, 1947*.

7. The woman in *Harlem, 1947* has a hat with ____flower____.

8. Her jewelry is beautiful, especially her ____earrings____. 宝石类

9. The man and woman in the photo *Harlem, 1947* are wearing fine ____clothes____. 格外的,特别的

10. Many ____artist____ and photographers live in New York City. 黑人住宅区

11. The ____life____ of famous artists are interesting to read.

12. I like photography. I'm taking two photography ____class____ at The New
School in New York. 照相老术

EXERCISE 5: Proper Nouns

(Grammar Note 5)

Change small letters to capital letters where necessary.

MIKE: Hi, are you ~~amy~~ *Amy* lan?

AMY: Yes, I am.

MIKE: I'm ~~mike cho~~ *Mike Cho*. I work with Doug.

AMY: Nice to meet you, ~~mike~~ *Mike*.

MIKE: It's nice to meet you. Your photos are great.

AMY: Thanks. So, ~~mike~~ *Mike*, are you from ~~phoenix~~ *Phoenix*?

MIKE: No, I'm not. I'm from ~~san francisco~~ *San Francisco*. I'm here for the Labor Day holiday.

AMY: Oh, ~~san francisco~~ *San Francisco* is beautiful. I was there last year.

MIKE: Doug says you travel a lot.

AMY: Yes, I do. I was in ~~india~~ *India* last year. And the year before that I was in almost every country in Central America.

MIKE: That's great.

AMY: Do you travel?

MIKE: When I can. I was in ~~mexico~~ *Mexico* last ~~november~~ *November* during the thanksgiving vacation, and I was in ~~canada~~ *Canada* with my family for a week last summer.

AMY: Any photos?

MIKE: No. My dad's brother sam is the photographer in our family.

EXERCISE 6: Editing

Correct the sentences. There are nine mistakes. The first mistake is already corrected. Find and correct eight more.

1. Henri Cartier-Bresson's photos are often of famous ~~person~~ *people*.

2. This is *a* photo of Henri Matisse.

3. Henri Matisse was *an* great artist.

4. Before Matisse was *a* artist, he was *a* lawyer.

5. Matisse's ~~paintings~~ *painting* ~~are~~ *is* in museum all over the world.

6. In this photo Matisse is in the south of ~~france~~ *France*.

7. We see four ~~bird~~ *birds* outside their cages.

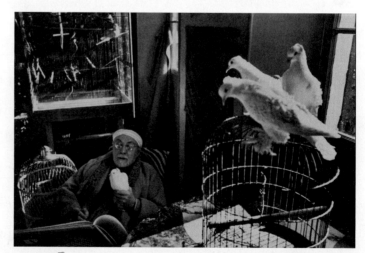

Matisse and His Doves, 1944

EXERCISE 7: Pronunciation

A | *Read and listen to the Pronunciation Note.*

Pronunciation Note
When **nouns are plural**, the **ending** can have one of three sounds: / s / , / z / , or / ɪz /.
EXAMPLES: students / s / teachers / z / buses / ɪz /

B | *Listen and complete each sentence with the correct word from the box. Then listen again and check the ending of the sound that you hear.*

artists	books	boxes	classes	glasses	~~photos~~	scissors

	/ s /	/ z /	/ ɪz /
1. The ___photos___ are ready.	☐	☑	☐
2. Her art ___classes___ are from 10:00 to 1:00.	☐	☐	☑
3. Be careful. The ___scissors___ are sharp.	☐	☑	☐
4. The ___boxes___ are full of old photos.	☐	☐	☐
5. The paintings are by different ___artists___.	☐	☐	☐
6. I need my ___glasses___ to see the names of the artists.	☐	☐	☑
7. I have some interesting ___books___ about Africa in that bookcase.	☐	☐	☐

C | *Listen again and repeat.*

EXERCISE 8: Listening

A | *Listen to a conversation between Doug and Lily. What is Lily telling Doug about? Circle the correct letter.*

a. a birthday party

b. a holiday

c. a family photo

1. Who are the people in the photo?

    a. Lily's family and friends   **b.** Lily's family

2. What is the holiday?

    a. Easter   b. Thanksgiving

3. Who is the photographer?

    a. a cousin   b. an uncle

4. When is Lily's birthday?

    a. before Thanksgiving   b. after Thanksgiving

5. What is in the boxes?

    a. gifts   b. games

EXERCISE 9: Game: Describing Things

PAIRS: Look at these things. You have 15 minutes. Together list as many nouns as you can. The pair with the most correct nouns wins.

EXERCISE 10: Game: Comparing Choices

A | *PAIRS: Name the following people, places, and things.*

an artist or a photographer	
an artist or a photographer	
a music band	
three countries	China Canada Japan
three things in your class	pen book paper box
three parts of the body	eye ear hand foot
two holidays	Christmas Thanksgiving
three occupations	doctor nurse Lawyer
two electronic items	TV computer

B | *Compare your choices with those of another pair. How many of the same choices do you have?*

EXERCISE 11: Writing

A | *Write a paragraph about a photo of a person you know. Tell about the person. Tell about the photo.*

EXAMPLE: This is a photo of my grandmother. She was born in China in 1945. She lives in Los Angeles now. She was a dancer. In this photo she's in her garden. It was her birthday. My grandmother is old, but she is still a striking woman.

B | *Check your work. Use the Editing Checklist.*

Editing Checklist

Did you . . . ?
☐ use singular and plural count nouns and proper nouns correctly
☐ check your spelling

UNIT 4 Review

Check your answers on page UR-1.

Do you need to review anything?

A | Complete the sentences. Use **a, an,** or ∅.

1. This is __a__ photo of my best friend.

2. He is __an__ actor.

3. He is __∅__ talented. 天才

4. His friends are __∅__ actors too.

5. They all are __∅__ hardworking.

B | Complete the sentences with the words from the box. Use the plural form.

city	clothes	fish	person	watch

1. My favorite ~~city~~ cities are Venice and Rio de Janeiro.

2. The two __watches__ in the photograph show midnight.

3. The __clothes__ in the photos are from the 1980s, so the photos are probably from that time. 大概的

4. We take photos of the __fish__ in the sea with our underwater camera.

5. We see three ~~person~~ people in the photo: a man and two women.

C | Add capital letters where necessary.

ALI: Hi, are you the photographer?

AMY: Yes, I'm Amy Lin.

ALI: Nice to meet you. I'm ali Mohammed.

AMY: Are you from london?

ALI: Yes, I am. I'm here for your thanksgiving Day holiday.

D | Correct the paragraph. There are six mistakes. 弄错

Melanie Einzig is artist and an photographer. She was born in Minnesota, but lives in New york. Einzig captures moments in time. Her photograph are striking. They are in museum in San francisco, Chicago, and Princeton.

Descriptive Adjectives
CAVE HOMES

STEP 1 GRAMMAR IN CONTEXT

Before You Read

Look at the photographs on this page. What words describe them?

beautiful   **boring**   **exciting**   **ordinary**   **ugly**   **unusual**

Read

Read the online article about an interesting place.

rock formations

underground caves

Cappadocia, a Place of Mystery

This place is like another world, but it is here on Earth. It's so **different**, it's **awesome**. What is this place? It's Cappadocia, in Turkey. Why is it so **different**? What's so **unusual** about it? **Beautiful** rock formations and **underground** cities make it a very **special** place.

Cappadocia has a **long** history. Many people lived in the **underground** cities to be **safe** from enemies.[1] These cities were **big**. One city, Derinkuyu, had room for more than 30,000 people.

Today only a few people live in these cave homes in **underground** cities. But many people from all over the world visit them. They are full of **interesting** things to see. From above, Cappadocia looks like another world, like a *Star Wars* movie.

The weather in Cappadocia is **comfortable** all year long. It has **warm**, **dry** summers and **cold**, **snowy** winters. There is a **big** difference between day and night temperatures. The **average** summer temperature is 73 degrees Fahrenheit, and the **average** winter temperature is 28 degrees Fahrenheit.

Awesome underground cities, **beautiful** rock formations, and an **interesting** history—these things make Cappadocia a place you won't forget.

---

[1] **enemies:** people who want to hurt you

After You Read

A | **Practice** *PAIRS: Now read the online article aloud. Take turns reading each paragraph.*

B | **Vocabulary** *Complete the sentences with the words from the box.*

average	awesome	comfortable	dry	safe	unusual

1. The _____average_____ of the numbers 20, 25, and 30 is 25.

2. Be careful. It is not _____safe_____ to walk there.

3. That rock formation looks like a camel. It is _____unusual_____.

4. Bring water. It is hot and _____dry_____ there.

5. We were happy with our hotel. It wasn't special, but it was

    _____comfortable_____.

6. I bought a(n) _____ rug in Turkey. It's very different

    from other rugs.

C | **Comprehension** *Read the questions. Circle the correct letter.*

1. Where is Cappadocia?
    a. not on this earth
    b. in Turkey

2. Why is Cappadocia so unusual?
    a. It has interesting rocks and cities under the ground.
    b. The people are awesome and the plants are beautiful.

3. How many people lived in Derinkuyu in the past?
    a. over 3,000
    b. over 30,000

4. Why does Cappadocia look like a scene from the movie *Star Wars*?
    a. The area looks like another world.
    b. It is a beautiful place with many rock formations.

5. How is the weather in Cappadocia?
    a. cool in summer and very cold in winter
    b. warm in summer and cold in winter

DESCRIPTIVE ADJECTIVES

Noun	Be	Adjective		Adjective	Noun
The room	is	**small**.	It is a	**small**	room.
The rooms	are		They are		rooms.

GRAMMAR NOTES

1	**Adjectives** describe nouns.	NOUN ADJECTIVE • **Cappadocia** is **beautiful**. ADJECTIVE NOUN • It's a **beautiful place**.
2	Adjectives can come • after the verb **be** • before a noun	• The room is **big**. • It's a **big** room. Not: It's a ~~room big.~~
3	**BE CAREFUL!** Do not add **-s** to adjectives.	• a **hot** summer, a **cold** winter • **hot** summers, **cold** winters Not: ~~colds winters~~
4	For **adjective** + **noun**: Use **a** before the adjective if the adjective begins with a **consonant sound**. Use **an** before the adjective if the adjective begins with a **vowel sound**.	• It's **a b**eautiful place. • It's **an u**nusual place.
5	Some adjectives end in **-ing**, **-ly**, or **-ed**.	• It's **interesting**. • They're **friendly**. • We're **tired**.

EXERCISE 1: Discover the Grammar

Maria is visiting Turkey. Read her travel blog about her hotel in Cappadocia. Underline eleven more adjectives.

maria.blogspot.com

I'm at a cave hotel in Cappadocia. Gamirasu Cave Hotel is in a <u>traditional</u> village. In the past it was a cave home. Now it's a hotel. The hotel is in a small village in the center of Cappadocia. My cave room is fun. It's old but has a modern bathroom and Internet service! The rooms are not expensive. The price of the room includes a delicious breakfast and dinner. The food is good. The service is good too—the people are helpful and friendly. Also, it's easy to visit all of Cappadocia from the hotel. It was a great choice.

EXERCISE 2: Word Order

(Grammar Notes 1–5)

Complete the conversations with the words in parentheses. Remember to use a capital letter at the start of each sentence.

1. **A:** Where are we?

   B: <u>We are at an old market.</u>
   (market / at / we / are / old / an)

2. **A:** <u>The carpets are awesome.</u> Are they for sale?
   (awesome / carpets / the / are)

   B: Yes, they are.

3. **A:** How are the prices? Are they expensive?

   B: No, <u>the prices are reasonable.</u>
   (the / prices / reasonable / are)

4. **A:** How's the weather?

   B: <u>It's warm and sunny.</u>
   (warm / it / and / sunny / is)

5. **A:** How are you?

   B: <u>I'm tired, but happy</u>
   (tired / happy / I'm / but)

   I'm happy but tired

EXERCISE 3: Sentences with Adjectives

(Grammar Notes 1–5)

Write sentences with the words in parentheses. Add the correct form of the verb **be**. Add **a** if necessary.

1. Ali Baba Kitchen is a good restaurant.
   (Ali Baba Kitchen / good restaurant)

2. The food is delicious
   (the food / delicious)

3. The waiters are friendly and helpful.
   (the waiters / friendly and helpful) 有帮助的

4. The Bilton is a comfortable hotel.
   (the Bilton / comfortable hotel)

5. The rooms are not expensive.
   (the rooms / not expensive)

6. The outdoor market is safe
   (the outdoor market / safe)

7. The carpets are expensive
   (the carpets / expensive)
   ['ka:pit] 地毯

8. That is a beautiful carpet
   (that / beautiful carpet)

9. The climate is mild.
   (the climate / mild) 温和的.
   ['klaimit] 气候 区域

10. The weather is comfortable all year round
    (the weather / comfortable all year round)

EXERCISE 4: Editing

Correct the conversation. There are five mistakes. The first mistake is already corrected. Find and correct four more.

A: Is that a ~~lamp new~~ new lamp?

B: Yes, it is. ~~It's~~ It is from Turkey.

A: The colors are ~~beautifuls~~ beautiful.

B: Thanks. I got it at an old market in Cappadocia.

A: Were there many interesting things to buy?

B: Yes. These plates are from the market too.

A: The colors are unusual. I like them a lot.

B: Here. This one is for you.

EXERCISE 5: Listening

A | *Listen to the conversation. Sun Hi is talking to her friend Russ. What are they talking about? Circle the correct letter.*

a. Russ and Sun Hi's vacation

b. Sun Hi's visit to a national park

c. unusual places

B | *Listen again. Complete the sentences. Circle the correct letter.*

1. Sun Hi says Mesa Verde is _____.

   (**a.**) awesome   **b.** awful

2. The homes in the mountains are very _____.

   a. cold   **b.** old

3. The hotel is _____.

   a. clean   **b.** nice

4. The weather is _____.

   a. warm   **b.** cold

5. The park is _____.

   a. crowded   **b.** not crowded

EXERCISE 6: Pronunciation

A | *Read and listen to the Pronunciation Note.*

> **Pronunciation Note**
>
> Words have one or more **syllables**.
>
> **EXAMPLES:** hat   happy
>
> **One syllable** in a word is always **stressed**. Stressed syllables are long and loud.
>
> **EXAMPLE:** happy

B | *Listen and repeat each adjective.*

One syllable	Two syllables	Three syllables	Four syllables
• cold	• boring	• usual	• traditional
		• beautiful	
		• expensive	
		• important	

C | *Listen and mark the stressed syllable in each word.*

1. ugly

2. warm

3. unusual

4. friendly

5. modern

6. cheap

7. unimportant

D | *PAIRS: Take turns. Name an adjective from Parts B and C. Your partner names the opposite.*

EXAMPLE: **A:** Ugly.
　　　　　　 B: Beautiful!

EXERCISE 7: Guided Conversation

GROUPS: Each student writes the name of a city or place he or she knows well. The group asks questions about the place. Use the adjectives in Exercise 6 and the rest of the unit.

EXAMPLE: **A:** Woodside, Queens, in New York City.
　　　　　　 B: Are the homes in Woodside expensive?
　　　　　　 C: Are the people friendly?
　　　　　　 D: Is the weather mild?

EXERCISE 8: Writing

A | *Write a paragraph about an interesting place. Use* **be** *and adjectives.*

EXAMPLE: JeJu Island is in South Korea. It is a popular vacation place. Many Koreans go to this island on their honeymoon. The people are friendly, and the climate is mild. It's a good place for hiking and horseback riding. It's safe and the beaches are awesome.

B | *Check your work. Use the Editing Checklist.*

Editing Checklist

Did you . . . ?

☐ use the correct form of descriptive adjectives

☐ use the correct word order with descriptive adjectives

☐ check your spelling

UNIT 5 Review

Check your answers on page UR-1.
Do you need to review anything?

A | Complete the sentences. Add **a, an, or Ø**.

1. Mesa Verde has __a__ long history.

2. We like to visit __Ø__ big cities.

3. Miami has __a__ hot, humid summers.
   [ˈhjuːmɪd]
   潮湿的

4. It is __a__ interesting place.

5. The Grand Canyon has __Ø__ beautiful rock formations. [fɔːˈmeɪʃən]
   大成造

B | Complete the sentences. Circle the correct letter.

1. We are at _____.

   a. a hotel small   **b.** small hotel   **c.** a small hotel

2. The hotel has _____.

   a. an interesting garden   **b.** an garden interesting   **c.** a garden interesting

3. Our room is _____.

   a. a big and a comfortable   **b.** big and comfortable   **c.** a big and comfortable

4. The people here are _____.

   a. kinds and helpful   **b.** kinds and helpfuls   **c.** kind and helpful

5. It was _____.

   a. a choice great   **b.** a great choice   **c.** great choice

C | Write sentences with the words in parentheses.

1. (museum / I'm / the / at / new) __I'm at the new museum__

2. (full of / to see / things / interesting / It is) __It is interesting things full of to see.__

3. (bowls / unusual / from / It has / long ago) __It has unusual bowls form long ago.__

4. (has / It / carpets / beautiful / too) __It has carpets beautiful too.__

5. (place / is / to visit / The museum / a great) __The museum is a great place to visit.__

D | Correct the paragraph. There are five mistakes.

The Grand Canyon National Park in Arizona is a ~~a~~ (an) awesome place to visit. Almost five million people visit this park ~~a~~ unusual each year. The weather is good in the late spring and summer, but it crowded is during those months. There are seven differents places to stay in the park. I like El Tovar. It is a old hotel with a great view.

UNIT 6 Prepositions of Place

LOCATIONS

STEP 1 GRAMMAR IN CONTEXT

Before You Read

PAIRS: Answer the questions. Look at the map to answer questions 1 and 2.

1. Where is the Chinese Garden? Where are the African Masks?

2. Where are the rest rooms?

3. Is there an art museum in your city? Where is it? What kind of art is there?

   艺术
   [a:t]

4. What kind of art do you like?

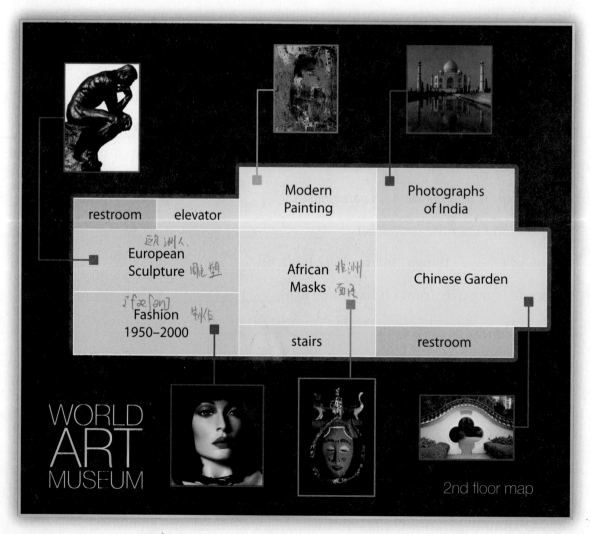

stair
楼梯；在楼上

Read

🎧 *Read Marina's posting and the conversation between Marina and a museum guard.*

WALL
FRIENDS
PHOTOS

Marina Olitskaya

 Marina Olitskaya Hey everyone. I want new glasses, and I need an eye exam. Any suggestions?[1] What's the best place to go?
September 3 at 10:16am · Comment · Like

 George Rami Try *Your Color Eyes*. It's **at** 7 East 89th Street, **between** Madison and Fifth Avenue. The doctor there is really good. His name is Dr. Green. And the glasses are a great deal.[2]
September 3 at 12:31pm · Like

 Marina Olitskaya So that's **near** the World Art Museum? Great! I'll go to the museum after I see the doctor. I want to see their African masks. Are you free then?
September 3 at 1:15pm · Like

AT THE MUSEUM

MARINA: Excuse me, where are the African masks?

GUARD: They're **on** the second floor. We're **on** the first floor.

MARINA: OK.

GUARD: So take the elevator or the stairs. The elevator is **on your left**, **behind** the gift shop. The stairs are **on your right**, **in back of** the information booth.[3] Then go up one flight.[4] The African Masks are just **up the stairs**. They're **between** the sculpture and the Chinese garden.

MARINA: Great. Oh, I'm sorry, one more thing. Where's . . .

GUARD: The restroom?

MARINA: No, the cafeteria. I'm starving.[5]

---

[1] **suggestions:** ideas
[2] **a great deal:** not very expensive
[3] **information booth:** a place where people ask questions
[4] **go up one flight:** go one floor upstairs.
[5] **I'm starving:** I'm very hungry.

After You Read

A | Practice *PAIRS: Now read the posting and the conversation aloud. Take turns reading each part.*

B | Vocabulary *Complete the conversations with the words from the box. Use the correct form.*

appointment	be free	cafeteria	flight	restroom	sculpture

1. **A:** I'm hungry. Where's the ___cafeteria___ ?

   B: Downstairs.

2. **A:** What do you make in your ___sculpture___ class?

   B: We make things from stone or metal.

3. **A:** Where is the garden with the unusual flowers?

   B: It's one ___restroom___ up, on the second floor.

4. **A:** Are you busy Thursday?

   B: No, I ___be free___ .

5. **A:** Where's Marina?

   B: At the eye doctor, I think. Her ___appointment___ is at 3:00.

6. **A:** Is the ___restroom___ in the back of the cafeteria?

   B: No, it's in the front, next to the elevator.

C | Comprehension *Write* **T** *(True),* **F** *(False), or* **?** *(it doesn't say) for each statement.*

__T__ **1.** Dr. Green's office is on 98th Street.

__F__ **2.** The glasses at *Your Color Eyes* are expensive.

__T__ **3.** The African masks are on the second floor.

__T__ **4.** The stairs are next to the elevator.

__F__ **5.** At the museum, Marina is hungry.

__F__ **6.** The cafeteria is closed.

PREPOSITIONS OF PLACE

 The glasses are **between** the book and the watch.

 The glasses are **next to** the newspaper.

 The glasses are **behind** the box.

 The glasses are **under** the table.

 The glasses are **in** his pocket.

 The glasses are **on** the table **near** the window.

 The man is **in back of** the woman.

 The man is **in front of** the woman.

GRAMMAR NOTES

1	**Prepositions of place** tell <u>where</u> something is. Some common prepositions of place are:	• My bag is **under** my seat. • Your umbrella is **near** the door.

in	on your left
in front of	behind
in back of	between
on	near
on your right	next to

(continued on next page)

2	For **prepositions in addresses**, use:	
	in before a country, a state, a province, a city, a room number	• He's **in** Canada. He's **in** British Columbia. • He's **in** Vancouver. He's **in** room 302.
	on before a street, an avenue, a road	• It's **on** Main Street. It's **on** 10th Avenue.
	at before a building number	• We're **at** 78 Main Street.
	on the before a floor	• We're **on the** second floor.
	on the corner of before a street or streets	• It's **on the corner of** Main Street.
	USAGE NOTE: In informal conversation, *street* or *avenue* is dropped.	• It's on the corner of **Main Street** and **Mott Avenue**. • It's on the corner of **Main** and **Mott**.
3	For **prepositions before places** use:	
	in school OR *at* school	• I'm **in** school from 9 to 11. • I'm **at** school now.
	at work	• She's **at** work right now.
	at home OR home	• No one is **at** home. OR No one is home.

REFERENCE NOTE

For lists of ordinal and cardinal numbers, see Appendix 3 on page A-3.

STEP 3 FOCUSED PRACTICE

EXERCISE 1: Discover the Grammar

Look at the eye chart. Then answer the questions to find the message. There are three words.

E
R T N
I L W O V
E G S L I P H

1. The first word has one letter. This letter is next to an *L*. It isn't a *W* or an *S*. What's the word? _____ I _____

2. The second word has four letters. The first letter is between the *S* and an *I*. The second letter is under the *N*. The third letter is a *V*. A *T* is under the last letter. What's the word? LOVE _____

3. The third word has seven letters. A *T* is under the first letter. The second letter is an *N*. The third letter is between an *E* and the *S*. The fourth letter is an *L*. The fifth letter

is an *I*. The sixth letter is between the *L* and the *G*. The last letter is an *H*. What's the word? English

4. What's the message? I L o v e E n g l i s h !

EXERCISE 2: Prepositions of Place

(Grammar Notes 1–2)

Look at the map. Complete the sentences with the words from the box.

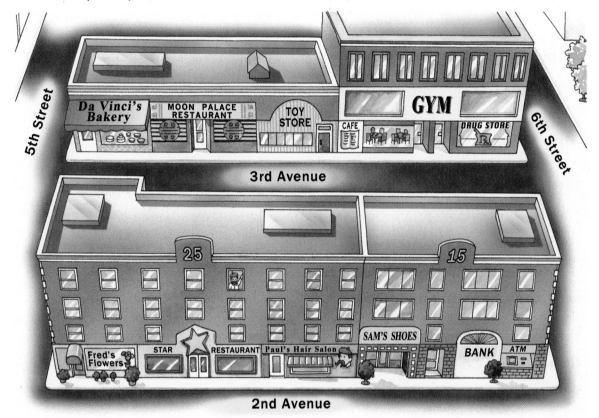

at	next to	on the	under
between	~~on~~	on the . . . of	

1. Fred's Flowers is _____ on _____ Second Avenue.

2. Paul's Hair Salon is _____ next to _____ Sam's Shoes.

3. Da Vinci's Bakery is _____ on the _____ corner _____ of _____ Third Avenue and Fifth Street.

4. The café is _____ between _____ the drugstore and the toy store.

5. Paul's apartment is _____ at _____ 25 Second Avenue.

6. His apartment is _____ on the _____ fourth floor.

7. The café and drug store are _____ under _____ a gym.

EXERCISE 3: Prepositions of Place

Complete the sentences. Choose from the words in the box. Use some words more than once.

at	between	in	of	on

1. My best friend lives in an apartment _____ *in* _____ Lakeville.

2. He lives _____ *at* _____ 435 East Water Street.

3. He lives _____ *on on* _____ the third floor.

4. His apartment is _____ *beteen* _____ a library and a bank.

5. The bank is _____ *on* _____ the corner of Lexington Avenue and 77th Street.

6. My friend is now _____ *in* _____ front _____ *of* _____ his building. He and a neighbor are talking.

7. His neighbor's little boy is _____ *at (in)* _____ school for the first time. It is a big step for him.

EXERCISE 4: Prepositions of Place .

(Grammar Notes 1–3)

Complete the sentences. Write true sentences.

1. I am _____ *in* _____ school.

2. I am _____ *at* _____ room _____ *333* _____ .

3. My classroom is _____ *on the third floor* _____ .
   (floor)

4. My school is _____ *on* _____ .
   (school address)

5. I am not _____ *at* _____ home. I'm not _____ *at* _____ work.

6. I am in _____ *San Francisoo* _____ , in _____ *Amincan* _____ .
   (your city) **(your country)**

EXERCISE 5: Editing

Correct the conversations. There are six mistakes. The first mistake is already corrected. Find and correct five more.

1. **A:** I'm in school until 2:00, but I'm free after that. Let's go to the Modern

   Art Museum.

   B: OK. Where is it?

   A: It's ~~in~~ *on* Fifth Avenue between Eight and Ninth Streets.

2. **A:** Excuse me. Are the masks ~~on~~ the third floor?

   B: I don't know. Ask at the Information Booth.

   A: Where is that?

   B: It's in front ~~of~~ the stairs, near ~~to~~ the gift shop.

   And the sculptures are on the second floor, in back ~~of~~ the paintings.

STEP 4 COMMUNICATION PRACTICE

EXERCISE 6: Pronunciation

A | *Read and listen to the Pronunciation Note.*

> **Pronunciation Note**
>
> **Stressed words** are longer and louder. Sometimes we stress words to make our meaning clear.
>
> **EXAMPLE:** I'm not at school. I'm at the museum.

B | *Listen and mark a dot (•) over the stressed words.*

1. I'm on the first floor. I'm not on the fifth floor.

2. I'm on the first floor. He's on the fifth floor.

3. The museum is on Fifth Street. It's not on Fifth Avenue.

4. The museum is on Fifth Street. The library is on Fifth Avenue.

5. Your glasses are on the table. Your gloves are in the drawer.

C | *Listen and repeat each sentence.*

EXERCISE 7: Listening

A | *Look at the world map in Appendix 1 on pages A-0–A-1. Listen to the locations of countries. Find the countries on the map. Write the countries.*

1. ___ ___ ___ ___ ___   3. ___ ___ ___ ___ ___ ___ ___ ___ ___ ___

2. ___ ___ ___ ___ ___ ___   4. ___ ___ ___ ___ ___

B | *Listen again. Then compare your answers with a partner's.*

bone 骨头、   tube
[bɑʊn]
nobe 长袍、

EXERCISE 8: Guessing Countries

A | *PAIRS: Write sentences about a country's location. Use the prepositions* **between,** **near, next to,** *and* **in.**

B | *Join another group. They guess the country. (See the map in Appendix 1, pages A-0—A-1.)*

> **EXAMPLE:** This country is in Central America. It is between Costa Rica and Colombia. What country is it?

EXERCISE 9: Game: Describing Locations

GROUPS: Name a place everyone knows. Each student describes its location in a different way. The group with the most correct sentences wins.

> **EXAMPLE:** **Central Park**
> **A:** It's between Fifth Avenue and Central Park West.
> **B:** It's in New York.
> **C:** It's near our school.
> **D:** It's between 59th Street and 110th Street.

EXERCISE 10: Writing

A | *Write an invitation to a party. Give the address and nearby places. Use prepositions with addresses and locations.*

> **EXAMPLE:**

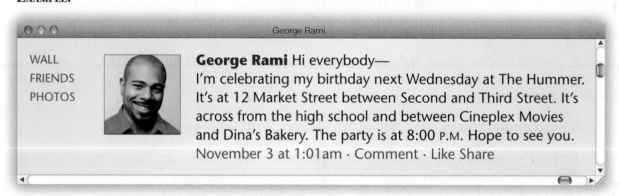

George Rami

WALL
FRIENDS
PHOTOS

George Rami Hi everybody—
I'm celebrating my birthday next Wednesday at The Hummer. It's at 12 Market Street between Second and Third Street. It's across from the high school and between Cineplex Movies and Dina's Bakery. The party is at 8:00 P.M. Hope to see you.
November 3 at 1:01am · Comment · Like Share

B | *Check your work. Use the Editing Checklist.*

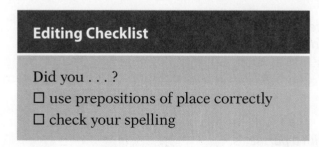

Editing Checklist

Did you . . . ?
☐ use prepositions of place correctly
☐ check your spelling

UNIT

6 Review

Check your answers on page UR-2.
Do you need to review anything?

A | *Look at the picture. Complete the sentences with the words from the box.*

behind	in front of	next to	on	under

1. The book is _____*on*_____ the table.

2. The glasses are _____*under*_____ the table.

3. The cup is _____*behind*_____ the book.

4. A watch is _____*next to*_____ the book.

5. A pencil is _____*in front of*_____ the book.

B | *Complete the sentences. Use prepositions.*

1. I'm _____*at*_____ work now, but I need to leave soon.

2. My appointment with Dr. McDonnell is _____*at*_____ 4:30 P.M.

3. The doctor's office is _____*at*_____ 235 West Second Street. He's

_____*on the*_____ second floor.

tour.

rest 台n.

C | *Follow the instructions. Draw in the space provided.*

circle   square   triangle

1. Draw a circle on the left.
2. Draw a square on the right.
3. Draw a triangle between the circle and square.
4. Draw an X inside the circle.
5. Draw a Y inside the triangle.
6. Draw a Z under the square.

does 第三人称单数现在式.

headache
I'hedeik] 头痛.

D | *Correct the conversation. There are five mistakes.*

A: Is Jon at the school?

B: No. He's *at* ~~in~~ home.

A: Where does he live?

B: He lives *on* ~~at~~ Oak Street, between First and Second Avenue *in* ~~at~~ Lakeville.

A: Does he live in an apartment?

B: Yes. He lives *on* ~~in~~ the third floor.

grad 毕业.
[græd]

From Grammar to Writing

CONNECTING WITH *AND* AND *BUT*

We use the word **and** to add information. We use the word **but** to show a surprise or contrast. We usually use a comma before **and** and **but** when they connect two sentences.

> **EXAMPLES:** The book is good, **and** it is easy to understand.
> The book is good, **but** it is difficult to understand.

We can use **and** or **but** to connect two descriptive adjectives.

> **EXAMPLES:** I am hungry **and** tired.
> He is tired **but** happy.

1 | *Complete the sentences with **and** or **but**.*

1. She's friendly _____*and*_____ popular.

2. She's friendly _____*but*_____ unpopular.

3. Her last name is long, _____*and*_____ it's hard to pronounce.

4. Her last name is long, _____*but*_____ it's easy to pronounce.

2 | *Use **and** or **but** to complete the story about Henry. Then on a separate piece of paper, write a story about someone who made a big change in his or her life.*

Five years ago Henry was a banker. His home was big _____*and*_____ expensive.
1.

His car was fast _____*and*_____ fancy. His workday was long, _____*and*_____
2.   3.

his work was stressful. He was rich, _____*but*_____ he was stressed and unhappy.
4.

Today Henry works in a flower shop. His home is small _____*and*_____
5.

inexpensive. His car is old _____*and*_____ small. His workday is short,
6.

_____*and*_____ his work is relaxing. He isn't rich, _____*but*_____ he's relaxed
7.   8.

and happy.

3 | *On a separate piece of paper, write a story about a big change you made in your life.*

4 | *Exchange papers with a partner. Did your partner follow the directions? Correct any mistakes in grammar and spelling.*

5 | *Talk to your partner. Discuss the mistakes you made. Then rewrite your own paper and make any necessary changes.*

IMPERATIVES AND
THE SIMPLE PRESENT

命令
普通的   现在的

UNIT 7

Imperatives; Suggestions with *Let's, Why don't we . . . ?*

LONG LIFE

STEP 1 GRAMMAR IN CONTEXT

Before You Read

Some people live very long lives. Discuss the questions.

1. Who is the oldest person you know? How old is he or she?
2. What do you think is important for a long life?

Read

Read the online article. Then read the conversation between Joe and Mary on page 73.

Secrets to a Long Life

Yiannis Karimalis was 40 years old. He was a bridge painter in the United States. He was sick. His doctor said, "I'm sorry. You have stomach cancer.[1] It is very bad." Yiannis moved back to his hometown in Greece, to the island of Ikaria.

Yiannis is in his 80s and still alive today. His doctor is dead.

Many people in Ikaria live long lives. What are their secrets? Scientist Dan Buettner studies the lifestyle[2] of older people in different parts of the world. As a result of his studies in Ikaria, he offers this advice:

- **Eat** a lot of green vegetables, fresh fruit, olive oil, fish, and Greek honey.
- **Drink** herbal tea and goat milk.
- **Don't worry**.
- **Take naps**.
- **Walk**. **Don't use** a car, a bus, or a train.
- **Call friends** often.
- **Pray**.

Ikaria, Greece

[1] *cancer:* serious illness in which a growth spreads
[2] *lifestyle:* the way you live

JOE: Interesting article. But it's too healthy for me.

MARY: Come on, Joe, these suggestions are easy to follow. **Let's try** some of them.

JOE: I have a better idea. **Let's move** to Ikaria!

MARY: Um, **why don't we** just **take** a trip to Greece?

JOE: Stop right there. I'm on the phone with the airlines.

After You Read

A | Practice *PAIRS: Now read the online article and the conversation aloud. Take turns reading each paragraph of the article.*

B | Vocabulary *Complete the sentences with the words from the box.*

advice	dead	island	nap	pray	secret

1. You look very tired. Why don't you take a ____nap____?

2. Don't tell him. It's a ____secret____.

3. The flowers are ____dead____ because nobody watered them.

4. The doctor's ____advice____ to Mark was, "Walk more. Eat less."

5. We ____pray____ for peace.

6. Ikaria is a Greek ____island____.

C | Comprehension *Circle the correct words to complete the sentences.*

1. At 40, Yiannis Karimalis was **sick** / **tired**.

2. Karimalis was a **house** / **bridge** painter.

3. Today Karimalis lives in **the United States** / **Greece**.

4. Dan Buettner is a **painter** / **scientist**.

5. Buettner tells people to **take it easy** / **work hard**.

6. **Mary** / **Joe** wants to follow Buettner's advice.

THE IMPERATIVE

Affirmative Statements		Negative Statements		
Base Form of Verb		*Don't*	Base Form of Verb	
Walk	to work.	Don't	take	a bus.

SUGGESTIONS

Affirmative Statements			Negative Statements			
Let's	Base Form of Verb		*Let's*	*Not*	Base Form of Verb	
Let's	use	olive oil.	Let's	not	use	butter.

[stand] 站立

Suggestions for You and Another Person			Suggestions for Another Person		
Why Don't We	Base Form of Verb		*Why Don't You*	Base Form of Verb	
Why don't we	go	on a bike tour?	Why don't you	get	the cameras?

[tur]
观光

RESPONSES TO SUGGESTIONS

[ə'griː] 同意去体·

手绝

Agree	Disagree
OK.	No, I don't feel like it.
That's a good idea. OR Good idea.	Why don't we . . . instead. 代替
That sounds good to me. OR Sounds good to me.	Sorry, not today.
Sounds like a plan.	I can't. I . . .

计划

GRAMMAR NOTES

1	The **imperative** uses the **base form of the verb**.	• **Walk** to work.
2	To make an imperative **negative**, use ***don't*** + **base form** of the verb.	• **Don't worry**. • **Don't be** late.
3	In an imperative statement, the subject is always *you*, but we don't say it or write it.	• (You) **Be** careful.
4	Use the **imperative** to a. give directions and instructions 指令 b. give orders 命令 c. give advice or suggestions 建议 d. give warnings 警告 e. make polite requests 请求 有礼貌的	• **Turn** right. • **Stand** there. • **Use** olive oil. **Don't use** butter. • **Be** careful! It's hot. • Please **call** before noon.

5	Use *please* to make orders, warnings, and requests more polite. *Please* can come at the beginning or the end of the sentence.	• **Please** be careful. • **Please** call before noon. • Call before noon, **please.**
6	Use *Let's* or *Let's not* + **base form** for suggestions that include you and another person.	• **Let's go.** • **Let's not eat** there.
7	Use *Why don't we* + **base form** for suggestions that include you and another person. Use *Why don't you* to make a suggestion or give advice to another person. Remember to put a question mark (?) at the end of sentences with *Why don't we* and *Why don't you.*	• **Why don't we go** to the pool? • **Why don't you look** on the Internet? • **Why don't we meet** at the gym? • **Why don't you call** home?

STEP 3 FOCUSED PRACTICE

EXERCISE 1: Discover the Grammar

Read the conversations. Next to **line A**, *write* **I** *for the imperative form and* **S** *for suggestions. Next to* **line B**, *write* **A** *when the person agrees. Write* **D** *when the person disagrees.*

  _S_   **1. A:** Let's buy yogurt.

  _D_   **B:** I don't like yogurt. Why don't we buy goat cheese?

  _I_   **2. A:** Please get more broccoli. It's on sale.

  _A_   **B:** OK. That's a good idea.

  _S_   **3. A:** Let's not drive to school. The weather is great.

  _D_   **B:** But it's late. Let's walk after school.

  _I_   **4. A:** Call Roberto and invite him to dinner.

  _A_   **B:** Good idea. What's his number?

  _S_   **5. A:** Why don't you take some time off? You look tired.

  _D_   **B:** Don't worry. I'm fine.

  _I_   **6. A:** Maria, don't get those flowers. Some are almost dead.

  _A_   **B:** OK. Thanks for telling me.

EXERCISE 2: Imperative and Suggestions: Affirmative and Negative *(Grammar Notes 1–6)*

Circle the correct words to complete the sentences.

1. The bread is still hot. **Eat / Don't eat** it now.

2. It's cold here. Please **close / don't close** the window.

3. It's a secret. Please **tell / don't tell** your brother about my plan.

4. For information about Dan Buettner, **check / don't check** the Internet.

5. **Let's walk / Let's not walk** to the store. It's not far.

6. **Let's buy / Let's not buy** those doughnuts. They're not very healthy.

7. Please **give / don't give** me directions to the gym. I want to go there today.

8. **Don't try / Try** this herbal tea. It's delicious.

9. **Take / Don't take** a nap now. Help me prepare dinner.

10. **Don't visit / Visit** that island in July. The weather is usually awful at that time.

EXERCISE 3: Imperative for Directions *(Grammar Notes 1, 3–4)*

A | *Read the conversation. Joe gives Mary directions to Gold's gym. Then look at the map and put an **X** on the gym.*

MARY: Excuse me . . . Where's Gold's Gym?

JOE: Um, sure . . . The gym is on Second Avenue between 70th and 71st Street.

We're on Third Avenue at 73rd Street. Walk down Third Avenue to 71st Street. That's two blocks from here. Turn left at 71st Street. Walk one block to Second Avenue. Then turn right on Second Avenue. It's right there, on your right.

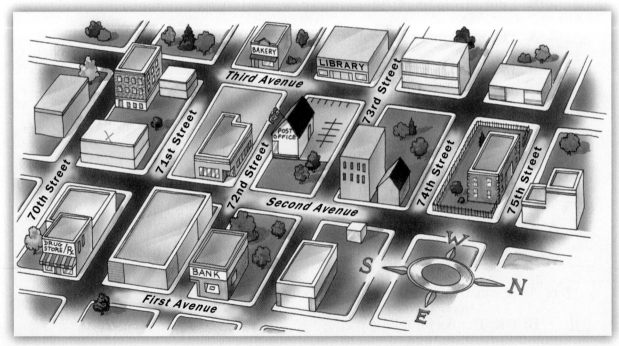

B | *Look at the map again. You are at the drug store. Continue the directions to the library.*

Walk down 71st Street to ___turn left___. ___Walk two block___
___turn right at the First Avenue. It's right there___
___on your right___

EXERCISE 4: Editing

Correct the conversation. There are six mistakes. The first mistake is already corrected.
Find and correct five more.

> **JOE:** Let's ~~to~~ go to the movies.
>
> **MARY:** Why we don't go to the park first? It's a beautiful day.
>
> **JOE:** OK. But first let have *eat* lunch. I'm hungry.
>
> **MARY:** I'm hungry too. Why don't we have a fruit salad with nuts?
>
> **JOE:** Good idea.
>
> **MARY:** But you don't use those apples. They're bad. Throws them away.
>
> **JOE:** OK.
>
> **MARY:** And why you don't add honey to the yogurt? It's delicious that way.
>
> **JOE:** You're right. This is really good.

STEP 4 COMMUNICATION PRACTICE

EXERCISE 5: Listening

A | *Listen. What kind of ad is this? Circle the correct letter.*

a. an ad for a spa

b. an ad for exercise classes

c. an ad for healthy eating

B | *Listen again and check (✓) what the spa offers.*

___✓___ **1.** yoga classes

_____ **2.** tai chi classes

_____ **3.** fresh vegetables

_____ **4.** healthy breakfast

_____ **5.** healthy dinner

_____ **6.** massage and shower

_____ **7.** three weeks free

_____ **8.** two weeks free

EXERCISE 6: Pronunciation

🎧 **A** | *Read and listen to the Pronunciation Note.*

> **Pronunciation Note**
>
> We often **link** *don't* + *you*. The two words sound like "doncha" / **doʊnʃə** /
>
> **EXAMPLE:** Why don't you try that yogurt?

🎧 **B** | *Listen to the conversations. Notice the pronunciation of* **don't you.**

1. A: He's never sick.

   B: Maybe it's his healthy lifestyle. Why don't you try his exercise routine?

2. A: It's my mother's birthday tomorrow. I want to get her something.

   B: Why don't you get her Greek soap with olive oil? They say it's really good for

   the skin.

3. A: I don't want fried chicken. It's too fattening.

   B: Why don't you have the fish? It's broiled.

🎧 **C** | *Listen again. Repeat the suggestions with* **why don't you.**

EXERCISE 7: Making Suggestions for Another Person

PAIRS: Take turns. Read a problem. Your partner makes suggestions with **"Why don't you . . ."** *Agree if you like the suggestion. Disagree if you don't like the suggestion.*

1. I'm thirsty.   **2.** I'm bored.   **3.** I'm hungry.   **4.** I'm tired.

EXAMPLE: **A:** I'm thirsty.
   B: Why don't you have a soda?
   A: Soda? That's not healthy.
   B: Well, why don't you have some pineapple juice?
   A: OK. That's a good idea.

EXERCISE 8: Making Suggestions for You and Another Person

PAIRS: **Student A,** *make a suggestion for a healthy lifestyle.* **Student B,** *agree or make another suggestion and give a reason why. Continue until you both agree. Take turns. Use the topics from the list.*

- exercise with friends
- go to the gym
- sign up for a dance class
- go on a diet together
- hang out with friends
- your idea: _____

EXAMPLE: **A:** Let's go to the gym.
   B: Why don't we study first?
   A: OK. Let's study for an hour and then go to the gym.

EXERCISE 9: Giving Advice

PAIRS: What advice can you give for a healthy lifestyle? Make a list. Use the verbs **drink, eat, meet, nap, pray, walk,** *and* **worry.** *Then read your list to the class.*

> EXAMPLE:
> - Don't eat a lot of meat.
> - Eat . . .

EXERCISE 10: Giving Directions

A | *PAIRS: Look again at the map on page 76. You are at the library. Ask your partner directions to the bank.*

B | *PAIRS: Now give directions to a place on the map from the bakery. Your partner names the place.*

EXERCISE 11: Writing

A | *Write an ad for a hotel on the island of Ikaria. Use imperatives.*

> EXAMPLE:
> For a vacation you won't forget, come to Jean's "Hotel for Life" on the beautiful island of Ikaria. Enjoy a comfortable room with an awesome view of the beach. Eat three delicious and healthful meals in our dining room or on your terrace. Swim in our pool. Jog on the beach. Relax in our jacuzzi. Everything is there for you. Don't delay. Book a room today.

B | *Check your work. Use the Editing Checklist.*

Editing Checklist

Did you . . . ?
- ☐ use imperatives correctly
- ☐ check your spelling

A | *Circle the correct words to complete the sentences.*

1. (**Let's get**) / Let's not get ice cream. It's on sale this week.

2. (**Why don't we invite**) / Let's not invite Bob? He's really nice.

3. Please buy / (**Don't buy**) peppers. I don't like them.

4. Let's meet / (**Let's not meet**) before 8. I have a lot of work.

5. Touch / (**Don't touch**) the wall. The paint is still wet.

[wet] 潮湿

B | *Complete the instructions with the verbs in parentheses. Use the imperative affirmative or negative form.*

1. _____wear_____ comfortable clothes to tai chi class. They're very important.
   (wear)   重要的

2. _____Don't wear_____ tight clothes.
   (wear)

3. _____bring_____ a mat and water.
   (bring)

4. _____Don't bring_____ coffee or soda inside the classroom. You can have those drinks in
   (bring)
   the nearby lounge.

5. Please _____pay_____ by check or cash. We don't accept credit cards.
              (pay)

C | *Write suggestions with the words in parentheses.*

1. _____Let's go to the gym._____
                    (go to the gym / let's)

2. _____Let's watch a movie this afternoon._____
                    (watch a movie this afternoon / let's)

3. _____why don't we take a trip together,_____
                    (take a trip together / why don't we)

4. _____why don't we hang out with Pietro this weeked._____
                    (hang out with Pietro this weekend / why don't we)

D | *Correct the sentences. There are six mistakes. Check for punctuation.*

1. Why you don't ask Andrij for help?
        why don't

2. You look really tired. You take a short nap.
                           why don't
                           we don't

3. Let's to walk to work. Let's not drive.
        go

   Let's

4. Don't ask Boris to fix the car. Asks Mickey.

   Let's go

5. I'm on a diet, so buy yogurt at the store. Don't to buy sour cream.

8 Simple Present: Affirmative and Negative Statements

SHOPPING

STEP 1 GRAMMAR IN CONTEXT

Before You Read

A | Kawaii *is the Japanese word for "cute." In Japan, girls like* kawaii *things. In the United States, teens want "cool" things. What do young people say in your country?*

B | *Circle what's true about you.*

1. I **often** / **don't often** shop for clothes.

2. I look for **bargains** / **comfortable clothes** / **trendy clothes**.

〔'baːgin〕
康价的

〔'trendi〕
时毛的

Read

Read the online article about teenage shoppers in Japan.

teen (十几岁的) trend 转向
短句

SWEET LIFE magazine

TEEN 悲伤的 *TRENDS*

SWEET LIFE magazine

Yumi **is** 17 years old. She**'s** a senior in high school in Japan. Yumi 高年级的 **wears** *kawaii* boots and jeans. She **carries** a *kawaii* phone. Sometimes Yumi dresses as her favorite cartoon character. She wears makeup and *kawaii* costumes. 〔'kostjuːm〕〔'kæəiktə〕特质
服饰

carry
〔'kæri〕
携带

Yumi **uses** the word *kawaii* a lot. She **doesn't buy** non-*kawaii* things.

Businesses **look** at Yumi and her friends. They **study** their clothes. Companies **know** that Yumi **is** not alone. There **are** many other teens like Yumi. Yumi and her friends **buy** cool clothes. Their clothes **don't** always **cost** a lot. But the number of teenage shoppers is big. And that **means** a lot of money for businesses. In the 1990s, college girls were the trendsetters.[1] Now it**'s** high school girls. Maybe in the future middle school girls will set trends. And it**'s** not just girls. Nowadays guys **shop** and **want** a certain "look" too.
〔'soːtən〕

This Japanese girl follows the fashion trend "anime." She is dressing as her favorite cartoon.

[1] *trendsetters:* people who start a new way of doing something

fashion
〔'fæʃən〕
(做成…的形状)

trend
转向

shoppers 顾客.

After You Read

A | Practice *PAIRS: Now read the article aloud. Take turns reading each paragraph.*

B | Vocabulary *Circle the letter of the best meaning for the words in* **blue**.

1. Yumi is a **senior**. She's in her __*c*__ year of high school.

   a. first **b.** second **c.** last

2. She's a **teenager** (or teen). She is between __*b*__ years old.

   a. 11 and 15 **b.** 13 and 19 **c.** 15 and 20

3. Her brother is in **middle school**. Middle school is between __*b*__.

   a. high school **b.** primary school **c.** kindergarten
      and college   and high school   and first grade

4. Many **companies** study teens. These __*b*__ believe that teenagers spend
   a lot of money.

   [spend]
   花费.
   浪费

   a. friends **b.** businesses **c.** families

5. You look **cute** in that photo. You look __*a*__.

   a. pretty **b.** serious **c.** funny

6. Many teens **are like** Yumi. They __*b*__ Yumi.

   a. are in love with **b.** are similar to **c.** are friends of

7. He lives **alone**. He lives __*a*__.

   a. by himself **b.** with friends **c.** with relatives

C | Comprehension *Write* **T** (**True**) *or* **F** (**False**) *for each statement.*

___T___ **1.** Yumi wears boots.

___F___ **2.** Yumi works for a company.

___T___ **3.** Yumi has friends.

___T___ **4.** *Kawaii* means "cute."

___F___ **5.** Yumi doesn't like costumes.

___F___ **6.** Teenage boys don't like clothes.

___F___ **7.** Middle school girls set clothes trends today.

SIMPLE PRESENT: AFFIRMATIVE AND NEGATIVE STATEMENTS

Affirmative Statements			Negative Statements			
Subject	**Verb**		**Subject**	*Do not / Does not*	**Base Form of Verb**	
I You* We They	**sell** **have**	jeans.	I You* We They	**do not** **don't**	**sell** **have**	jeans.
He She It	**sells** **has**		He She It	**does not** **doesn't**		

You is both singular and plural.

GRAMMAR NOTES

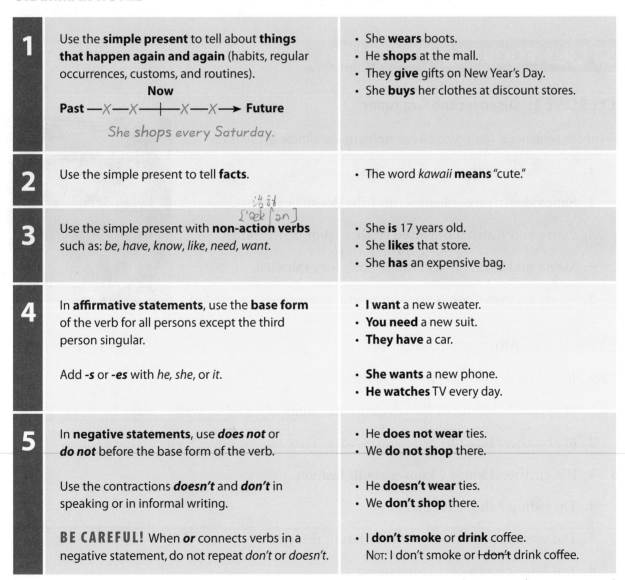

1 Use the **simple present** to tell about **things that happen again and again** (habits, regular occurrences, customs, and routines).

```
                    Now
Past —X—X—+—X—X—→ Future
      She shops every Saturday.
```

- She **wears** boots.
- He **shops** at the mall.
- They **give** gifts on New Year's Day.
- She **buys** her clothes at discount stores.

2 Use the simple present to tell **facts**.

- The word *kawaii* **means** "cute."

3 Use the simple present with **non-action verbs** such as: *be, have, know, like, need, want.*

- She **is** 17 years old.
- She **likes** that store.
- She **has** an expensive bag.

4 In **affirmative statements**, use the **base form** of the verb for all persons except the third person singular.

Add **-s** or **-es** with *he, she,* or *it.*

- **I want** a new sweater.
- **You need** a new suit.
- **They have** a car.

- **She wants** a new phone.
- **He watches** TV every day.

5 In **negative statements**, use *does not* or *do not* before the base form of the verb.

Use the contractions *doesn't* and *don't* in speaking or in informal writing.

BE CAREFUL! When *or* connects verbs in a negative statement, do not repeat *don't* or *doesn't.*

- He **does not wear** ties.
- We **do not shop** there.

- He **doesn't wear** ties.
- We **don't shop** there.

- I **don't smoke** or **drink** coffee.
  Not: I don't smoke or ~~I don't~~ drink coffee.

(continued on next page)

6	The **third person singular affirmative** forms of *have*, *do*, and *go* are <u>irregular</u>.	• She **has** a new coat. • He **does** the laundry on Saturday. • He **goes** to the gym at 10:00.
	The **third person singular negative forms** of *have*, *do*, and *go* are <u>regular</u>.	• She **doesn't have** a new hat. • He **doesn't do** laundry on Sunday. • He **doesn't go** to the gym at 11:00.

7	**BE CAREFUL!** The verb *be* **is irregular.** It has three forms in the present: *is, am,* and *are.*	**Be** • I **am** tired. • You **are** tall. • He **is** bored.	**Regular Verb** I **look** tired. You **look** tall. He **looks** bored.

REFERENCE NOTES
For a fuller discussion of **non-action verbs**, see Unit 17, page 188.
For **spelling and pronunciation rules for the third-person singular** in the **simple present**,
see Appendix 6, pages A-6–A-7.
For a complete presentation of the **present tense of verb *be***, see Unit 1, page 5.

STEP 3 FOCUSED PRACTICE

EXERCISE 1: Discover the Grammar

Read the sentences. Underline all examples of the simple present.

1. Sometimes clothes <u>send</u> a message.

2. Sandy doesn't wear leather, and she doesn't eat meat.

3. Pierre and Katrina <u>buy</u> used clothes from thrift shops.

4. Marta <u>makes</u> her own clothes. She's very talented.

5. Ali <u>wears</u> gym clothes every day, and he <u>exercises</u> every day.

EXERCISE 2: Affirmative Sentences

(Grammar Notes 1–4)

Circle the correct word to complete the sentence.

1. My grandfather **work** /(**works**) for a big company, and he **wear** /(**wears**) a suit to work.

2. My brothers (**like**) / **likes** casual clothes. They almost never (**wear**) / **wears** suits.

3. His girlfriend **know** /(**knows**) about fashion.

4. They (**shop**) / **shops** online.

5. The word *cool* **mean** /(**means**) different things.

6. You (**have**) / **has** a cute hairstyle.

EXERCISE 3: Negative Statements

(Grammar Notes 5, 7)

Underline the verb in the first sentence. Complete the second sentence in the negative.
Use the same verb.

1. He <u>shops</u> at flea markets. He _____doesn't shop_____ at chain stores.

2. We buy name brands. They _____don't buy_____ name brands.

3. I like jeans. I _____don't like_____ suits.

4. I need a new jacket. I _____don't need_____ a new raincoat.

5. My mother wears high heels. She _____doesn't wear_____ sneakers.

6. That dress looks good. It _____doesn't look_____ too tight.

7. We are 20 years old. We _____aren't_____ teenagers.

8. He is in middle school. He _____isn't_____ in high school.

EXERCISE 4: Affirmative and Negative Statements

(Grammar Notes 1–6)

Complete the sentences with the verbs in parentheses. Use the affirmative or negative
form.

1. (cost) **a.** It's expensive. It _____costs_____ a lot.

   b. It's cheap. It _____doesn't cost_____ a lot.

2. (need) **a.** I'm hot. I _____need_____ a sweater.

   b. I'm cold. I _____don't need_____ a sweater.

3. (want) **a.** His jacket is old. He _____wants_____ a new one.

   b. His jacket is new. He _____doesn't want_____ a new one.

4. (like) **a.** We _____like_____ window shopping. We often look at store windows.

   b. They _____don't like_____ window shopping. They never

   look at store windows.

5. (have) **a.** He's rich. He _____has_____ a lot of money.

   b. She's poor. She _____doesn't have_____ a lot of money.

6. (go) **a.** He doesn't like that new department store. He

   _____doesn't go_____ there.

   b. She loves that new department store. She _____goes_____ there

   every week.

prefer [pri'fə:] 守覺

EXERCISE 5: Affirmative and Negative Statements

(Grammar Notes 1–7)

A | *Read this letter from a parent to an advice columnist. Complete the sentences with the verbs in parentheses. Use the correct form.*

Our son _____is_____ 14 years old. He _____'s_____ a good student at his
   1. (be)   **2. (be)**

middle school, and he _____has_____ a lot of friends. But we _____have_____ a
                        3. (have)   **4. (have)**

problem with him. He _____loves_____ clothes. He _____wears_____ trendy jeans
                      5. (love)   **6. (wear)**

with chains on them. And he _____prefers_____ expensive hoodies and brand names.
                            7. (prefer)

We _____aren't_____ poor, but I _____think_____ it is wrong to spend a lot of
     8. (be / not)   **9. (think)**

money on clothes, especially for a growing boy. We _____give_____ him spending
                                                    10. (give)

money, but he _____doesn't have_____ enough to buy all the clothes he wants. Now he
               11. (have / not)

_____wants_____ to get a part-time job. I _____dont want_____ him to work, but my
 12. (want)   **13. (want / not)**

husband _____thinks_____ it's OK. What do you think?
         14. (think)

Rosa Alvarado

B | *Complete the answer to the parent with the words from the box. Use the correct form.*

agree	sound	think	~~want~~	work

Your son is not alone. Most teens _____want_____ to look like other teens. It's very
                                   1.

normal. And I _____agree_____ with your husband. When a person _____works_____,
              2.   **3.**

that person _____thinks_____ about the cost of things. A job for your son
            4.

_____sounds_____ fine to me.
 5.

86   UNIT 8

EXERCISE 6: Editing

Correct the paragraph. There are eight mistakes. The first mistake is already corrected.
Find and correct seven more.

anime = cartoons

> Miyuki Miyagi is a teenager. She ~~live~~ *lives* in Japan. She ~~like~~ *likes* clothes, and she shops in the Harajuku
>
> District in Tokyo. She say,ͨ"My friends and I love fashion. We ~~goes~~ *go* to the stores, but we ~~doesn't~~ *don't*
>
> always buy much. Clothes are expensive. But we still look good. My friends and I know
>
> inexpensive ways to dress "kawaii." For example, sometimes we ~~are~~ make our own clothes. And
>
> we mix styles. Sometimes we put on gothic clothes with punk clothes or schoolgirl uniforms.
>
> Sometimes we wear~~s~~ lots of makeup. And sometimes we dresse~~s~~ like dolls, or like anime.

STEP 4 COMMUNICATION PRACTICE

EXERCISE 7: Pronunciation

A *Read and listen to the Pronunciation Note.*

> **Pronunciation Note**
>
> In English, we pronounce the **third person singular ending / s /**, **/ z /**, or **/ ɪz /**.
>
> **EXAMPLES:**
>
> He lik**es** music. **/ s /**
>
> She pla**ys** golf. **/ z /**
>
> He watch**es** TV every day. **/ ɪz /**

B *Underline the verb in each sentence. Then listen to each sentence and check (✓) the sound of the verb ending.*

	/ s /	/ z /	/ ɪz /
1. He <u>shops</u> a lot.	✓		
2. She uses that word a lot.		✓	
3. She buys clothes at discount stores.		✓	
4. He knows his business.		✓	
5. It costs a hundred dollars.	✓		
6. He misses her.			✓
7. She watches fashion shows on TV.			✓
8. He thinks about his clothes.	✓		

EXERCISE 8: Listening

A | *Listen to the conversation between Elvia and Pedro. What does Elvia want?*

    a. something new

    b. something black

mannequin

B | *Listen to the conversation again. Complete the sentences.*

1. Elvia wants something for _____ *Bill's party* _____.

2. There's a(n) _____ at the Wrap.

3. She wants a(n) _____ in a(n)

    _____.

4. It costs _____.

5. Pedro thinks Elvia is a(n) _____.

EXERCISE 9: Conversation

A | *Check (✓) the sentences that are true for you.*

1. _____ I wear colorful clothes.   __✓__ I don't wear colorful clothes.

2. _____ I like leather jackets.   __✓__ I don't like leather jackets.

3. __✓__ I buy designer clothes.   _____ I don't buy designer clothes.
设计家

4. __✓__ I read fashion magazines.   _____ I don't read fashion magazines.
流行   杂志

5. __✓__ I like unusual clothes.   _____ I don't like unusual clothes.
与众不同的

6. _____ I wear traditional clothes.   __✓__ I don't wear traditional clothes.
传统的

7. __✓__ I have more than three pairs   _____ I don't have more than three pairs
    of jeans.   配对   of jeans.

B | *PAIRS: Discuss the ways you and your partner are alike or different.*

    EXAMPLE: We don't wear colorful clothes. We like dark colors such as black and gray.

EXERCISE 10: Discussion

GROUPS: Talk about clothes customs in different parts of the world.
For example, do people wear traditional clothes or Western clothes? Do
people remove their shoes when they enter a home? Do people cover
their heads?

> EXAMPLE: **A:** In my country, Peru, some people wear colorful woven
> clothes.
> **B:** What do they look like?
> **A:** They have wide sleeves and full skirts.
> **B:** In Argentina some men who work in the country wear
> "gaucho" clothing. They wear wide brimmed hats,
> ponchos, and loose pants in their boots.

EXERCISE 11: Writing

A | *Write about the way you and a relative dress. Use the simple present.*

> EXAMPLE: I usually wear polo shirts and matching slacks to school. Sometimes I wear sneakers,
> and sometimes I wear boots. I have five polo shirts. They're blue, black, brown, beige,
> and green. Every day I wear a different shirt. My sister wears bright colors, and her
> clothes are very unusual. She's pretty, so everything looks great on her.

B | *Check your work. Use the Editing Checklist.*

Editing Checklist
Did you . . . ? ☐ use the simple present correctly ☐ remember to add **-s** or **-es** to the third person singular ☐ use correct spelling

A | Circle the correct words to complete the sentences.

1. John **shop** / **shops** at The Wrap.

2. He **like** / **likes** their clothes.

3. My sister and I **don't like** / **am not like** the clothes at The Wrap.

4. We **go** / **goes** to Blooms.

5. Blooms **has** / **have** interesting clothes.

B | Complete the sentences with the verbs in parentheses. Use the affirmative or negative form.

1. It's hot today. We ___don't need___ jackets.
   (need)

2. It's cold and windy today. They ___need___ jackets and sweaters.
   (need)

3. They ___play___ soccer. They enjoy the sport.
   (play)

4. He ___doesn't like___ sports. He prefers to watch movies or read books.
   (like)

C | Complete the sentences with the words from the box. Use the correct form.

be	be	not wear	wear	work

1. My brother ___is___ a fashion designer.

2. He ___works___ for a magazine.

3. He ___wears___ a lot of trendy clothes. People always notice his clothes.

4. I ___don't wear___ trendy clothes. I wear old jeans and a white T-shirt.

5. My brother and I ___are___ different in other ways too.

D | Correct the sentences. There are six mistakes.

1. My son doesn't ~~has~~ have a suit.

2. He always wears jeans, T-shirts, and hoodies.

3. He needs a suit for my brother's wedding.

4. Suits ~~is~~ are expensive, and my son ~~don't~~ doesn't like to wear them.

5. We ~~wants~~ doesn't to rent or borrow a suit for him.

Simple Present: *Yes / No* Questions and Short Answers

ROOMMATES

STEP 1 GRAMMAR IN CONTEXT

Before You Read

GROUPS: Do you live alone? Do you have a roommate? Do you share a room with someone? Imagine you are looking for a roommate. What questions are important to ask?

Read

Colleges often use questionnaires to help students find the right roommate. Read the roommate questionnaire. Are Dan and Jon a good match? Why or why not?

Roommate Questionnaire[1]

	Dan		Jon	
	YES	**NO**	**YES**	**NO**
1. Do you **wake up** early?		✓		✓
2. Do you **stay up** late?	✓		✓	
3. **Are** you neat?	✓		✓	
4. **Does** a messy room **bother** you?	✓		✓	
5. **Are** you quiet?		✓	✓	
6. **Are** you talkative?	✓			✓
7. **Does** noise **bother** you?		✓		✓
8. **Are** you outgoing?	✓			✓
9. **Are** you a private person?		✓	✓	
10. **Are** you easygoing?	✓		✓	
11. Do you **listen** to loud music?	✓		✓	
12. Do you **watch** a lot of TV?	✓		✓	
13. Do you **study** and **listen** to music at the same time?	✓		✓	
14. Do you **study** with the TV on?	✓		✓	

[1]***questionnaire:*** a list of questions

['prɑivit]

A | Practice PAIRS: Now read the questionnaire aloud. Take turns reading the questions.

B | Vocabulary Complete the statements with the words from the box. Use the correct form.

bother	messy	outgoing	stay up
easygoing	neat [ni:t]	private	wake up

1. The room was ___private___, so we helped put things away. Now it is ___neat___.

2. That smell _____ me. I feel a little sick.

3. We ___stay up___ late on Friday and Saturday nights.

4. She _____ at seven o'clock on weekdays.

5. He is pretty _____. He doesn't get upset about most things.

6. I don't know very much about my roommate. He's a very _____ person.

7. That little girl is very _____. She's not afraid to talk to anyone.

C | Comprehension Write **T** (True) or **F** (False) for each statement.

_____ 1. Dan and Jon wake up late.

_____ 2. Dan is neat, but Jon isn't.

_____ 3. Dan and Jon are quiet.

_____ 4. Dan is outgoing, but Jon isn't.

_____ 5. Jon is a private person.

_____ 6. Dan and Jon are both easygoing.

_____ 7. Dan and Jon listen to loud music.

_____ 8. Dan and Jon don't watch TV.

_____ 9. Dan and Jon study and listen to music at the same time.

STEP 2 GRAMMAR PRESENTATION

SIMPLE PRESENT: YES / NO QUESTIONS AND SHORT ANSWERS

Yes / No Questions			Short Answers					
Do / Does	**Subject**	**Base Form of Verb**	**Affirmative**			**Negative**		
Do	I you* we they	**work?**	Yes,	you I / we you they	**do.**	No,	you I / we you they	**don't.**
Does	he she it			he she it	**does.**		he she it	**doesn't.**

* *You* is both singular and plural.

GRAMMAR NOTES

1	For **yes / no questions** in the **simple present**, use **do** or **does** before the subject. Use the base form of the verb after the subject.	SUBJECT • **Do** you **need** a roommate? • **Does** he **have** a roommate?
2	We usually use **short answers** in conversation. Sometimes we use **long answers**.	**A:** Do you need a roommate? **B:** **Yes.** OR **Yes, I do.** OR 　　**Yes, I need a roommate.** **A:** Does he have a roommate? **B:** **Yes.** OR **Yes, he does.** OR 　　**Yes, he has a roommate.**
3	**BE CAREFUL!** Do not use *do* or *does* for *yes / no* questions with **be**.	• **Are** you from Ecuador? • **Is** he from France? 　NOT: ~~Do are you~~ from Ecuador? 　　　 ~~Does is he~~ from France? 　　　 ~~Does you~~ from Ecuador?

REFERENCE NOTE
For a discussion of **yes / no questions with be**, see Unit 2, page 17.

STEP 3 FOCUSED PRACTICE

EXERCISE 1: Discover the Grammar

Read about Dan and Jon. Then match the questions and answers on the next page.

In many ways Dan and Jon are alike. Both Dan and Jon like music and sports, but Dan likes popular music, and Jon likes hip-hop. Both Dan and Jon like basketball, but Jon likes soccer and Dan doesn't. Dan and Jon are both neat. They don't like a messy room. They both like to go to bed late—after midnight. They watch about two hours of TV at night, and they study with the TV on. But in one way Dan and Jon are completely different. Dan is talkative, but Jon is quiet. Dan says, "We're lucky about that. It works out nicely. I talk, he listens." Jon says, "Uh-huh."

(continued on next page)

_b_ **1.** Do they both like music and sports?   **a.** It doesn't say.

____ **2.** Do they like to go to bed early?   **b.** Yes, they do.

____ **3.** Does Dan like popular music?   **c.** Yes, he does.

____ **4.** Dan is talkative. Jon is quiet. Does it matter?   **d.** No, they don't.

____ **5.** Do Dan and Jon like movies?   **e.** No, it doesn't.

EXERCISE 2: *Yes / No* Questions and Short Answers   *(Grammar Notes 1–2)*

Complete the questions with **Do** *or* **Does** *and the verbs in parentheses. Then complete the short answers.*

1. (listen)   **A:** _____ *Do* _____ you _____ *listen* _____ to music?

   B: Yes, _____ *we do* _____. OR Yes, _____ *I do* _____.

2. (have)   **A:** _____ your roommate _____ a TV?

   B: No, she _____.

3. (wake up) **A:** _____ he _____ early?

   B: No, _____.

4. (stay up) **A:** _____ they _____ late?

   B: Yes, _____.

5. (bother) **A:** _____ the TV _____ you?

   B: No, _____.

6. (have)   **A:** _____ your room _____ a big window?

   B: Yes, _____.

7. (rain)   **A:** _____ it _____ a lot in your city?

   B: No, _____.

8. (have)   **A:** _____ I _____ Internet access?

   B: Yes, _____.

9. (go)   **A:** _____ she _____ to parties all the time?

   B: No, _____.

10. (need)   **A:** _____ we _____ another lamp?

   B: Yes, _____.

11. (sell)   **A:** _____ they _____ gum here?

   B: Yes, _____.

EXERCISE 3: *Yes / No* Questions and Short Answers

(Grammar Notes 1–3)

*Complete the **yes / no** questions with **Do, Does, Am, Is,** or **Are**. Then complete the short answers.*

1. **A:** _____ *Am* _____ I late?   **B:** No, ___ *you aren't* ___ .

2. **A:** _____ he come late?   **B:** Yes, _____ .

3. **A:** _____ you busy?   **B:** Yes, we _____ .

4. **A:** _____ they have a lot of work?   **B:** No, _____ .

5. **A:** _____ they roommates?   **B:** No, _____ .

6. **A:** _____ they live in a dormitory?   **B:** Yes, _____ .

7. **A:** _____ she your sister?   **B:** No, _____ .

8. **A:** _____ you live at home?   **B:** Yes, I _____ .

9. **A:** _____ your roommate play baseball?   **B:** No, he _____ .

10. **A:** _____ we in the right room?   **B:** Yes, you _____ .

11. **A:** _____ you friends?   **B:** Yes, _____ .

12. **A:** _____ you cook well?   **B:** No, I _____ .

EXERCISE 4: *Yes / No* Questions and Short Answers

(Grammar Notes 1–2)

*Complete the conversation. Write questions with the words in parentheses. Then write short answers with **do, does, don't** or **doesn't**.*

A: So tell me about your new roommate, Edward. ___ *Do you like* ___ him?
　　　　　　　　　　　　　　　　　　　　　　　　　1. (you / like)

B: ___ *Yes, I do* ___ . He's a really nice guy.
　　　　2.

A: Where is he from? He sounds like a native speaker. _____ from England?
　　　　　　　　　　　　　　　　　　　　　　　　　　　　　　　3. (he / come)

B: _____ . He comes from Australia.
　　　　4.

A: Cool. What's he studying?

B: Music.

A: Oh, he's a music major. _____ an instrument?
　　　　　　　　　　　　　　5. (he / play)

B: Of course. He plays three instruments: violin, cello, and piano.

A: Wow. _____ with him?
　　　　　　　6. (you / play)

B: _____ . I'm not a good musician. But sometimes his cousin plays with him.
　　　　7.

(continued on next page)

A: _____ a lot of family close by?
    8. (he / have)

B: _____. His uncle, his aunt, three cousins, and his grandmother are
    9.

10 minutes away. I was at their home last night.

A: Really? _____ them often?
    10. (you / see)

B: _____. They invite us for a meal at least once a month. They all play music,
    11.

and they're interesting people. His uncle is a conductor, and she is an opera singer.

A: _____ them a small gift when you visit?
    12. (you / bring)

B: _____. I'm a poor student.
    13.

A: Hey, you're not that poor.

EXERCISE 5: Editing

Correct the conversations. There are eight mistakes. The first mistake is already corrected. Find and correct seven more.

1. **A:** Does she ~~goes~~ go to school?

   B: Yes, she ~~goes.~~ does

2. **A:** Does he ~~needs~~ need help?

   B: Yes, he does.

3. **A:** Do they ~~are~~ like rock music?

   B: Yes, they do.

4. **A:** ~~Do~~ Does she live near the museum?

   B: Yes, she ~~lives.~~ does

5. **A:** Does he ~~has~~ have a roommate?

   B: Yes, he does.

6. **A:** Are you friends?

   B: Yes, we ~~do.~~ are

STEP 4 COMMUNICATION PRACTICE

EXERCISE 6: Pronunciation

A | *Read and listen to the Pronunciation Note.*

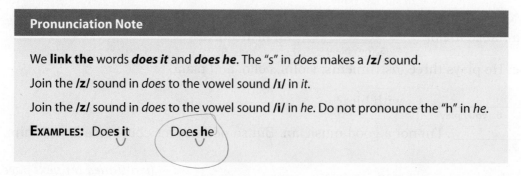

> **Pronunciation Note**
>
> We **link the** words **does it** and **does he**. The "s" in *does* makes a **/z/** sound.
>
> Join the **/z/** sound in *does* to the vowel sound **/ɪ/** in *it*.
>
> Join the **/z/** sound in *does* to the vowel sound **/i/** in *he*. Do not pronounce the "h" in *he*.
>
> **EXAMPLES:** Does it   Does he

B | *Listen to questions and repeat each question.*

1. Does it have Internet service?
2. Does it come with a desk?
3. Does it have two closets?
4. Does it have windows?

5. Does it have air conditioning?
6. Does he have a roommate?
7. Does he have a test?
8. Does he have a cold?

C | *PAIRS: Take turns. Look at Serge Lafitte's answers to a questionnaire. Ask your partner questions about Serge Lafitte. Remember to link **Does + he.***

EXAMPLE: **A:** Does he like movies?
B: Yes, he does.

NAME: *Serge*		
Do you _____?	**YES**	**NO**
1. like movies	✓	
2. stay up late	✓	
3. have a part-time job		✓
4. study and listen to music	✓	
5. like a clean, neat room		✓

EXERCISE 7: Listening

A | *Listen to the conversation. Why is Andrea talking to Valentina Gold?*

a. to find a roommate   **b.** to work out a problem with her roommate

B | *Listen again. Complete the chart with Andrea's answers.*

	Andrea	**Leyla**
parties		likes parties
music		likes rock
sports		plays basketball, soccer, swims
study habits		studies at night in her room

C | *Compare Andrea and Leyla. Are they a good match? Why or why not?*

_____

_____

EXERCISE 8: Discussion: Comparing Habits and Personality

PAIRS: Look at the roommate questionnaire again. Answer the questions for yourself. Then compare your answers with a partner's.

	YOU	
	YES	NO
1. Do you **wake up** early?	☐	☐
2. Do you **stay up** late?	☐	☐
3. Are you neat?	☐	☐
4. Does a messy room **bother** you?	☐	☐
5. Are you quiet?	☐	☐
6. Are you talkative?	☐	☐
7. Does noise **bother** you?	☐	☐
8. Are you outgoing?	☐	☐
9. Are you a private person?	☐	☐
10. Are you easygoing?	☐	☐
11. Do you **listen** to loud music?	☐	☐
12. Do you **watch** a lot of TV?	☐	☐
13. Do you **study** and **listen** to music at the same time?	☐	☐
14. Do you **study** with the TV on?	☐	☐

EXERCISE 9: Game: Find Someone Who . . .

Find out about your classmates. Ask these questions and add your own. Take notes. Tell the class something new about three classmates.

Do you . . . ?	Are you . . . ?
cook well	messy
text every day	outgoing
play a musical instrument	a private person
like sports	athletic
watch sports on TV	handy (good at fixing things)
have a lot of brothers and sisters	an only child
have a lot of electronics	interested in art
Your question:	*Your question:*

EXAMPLE: Ali is handy. He fixes things.
Sara plays the violin. She was in a concert last month.
Mi Young watches sports on TV. She loves the New York Yankees.

EXERCISE 10: Game: What's in Your Backpack?

Work in small groups. Ask questions. Check (✓) the items you have. The first group to check 10 items wins.

EXAMPLE: Do you have keys? OR Does anyone have keys?

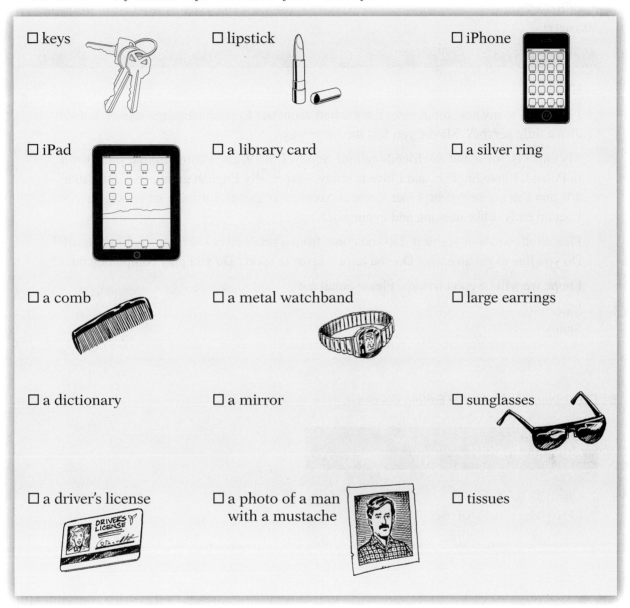

☐ keys

☐ lipstick

☐ iPhone

☐ iPad

☐ a library card

☐ a silver ring

☐ a comb

☐ a metal watchband

☐ large earrings

☐ a dictionary

☐ a mirror

☐ sunglasses

☐ a driver's license

☐ a photo of a man with a mustache

☐ tissues

EXERCISE 11: Writing

A | *Imagine you plan to study English at a school for international students. The school has chosen a roommate for you. You do not know the roommate. Write your new roommate an email. Tell about yourself and ask your roommate questions. Use the simple present.*

EXAMPLE:

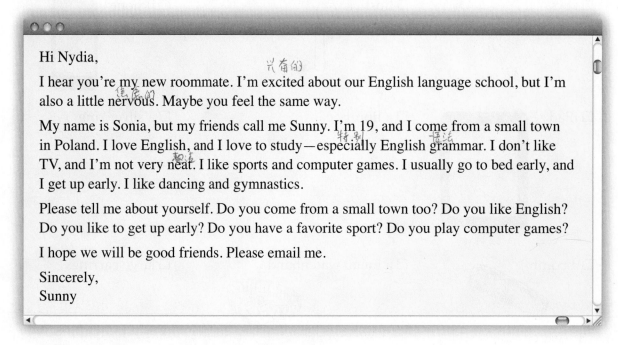

Hi Nydia,

I hear you're my new roommate. I'm excited about our English language school, but I'm also a little nervous. Maybe you feel the same way.

My name is Sonia, but my friends call me Sunny. I'm 19, and I come from a small town in Poland. I love English, and I love to study—especially English grammar. I don't like TV, and I'm not very neat. I like sports and computer games. I usually go to bed early, and I get up early. I like dancing and gymnastics.

Please tell me about yourself. Do you come from a small town too? Do you like English? Do you like to get up early? Do you have a favorite sport? Do you play computer games?

I hope we will be good friends. Please email me.

Sincerely,
Sunny

B | *Check your work. Use the Editing Checklist.*

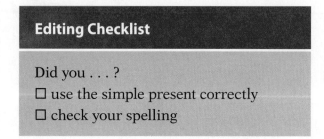

Editing Checklist

Did you . . . ?
☐ use the simple present correctly
☐ check your spelling

9 Review

Check your answers on page UR-2.
Do you need to review anything?

A | Complete the sentences with the words from the box.

| Am | Are | Do | Does | Is |

1. _____Do_____ you know his brother?

2. _____Does_____ his brother messy?

3. _____Is_____ he have a lot of friends?

4. _____Are_____ they easygoing?

5. _____Am_____ I your best friend?

B | Complete the questions with the verbs in parentheses. Use the correct form.

1. (have) _____ you _____ a roommate?

2. (speak) _____ his roommate _____ English fluently?

3. (watch) _____ your roommate _____ TV at night?

4. (be) _____ your roommate talkative?

5. (be) _____ your roommates' parents in the United States?

C | Write questions about an apartment. Use the words in parentheses.

1. _____?
   (be / the neighbors / noisy)

2. _____?
   (the apartment building / have / an elevator)

3. _____?
   (be / the apartment / near trains or buses)

4. _____?
   (the bedroom / have / two closets)

5. _____?
   (be / the bedroom / big)

D | Correct the conversations. There are five mistakes.

1. **A:** Does he have a big TV in his room?
   B: Yes, he has.

2. **A:** Does she needs help?
   B: No, she don't.

3. **A:** Do you are friends?
   B: Yes, we aren't.

Unit 9 Review: Simple Present: *Yes / No* Questions and Short Answers **101**

10 Simple Present: *Wh-* Questions
DREAMS

STEP 1 GRAMMAR IN CONTEXT

Before You Read

PAIRS: Do you dream? Do you remember your dreams? What do you dream about?

Read

Ask the Expert *is a radio talk show. Today Rob Stevens is talking to dream expert Helena Lee. Read the conversation.*

Dreams

RS: Good afternoon. I'm Rob Stevens. Welcome to *Ask the Expert*. This afternoon my guest is Helena Lee. She's the author of *Sleep and Dreams*. Thank you for coming.

LEE: Thanks, Rob. It's great to be here.

RS: Helena, we have a lot of questions about dreams. Our first question is from Carolina Gomes. She asks, "**Why do we dream?**"

LEE: That's a good question. Actually, nobody really knows why. But I think dreams help us understand our feelings.

RS: OK. . . . Our next question is from Jonathan Lam. He asks, "**Who dreams?** Does everyone dream?"

LEE: Yes, everyone dreams. People dream in every part of the world. And what's more, scientists believe animals dream too.

RS: Wow! That's really interesting. **How do we know?**

LEE: We have machines. They show when people or animals dream. But, of course, no one knows what animals dream about.

RS: Our next question is from Pablo Ortiz. He writes, "People don't remember *all* their dreams. **What dreams do they remember?**"

LEE: People remember their unusual dreams. And, unfortunately, people remember their bad dreams, or nightmares.

RS: Beata Green says, "I have the same dream again and again. **What does that mean?**"

LEE: That dream has special meaning for you. You need to think about it.

RS: Here's a question from Samuel Diaz. "**When do people dream?**"

LEE: They dream during deep sleep. It's called REM sleep. REM means *rapid eye movement*.

RS: I hear REM sleep is important. **Why do we need it?**

LEE: Without it, we can't remember or think clearly.

RS: Our last question for today is from Mike Morgan. He writes, "My roommate doesn't remember his dreams. **Why do I remember my dreams?**"

LEE: Well, a University of Iowa professor says, "Creative[1] people remember their dreams."

RS: Thank you so much, Helena. We look forward to reading your new book.

---
[1] ***creative:*** able to see things in a new way

After You Read

A | Practice *PAIRS: Now read the conversation aloud.*

B | Vocabulary *Complete the conversations with the words from the box.*

author	guest	nightmares	remember	unfortunately

1. **A:** Who's the ____author____ of that book?

   B: Helena Lee. She was a(n) ____guest____ on *Ask the Expert*.

2. **A:** Do you ____remember____ your dreams?

   B: No, I don't. ____unfortunately____, I remember my ____nightmares____ because they

   wake me up.

C | Comprehension *Write* **T** (**True**), **F** (**False**), *or* **?** (**it doesn't say**) *for each statement.*

___F___ 1. Only creative people dream.

___F___ 2. Animals dream about food.

___T___ 3. People dream during REM sleep.

___F___ 4. REM stands for real eye movement.

___F___ 5. A professor believes that smart people remember their dreams.

SIMPLE PRESENT: *WH-* QUESTIONS; SHORT AND LONG ANSWERS

Wh- Questions				Answers	
Wh- Word	**Do / Does**	**Subject**	**Base Form of Verb**	**Short**	**Long**
When		I		From 10:00 P.M. to 5:00 A.M.	You sleep from 10:00 P.M. to 5:00 A.M.
Where	**do**	you	**sleep?**	On the futon.	I sleep on the futon.
Why		we		Because we're tired.	We sleep because we're tired.
What		they	**need?**	Two pillows.	They need two pillows.
Who	**does**	she	**know?**	My brother.	She knows my brother.
How		it	**feel?**	Good.	The blanket feels good.

Wh- Questions about the Subject			Answers
Wh- Word	**Verb**		
Who	**dreams?**		Everyone does.
What	**happens**	during REM sleep?	People dream.

GRAMMAR NOTES

1 *Wh-* **questions** ask for <u>information</u>. Most questions use **wh- word** + **do** or **does** + **subject** + **base form of the verb**.

WH- WORD	DO / DOES	SUBJECT	BASE FORM	
• **When**	**do**	you	**go**	to bed?
• **What**	**does**	he	**dream**	about?

2 To ask a **question about the subject**, use **who** or **what** + **third-person singular form of the verb**.

SUBJECT
• **My brother** sleeps on the sofa.
• **Who sleeps** on the sofa?

SUBJECT
• **Milk** helps me fall asleep.
• **What helps** you fall asleep?

BE CAREFUL! Do not use **do** or **does** with questions about the subject. Do not use the base form of the verb.

NOT: Who ~~does~~ sleeps on the sofa?
NOT: Who ~~do~~ sleeps on the sofa?
NOT: Who ~~sleep~~ on the sofa?

3

Who asks questions about a *subject*.
Who and *whom* ask questions about an *object*.

USAGE NOTE: *Whom* is very formal.

SUBJECT
· **Who helps** John? Mary does.

OBJECT
· **Who does** Mary **help**? John.

OBJECT
· **Whom does** Mary **help**? John.

REFERENCE NOTE
For more about *who*, *what*, *where*, *when*, and *why*, see Unit 2, page 17.

STEP 3 FOCUSED PRACTICE

EXERCISE 1: Discover the Grammar

Night owls like to stay up late at night. Early birds get up early. Read about a night owl and an early bird. Then match the questions and answers.

Felix is a night owl. He hates to get up in the morning. On weekends he goes to bed at 1:00 A.M. and gets up at noon. Unfortunately for Felix, during the week his first class starts at 8:15, and he needs to get up early.

At 7:00 A.M. Felix's alarm rings. He wakes up, but he doesn't get up. He stays in bed and daydreams. At 7:20 his mom comes in. She has a big smile. She says, "Felix, it's time to get up."

Felix's mother is an early bird. Even on vacations she is up at 6:00 A.M. When his mom wakes him, Felix says, "Leave me alone. I'm tired."

Finally, at about 7:30, Felix gets up. He jumps out of bed, showers, and gets dressed. At 7:50 he drinks a big glass of juice, takes a breakfast bar, and runs to the bus stop. The bus comes at 8:00.

__f__ **1.** Who hates to get up in the morning?

_____ **2.** How does Felix feel in the morning?

_____ **3.** Why does Felix run to the bus stop?

_____ **4.** What does Felix have for breakfast?

_____ **5.** When does Felix sleep late?

_____ **6.** What happens at 7:00?

a. On weekends.

b. Tired.

c. Felix's alarm rings.

d. A glass of juice and a breakfast bar.

e. Because he doesn't want to be late for school.

f. Felix does.

EXERCISE 2: Word Order of *Wh-* Questions

(Grammar Notes 1–3)

Complete the conversations. Read the answers. Then write questions with the words in parentheses.

1. (do / you / usually get up / When)

   A: _When do you usually get up?_

   B: At 7:00 on weekdays.

2. (Where / come from / your guest / does)

   A: _____

   B: She's from Sydney.

3. (at night / they / How / do / feel)

   A: _____

   B: They're never tired at night. They're night owls.

4. (does / Who / he / dream about)

   A: _____

   B: He dreams about me.

5. (What / she / dream about / does)

   A: _____

   B: Actually, she never remembers her dreams.

EXERCISE 3: *Wh-* Questions about the Subject

(Grammar Note 3)

Complete the conversations. Read the answers. Then write questions with the words in parentheses. Use the correct form.

1. (Who / daydream)

   A: _Who daydreams?_

   B: John does.

2. (Who / have / nightmares)

   A: _____

   B: Her brother Sam does. What's more, he sometimes screams during a nightmare.

3. (Who / get up / before 6:00 A.M.)

    A: _____

    B: Grandma Ilene does.

4. (Who / hate / early morning classes)

    A: _____

    B: Bob, Emiko, and Jill do.

5. (Who / need / more than eight hours of sleep)

    A: _____

    B: Feng does.

EXERCISE 4: *Wh-* Questions

(Grammar Notes 1–3)

Read the answers. Then ask questions about the underlined words.

1. <u>Sabrina</u> daydreams.

    Who _daydreams_ _____?

2. Sabrina daydreams <u>during her math class</u>.

    When _____?

3. Sabrina daydreams about <u>her boyfriend</u>.

    Who _____?

4. Sabrina daydreams during math <u>because she doesn't like the class and doesn't</u>

    <u>understand the teacher</u>.

    Why _____?

5. Sabrina's boyfriend is <u>3,000 miles away in Alaska</u>.

    Where _____?

6. Sabrina feels <u>lonely</u>.

    How _____?

7. <u>Sabrina's boyfriend</u> has a good job.

    Who _____?

8. <u>He works for an oil company.</u>

    What _____?

EXERCISE 5: *Wh-* Questions: Subject and Object *(Grammar Notes 2–3)*

*Label the subject (**S**) and object (**O**) in each sentence. Write one question about the subject and one question about the object. Then answer the questions. Use short answers.*

                 S   O

1. My mother wakes me on weekdays.

    Q: *Who wakes you on weekdays?*   **Q:** *Who does your mother wake on weekdays?*

    A: *My mother.*   **A:** *She wakes me.*

2. In a dream Jake meets his boss at a party.

    Q: _____   **Q:** _____

    A: _____   **A:** _____

3. In a nightmare two giants hit Maya.

    Q: _____   **Q:** _____

    A: _____   **A:** _____

EXERCISE 6: Editing

Correct the questions. There are ten mistakes. The first mistake is already corrected. Find and correct nine more.

1. Where do they ~~sleeps~~? *sleep*

2. Why they need two pillows?

3. Who sleep on the sofa?

4. When does she goes to bed?

5. Who wake you?

6. Who does you dream about?

7. How he feels about that?

8. What you dream about?

9. Where he sleep?

10. How long does she sleeps at night?

EXERCISE 7: Listening

A | *Mia often has the same dream. She tells a doctor about her dream. Listen to their conversation. What is Mia looking for?*

_____

B | *Listen again to Mia's dream. Answer the questions.*

1. What important event does Mia have?   *She has an important test.*_____

2. What does the man in the dream say?   _____

3. What does Dr. Fox think Mia has?   _____

4. What do the two buildings symbolize?   _____

5. What does Mia's father want her to study?   _____

EXERCISE 8: Pronunciation

A | *Read and listen to the Pronunciation Note.*

> **Pronunciation Note**
>
> Some English words have an *r* or *l* after another consonant. For example, **/ pr /** as in **price** or **/ gl /** as in **glad**. If it is hard for you to pronounce these two consonants together, try saying the word with the second consonant and then add the first one.
>
> **EXAMPLES:** rice → **price**
>   lock → **clock**

B | *Listen and repeat the words.*

black	bright	dream	free	price
blue	clock	dress	great	three

C | *PAIRS: Read a word from Part B. Your partner writes the word in his or her notebook. Take turns.*

🎧 **D** | *Listen and read about Olivia's dream. Underline the words with consonant groups that have an / r / or / l / .*

> It was a great dream. Listen. I buy a black dress. The price is only thirty-three dollars. There's a problem with the dress. I bring it back. The salesperson says she's sorry.
>
> She gives me a bright blue dress instead. I try it on. The dress is perfect. I wear the dress to a party. I have a great night out.

EXERCISE 9: Interview

Answer the questions. Then work with a partner. Ask your partner the questions.

	You	Your Partner
When do you go to bed?		
What days do you sleep in?		
Does anyone wake you? If so, who?		
Do you dream? If so, what do you dream about?		
Are you an early bird or a night owl?		

EXERCISE 10: Group Interview

A | *Ask five students these questions about sleep. Take notes on a separate piece of paper.*

EXAMPLE: **YOU:** Juan, do you snore?
JUAN: No, I don't, but my sister Bianca snores.

1. Who snores?

2. Who gets up before 6:00 A.M.?

3. Who goes to bed after midnight?

4. Who needs more than eight hours of sleep?

5. Who needs less than five hours of sleep?

6. Who dreams in English?

7. Who daydreams?

8. Who has insomnia? (trouble sleeping)

9. Who falls asleep during the day?

B | *Tell the class interesting results.*

EXAMPLE: Juan's sister snores.
Nobody gets up before 6:00 A.M., but sometimes Hasan goes to bed at 5:00 A.M.

EXERCISE 11: Information Gap: Understanding Dreams

PAIRS: **Student A,** *follow the instructions on this page.* **Student B,** *turn to page 112 and follow the instructions there.*

1. Student B often has the same dream. Find out about Student B's dream. Ask these questions.

   In your dream:

   - Where are you?
   - Who do you see?
   - Is the person big? little?
   - Are you big? little?
   - What does the person say?
   - What do you do?

2. You have the following dream again and again. Read about your dream. Then answer Student B's questions about it.

   > You are on an airplane. The pilot comes to you. He says, "I need your help." You go with the pilot. You fly the plane. You land the plane. Everyone claps. You feel good. You wake up.

3. Talk about your dreams. What do they mean?

EXERCISE 12: Writing

A | *Write about a dream or daydream you often have. Answer the questions:*
   - What do you dream or daydream about?
   - Where does it take place?
   - What happens?
   - How often do you have this dream?
   - What do you think? Why do you have this dream or daydream?

   EXAMPLE: I often daydream about my family. I daydream about my birthday. I am 14 years old. We are at my grandparents' home. My grandparents' friends are there. They have a granddaughter. She is beautiful. I want to talk to her, but I get nervous. I can't talk. I turn red. Everyone looks at me. Then I run home. I feel very embarrassed.

B | *Check your work. Use the Editing Checklist.*

Editing Checklist
Did you . . . ?
☐ use the simple present correctly
☐ check your spelling

1. You often have the following dream. Read about your dream. Then answer Student A's questions about it.

> You are in the third grade. You see your third grade teacher. Your teacher is very big. You are small. Your teacher says, "Your schoolwork is great. You are my favorite student." You smile. Then you laugh. Then you wake up.

2. Student A often has the same dream. Find out about Student A's dream. Ask these questions.

   In your dream:

   - Where are you?
   - Who comes to you?
   - What does he say?

   - What do you do?
   - How do you feel?
   - What happens?

3. Talk about your dreams. What do they mean?

Check your answers on page UR-2.

Do you need to review anything?

A | Complete the **wh-** questions with the words from the box.

how	when	where	who	why

1. **A:** _____ does she snore?   **B:** I don't know why.

2. **A:** _____ do they get up?   **B:** At about 9:00 or 10:00.

3. **A:** _____ sleeps on the sofa?   **B:** Their uncle does.

4. **A:** _____ do you feel?   **B:** Sleepy.

5. **A:** _____ do you buy sheets?   **B:** At Bloom's department store.

B | Write questions with the words in parentheses. Use the correct form.

1. _____
   (Who / snore / in your family)

2. _____
   (What / you / dream about)

3. _____
   (What time / your mother / get up)

4. _____
   (What time / you / go to bed)

5. _____
   (Where / your brother / sleep)

C | Read the statement and answers. Then write the questions.

John meets his uncle at the diner on Saturdays.

1. **A:** _____   **B:** John does.

2. **A:** _____   **B:** His uncle.

3. **A:** _____   **B:** At the diner.

4. **A:** _____   **B:** On Saturdays.

D | Correct the questions. There are six mistakes.

1. Where you live and who you live with?

2. Why he daydreams in class?

3. When does she gets up?

4. How they feel about sleeping pills?

5. Who does you dream about?

From Grammar to Writing

TIME WORD CONNECTORS: *FIRST*, *NEXT*, *AFTER THAT*, *THEN*, *FINALLY*

1 | *Which paragraph sounds better,* **A** *or* **B**? *Why?*

Paragraph A

I like to watch my roommate prepare tea. She boils water and pours the boiling water in a cup with a teabag in it. She removes the teabag and adds sugar. She adds lemon. She adds ice. She sips the tea and says, "Mmm. This tea is just the way I like it."

Paragraph B

I like to watch my roommate prepare tea. First, she boils some water and pours the boiling water in a cup with a teabag in it. Next, she removes the teabag and adds some sugar. After that, she adds some lemon. Then she adds some ice. Finally, she sips the tea and says, "Mmm. This tea is just the way I like it."

You can make your writing clearer by using **time word connectors**. They show the order in which things happen. Some common ones are *first*, *next*, *after that*, *then*, and *finally*. We usually use a **comma** after these connectors.

> **EXAMPLE:** **First**, you add the water. **Next**, you add the sugar.

2 | *Add time word connectors to show the order of things in this paragraph.*

I take a shower. I have breakfast. I drive to the train station. I take a train and a bus. I get to work.

Now write a paragraph about a routine you follow. Use time word connectors. Here are some ideas:

> **EXAMPLE:** Every Saturday morning . . .
> Every New Year's Day . . .
> Every year on my birthday . . .

3 | *Exchange papers with a partner. Did your partner follow directions? Correct any mistakes in grammar and spelling.*

4 | *Talk to your partner. Discuss the mistakes you made. Then rewrite your own paper and make any necessary changes.*

There is / There are; Possessives; Modals: Ability and Permission

There is / There are

SHOPPING MALLS

Before You Read

PAIRS: Discuss the questions.

1. Do you like big malls? Why or why not?
2. Is there a mall near your school? Where is it? Do you go there? Why or why not?

Read

Read an advertisement for the West Edmonton Mall in Canada.

Come to Edmonton and see its top attraction,

West Edmonton Mall

West Ed Mall is a shopper's dream. **There are** more than 800 stores. They include everything from Old Navy® to Godiva® Chocolates to one-of-a-kind stores. Enjoy the mall's international flavor. **There's** Chinatown, where you can shop in a traditional Chinese marketplace. **There's** Europa Boulevard with its many European specialties. West Ed Mall also has over 110 eating places. And for the young and the young-at-heart **there are** seven world-class attractions including a water park, an amusement park, and an indoor skating rink. So make your travel plans now. **There isn't** a better time to get away.

After You Read

A | **Practice** *PAIRS: Now read the advertisement aloud. Take turns reading sentences.*

B | **Vocabulary** *Complete the conversations with the words from the box.*

amusement park	include	market
attraction	indoor	one of a kind
get away	international	

1. **A:** Why do you like that store?

   B: It's _____. It has unusual things for sale.

2. **A:** Does the bill _____ the tip at this restaurant?

   B: No. The tip is extra.

3. **A:** What kind of school is it?

   B: It's a(n) _____ school. Students come from all over the world.

4. **A:** There's a big _____ in the center of town. You can buy fresh fruit,

   vegetables, and handmade clothes.

   B: Let's go. It sounds great.

5. **A:** What's the main _____ at that mall?

   B: The prices. Everything is cheap.

6. **A:** What's your favorite ride at the _____?

   B: The Hurricane. It's fast and scary. I love it.

7. **A:** Does the school have a(n) _____ swimming pool?

   B: Yes, it does. The students can swim every day of the year.

8. **A:** He's tired and bored with his job.

   B: He needs to _____.

C | Comprehension *Read each question about the advertisement. Circle the correct letter.*

1. How many stores are there at the West Edmonton Mall?

   a. more than 80

   b. more than 100

   c. more than 800

2. What does the ad say about the mall?

   a. It has a chocolate flavor.

   b. It has a Canadian flavor.

   c. It has an international flavor. 特色

(Top) Spinner and *(Bottom)* statue at West Edmonton Mall

3. What kind of traditional market is there?

   a. a Mexican market

   b. a Chinese market

   c. a Turkish market

4. How many eating places are there?

   a. more than 80

   b. more than 100

   c. more than 7

5. What does West Edmonton Mall include?

   a. a water park

   b. schools

   c. a golf course

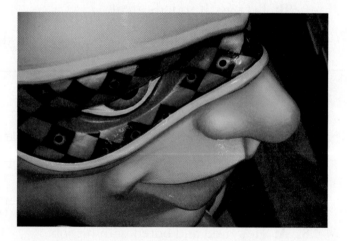

THERE IS / THERE ARE

Affirmative Statements			
There	*Be*	Subject	Place / Time
There	is	a restaurant	on this level.
		a movie	at 6:30.
There	are	two restaurants	near the entrance.
		shows	at 7:00 and 9:00.

ʃ ˈɛntrəns ʌ口

Negative Statements			
There	*Be + Not*	Subject	Place / Time
There	isn't	a restaurant	on the second level.
There	aren't	any movies	at 8:00.

Contractions
there is ⟶ there's
there is not ⟶ there isn't
there are not ⟶ there aren't

Yes / No Questions			
Be	*There*	Subject	Place
Is	there	a pizza place	on Second Street?
Are	there	any banks	nearby?

Short Answers			
Affirmative		Negative	
Yes,	there is.	No,	there isn't.
	there are.		there aren't.

GRAMMAR NOTES

concent i
音乐会

1	Use ***there is*** or ***there's*** to state facts about a **person** or **thing**.	• **There is a salesperson** near the door. • **There's a bookstore** next to the electronics store.
2	Use ***there are*** to talk about people or things. We often use *there is* or *there are* to tell the **location** of people or things or the **time** of events. *位置* **BE CAREFUL!** Don't confuse *there are* and *they are*.	• **There are five shoe stores** at the mall. • There's a woman's shoe store **on the second level**. (location) • There are concerts **on Friday and Saturday nights**. (time) • **There are two good restaurants.** **They are** on the third level.
3	In the negative, use the contractions ***isn't*** and ***aren't***. The full forms, *is not* and *are not*, are rarely used with *there*. **BE CAREFUL!** Don't confuse *there aren't* with *they aren't*.	• **There isn't** a cloud in the sky. • **There aren't** any gyms near our school. • **There aren't any** gyms here. **There are** three restaurants nearby, but **they aren't** open this late.
4	We often use ***any*** with *yes / no* questions about plural nouns.	• Are there **any** malls nearby?
5	**BE CAREFUL!** ***Here*** and ***there*** are adverbs of place. *Here* is for something nearby, and *there* is for something far. Don't confuse the adverb of place *there* with *there is* or *there are* or with the possessive adjective *their*.	• Last summer we exchanged homes with friends near Banff. We went **there**, and they came **here**. • Banff National Park is good for hiking. **There are** high mountains **there**. • **Their** home is in the mountains.
6	We often use ***There is*** or ***There are*** the first time we talk about people or things. We use ***he***, ***she***, ***it***, or ***they*** to tell more about the people or things.	• **There's a package** in the mail. **It's** heavy. • **There's a man** at the door. **He** wants to speak to you. • **There are three girls** in the dress store. **They** are choosing dresses for a party.

EXERCISE 1: Discover the Grammar

*Look at the mall directory. Write **T** (**True**) or **F** (**False**) for each statement.*

Mall Directory

Third Level	3a	3b	3c	3d	3e	
	Food Court	Thai food	Chinese food	Burgers	Sushi bar	Café
Second Level	2a	2b	2c	2d	2e	2f
	Women's clothes	Shoe store	Art supply store	Furniture store	Children's clothes	Cosmetics store
First Level	1a	1b	1c	1d	1e	1f
	Flower shop	Gift shop	Bookstore	Unisex hair salon	Electronics store	Women's clothes

_T_ **1.** There's a flower shop on the first level.

_F_ **2.** There's a café on the second level.

_T_ **3.** There aren't any toy stores.

_T_ **4.** There are five places to eat.

_F_ **5.** There isn't any Thai food at this mall.

_T_ **6.** There's a bookstore on the first level.

_T_ **7.** There aren't any office supply stores at the mall.

_T_ **8.** There aren't any jewelry stores at the mall.

_T_ **9.** There isn't an amusement park at this mall.

_T_ **10.** There's an art supply store at the mall.

EXERCISE 2: Affirmative and Negative Statements

(Grammar Notes 1–3)

Check (✓) each correct sentence. Change the sentences that don't make sense.

_____ **1.** There's a mall in the Chinese restaurant. _There's a Chinese restaurant in the mall._

_____ **2.** There's a second level on the shoe store. _There's a shoe store on the second level_

✓ **3.** There are two women's clothing stores at the mall. _There are mall at two women's_

✓ **4.** There's an electronics store on the first level. _There are first level_

_____ **5.** There isn't a mall in the men's clothing store. _____

✓ **6.** There aren't any furniture stores in the desks. _____

EXERCISE 3: Affirmative and Negative Statements

(Grammar Notes 1–4, 6)

Complete the conversation. Use **there is, there isn't, there are, there aren't, they are,** *or* **they aren't.**

A: This pizza place is awful. _____There aren't_____ any tablecloths, and the
                                        1.

placemats are dirty.

B: You're right. _____There aren't_____ any napkins either.
                          2.

A: Where is the busboy?

B: I don't know. _____There isn't_____ anyone here now except us.
                          3.

A: _____There is_____ a busboy here somewhere, but I don't see him now.
            4.

Well, I need a fork and knife.

B: _____There aren't_____ some forks and knives on that table. Oh.
            5.

_____There is_____ clean.
      6.

A: Oh my gosh. You won't believe this.

B: What is it? Boy, it's hot in here. _____There is_____ even a fan.
                                               7.

A: _____There is_____ a mouse over there, near the wall!
            8.

B: What? Ugh, _____There are_____ two mice! Let's leave!
                      9.

A: What about our food?

B: Let the mice have it. _____There is_____ hungry, too!
                                 10.

EXERCISE 4: There is / There are, There, and They are   (Grammar Notes 1–2, 5)

Complete the conversation. Use **there's**, **there are**, **there**, *and* **they're***. Remember to start sentences with a capital letter.*

A: How about some Chinese food?

B: Well, _____ there's _____ only one Chinese food restaurant nearby, but
                                1.

   it's not very good. _____ There are _____ a lot of other restaurants though.
                                2.

A: Today is Sunday. Are they open?

B: _____ There are _____ all open seven days a week.
                        3.

A: Well, _____ there is _____ a nice Mexican place over
                        4.

   _____ there _____ .
                        5.

B: Where?

A: Over _____ there _____ next to the diner.
                        6.

B: That's right. I know the place. I was _____ a few months
                                                            7.

   ago. Let's go.

EXERCISE 5: Agreement with *There is / There are*   (Grammar Notes 1–2, 6)

Complete the sentences. Use **There's** *or* **There are** *in the first sentence. Use* **He's, She's, It's,** *or* **They're** *in the second sentence.*

   1. _____There's_____ a good café over there. _____It's_____ next to the bookstore.

   2. _____ a salesman behind the counter. _____ talking to that woman.

   3. _____ a lot of wool sweaters. _____ in the back of the store.

   4. _____ a scarf on the floor. _____ your new one, isn't it?

   5. _____ some indoor parking spaces over there. _____ near the exit.

   6. _____ a small mall on Route 4. _____ next to the amusement park.

   7. _____ a lot of people in that line. _____ buying tickets for the movie.

EXERCISE 6: *Yes / No* Questions with *Is there / Are there* (Grammar Notes 1–4, 6)

Look at the calendar. Complete the questions with **is there** or **are there**. *Then write answers. Remember to start sentences with a capital letter.*

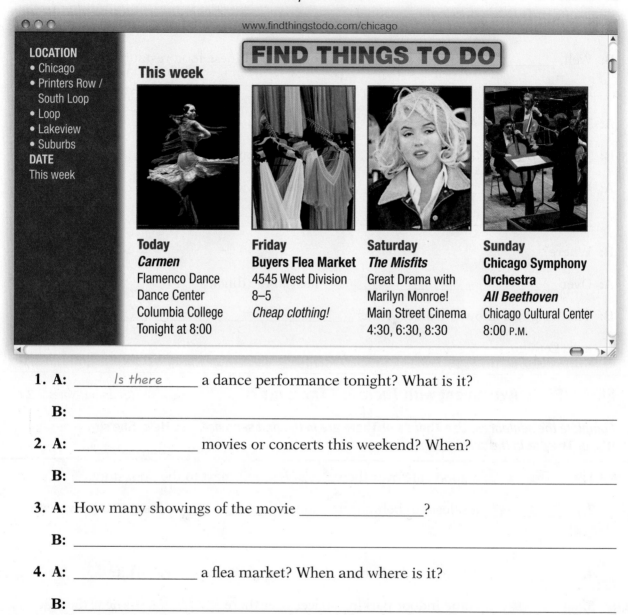

1. **A:** _____*Is there*_____ a dance performance tonight? What is it?

   B: _____

2. **A:** _____ movies or concerts this weekend? When?

   B: _____

3. **A:** How many showings of the movie _____?

   B: _____

4. **A:** _____ a flea market? When and where is it?

   B: _____

EXERCISE 7: Editing

Correct the paragraph. There are six mistakes. The first mistake is already corrected.
Find and correct five more.

>   *are*
>   There ~~be~~ pizza places at almost every mall. The pizzas come in all shapes and sizes. are
> traditional pizzas with mushrooms, pepperoni, and broccoli. There is also pizzas with curry, red
> herring, and coconut. In the United States they are over 61,000 pizza places. There represent
> 17 percent of all restaurants. There are popular with young and old.

EXERCISE 8: Pronunciation

🎧 **A** | *Read and listen to the Pronunciation Note.*

Pronunciation Note
The words *there*, *their*, and *they're* have the same sound.

🎧 **B** | *Listen to the sentences. Circle the correct letter of the word or words the speaker uses.*

1. **(a.)** there **b.** their

2. **a.** There **b.** There's

3. **a.** They are **b.** There are

4. **a.** There **b.** There's

5. **a.** There are **b.** They are

6. **a.** There **b.** They're

EXERCISE 9: Listening

🎧 **A** | *Listen to this conversation between two drivers. What is the speaker's first question?*

Excuse me, _____?

🎧 **B** | *Listen again. Mark the sentences Y (Yes), N (No), or ? (it doesn't say).*

___Y___ **1.** Is there a mall up ahead?

_____ **2.** Is the mall crowded?

_____ **3.** Is there a pizza place at the mall?

_____ **4.** Is the food court on the second level?

_____ **5.** Are there at least 10 places where you can eat?

EXERCISE 10: Comparing Pictures

PAIRS: Find 10 differences between Picture A and Picture B.

EXAMPLE: In Picture A there's a shoe repair shop between the bakery and the pizza place. In Picture B there isn't a shoe repair shop between the bakery and the pizza place. The shoe repair shop is between the pizza place and the flower shop.

Picture A

Picture B

EXERCISE 11: Game: Tic Tac Toe

Use the phrases in the boxes to ask your classmates questions. Begin with **Is there** *or* **Are there any.** *If a student says "yes," write his or her name in the box. When you have three across, down, or diagonally, call out, "Tic Tac Toe!"*

a big mall near your home	an amusement park near your home	an international club in your school
twins in your family	an Italian restaurant near your home	a skating rink near your home
a pizza place on your street	credit cards in your purse or pocket	an indoor pool near your home

EXERCISE 12: Writing

A | *Write about a place where you like to shop. Use* **There is, There isn't, There are,** *or* **There aren't.**

EXAMPLE: There's a small store near my home. It's called "Village Gifts." It's on a street with two other small shops. The owners are a husband and wife. Their gifts include unusual crafts from all over the world. There are some great things to buy—colorful pottery from Mexico, beautiful jewelry from Thailand, traditional rugs from China, and baskets from Jamaica. The owners love the things they sell. There's a story behind every item. That's why I like to shop there. There aren't many shops like that.

B | *Check your work. Use the Editing Checklist.*

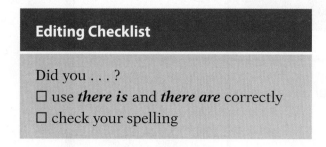

Editing Checklist

Did you . . . ?
- ☐ use *there is* and *there are* correctly
- ☐ check your spelling

Check your answers on page UR-2.
Do you need to review anything?

A | *Circle the correct words to complete the* **yes / no** *questions and short answers.*

1. **A: Are there / Are they** any soda machines in the building?

   B: Yes, **there are / they are**.

2. **A: Are there / Are they** any amusement parks near your school?

   B: No, **there aren't / they're not**.

3. **A: Is it / Is she** the teacher?

   B: Yes, **she's / she is**.

4. **A: Are there / Are they** new students?

   B: No, **they aren't / she isn't**.

5. **A: Are there / Is there** a men's room on this floor?

   B: No, **they aren't / there isn't**.

B | *Complete the sentences with* **There's, There are, She's, It's,** *or* **They're.**

1. ____There's____ a new pizza place on Elm Street. ____They're____ next to the post office.

2. ____There are____ a lot of people outside the pizza place. ____They're____ in a long line.

3. ____She's____ a great pizza chef there. ____It's____ funny, and her pizzas are delicious.

C | *Correct the paragraph. There are four mistakes.*

Visit the new Shopper's Mall on Route 290. There's over 100 stores. There a movie theater, and they are ten great places to eat. Come early. Every morning at 10:30 there are a free show for children. The mall is three miles from the Tappan Bridge on Route 290.

Possessives: Nouns, Adjectives, Pronouns; Object Pronouns; Questions with *Whose*

POSSESSIONS

STEP 1 GRAMMAR IN CONTEXT

Before You Read

A | *Is your handwriting neat? Is it difficult to read?*

B | *Look at Michelle and Rick's handwriting. Whose handwriting is neat? Whose is messy?*

My name is Michelle Young.

Read

A teacher is returning student compositions. Read the conversation.

TEACHER: **Whose** composition is this?

BORIS: Is it a good paper?

TEACHER: It's excellent.

BORIS: It's **my** composition.

YOLANDA: No, that's not **your** handwriting. It's **Kim's** composition. **Her** name is right there. She's absent today.

TEACHER: Thanks, Yolanda. **Whose** paper is *this*?

BORIS: Is it a good paper?

TEACHER: It's OK.

BORIS: Then it's **mine**.

JUAN: It's not **yours**. It's **mine**. See, **my** name is on the back.

TEACHER: You're right, Juan. I recognize your handwriting. Here, Boris. *This* is **your** composition.

BORIS: Is it a good paper?

TEACHER: It needs some work.

BORIS: I don't think it's **mine**.

TEACHER: Uh . . . I think it is. I have a grade for everyone else.

After You Read

A | Practice *GROUPS OF 4: Now read the conversation aloud.*

B | Vocabulary *Complete the sentences with the words from the box.*

back	composition	grade	handwriting	recognize

1. It's his letter. I can ___recognize___ the ___handwriting___.

2. We had to write a ___composition___ about a favorite childhood possession. Mine was about my blue blanket.

3. Are the answers in the ___back___ of the book?

4. What was your ___grade___ in English? Mine was an A+.

C | Comprehension *Whose compositions are these? Write **Kim, Juan,** and **Boris** below the correct composition.*

1. _____   2. _____   3. _____

POSSESSIVES, OBJECT PRONOUNS; QUESTIONS WITH *WHOSE*

Possessive Nouns	
Singular Nouns	**Plural Nouns**
John's last name is Tamez. **Russ's** last name is Stram.	The **girls'** gym is on this floor.
My **mother's** name is Rita. The **woman's** name is Carmen.	My **parents'** car is in the garage. The **women's** restroom is on the first floor.

Subject Pronoun	Possessive Adjective	Possessive Pronoun	
I	**my**	**mine**	That is **my** book. That book is **mine**.
You*	**your**	**yours**	Do you have **your** key? Do you have **yours**?
He	**his**	**his**	This is **his** car. This car is **his**.
She	**her**	**hers**	That's **her** house. That house is **hers**.
It	**its**		Look at that bird. **Its** feathers are red and gold.
We	**our**	**ours**	We lost **our** notes. We lost **ours**.
They	**their**	**theirs**	They can't find **their** tickets. They can't find **theirs**.

*You can be singular or plural.

	Object Pronoun (Singular)		Object Pronoun (Plural)
Raul likes	me.	Sarah knows	us.
	you.		you.
	him.		them.
	her.		

Questions with *Whose*	
Questions	**Answers**
Whose hair is long?	Carmen's. Carmen's is. Carmen's hair is long.
Whose eyes are green?	Igor's. Igor's are. Igor's eyes are green.
Whose compositions are finished?	Yoko's and Kaori's. Yoko's and Kaori's are. Yoko's and Kaori's compositions.

GRAMMAR NOTES

1	**Possessive nouns** and **possessive adjectives** show belonging or a relationship.	• **Kim's car** (the car belongs to Kim) • **her aunt** (relationship)
2	To show possession, add: **apostrophe (')** + **s** to a **singular noun**. **apostrophe (')** to a **plural noun** ending in **-s**. **apostrophe (')** + **s** to an **irregular plural noun**.	• That's **Juan's** composition. • My **parents'** home is near my home. • The **women's** restroom is on the first floor.
3	**Possessive adjectives** replace **possessive nouns**. Possessive adjectives agree with the possessive noun they replace.	**His** • ~~My father's~~ sisters are in Busan and Daegu. **Her** • ~~My mother's~~ brother is in Seoul.
4	A **noun** always follows a possessive noun or a possessive adjective.	• Bekir's **book** is new. • His **book** is new.

5	A **possessive pronoun** can replace a **possessive adjective** and **noun**.
	
	BE CAREFUL! A noun never follows a possessive pronoun.
	
	BE CAREFUL! The verb after a possessive pronoun agrees with the noun it replaces.
		• This isn't **my** umbrella. **Mine** is blue.
		  (My umbrella is blue.)
		
		• This is my hat. This is **mine**.
		  Noт: This is mine ~~hat~~.
		
		• Her **notebook** is blue. = **Hers is** blue.
		• Her **notebooks** are red. = **Hers are** red.

6	Use *whose* for questions about possessions. **BE CAREFUL!** *Who's* is short for *who is*.	• **Whose** notebook is this? • **Who's** absent?
7	**BE CAREFUL!** Don't confuse possessive pronouns with **object pronouns**. Object pronouns come after a verb.	• Do you need to see **me**? • The baby loves baths. We give **him** a bath every day.
8	**BE CAREFUL!** A noun + apostrophe (') + s may be short for *is* in conversation and very informal writing. Do not confuse *its* and *it's*. *its* = possessive adjective; *it's* = *it is*	• "**Anna's** late." (Anna **is** late.) • This is my turtle. **Its** name is Tubby. • **It's** a hot day.

REFERENCE NOTES

For more rules about possessive nouns, see Appendix 7 on page A-7.
For more about irregular plural nouns, see Appendix 5 on pages A-5–A-6.

EXERCISE 1: Discover the Grammar

Read the conversations. Then complete the sentences. Circle the correct letter.

Conversation 1:

FENG: Whose book is on the table next to the printer?

LI: It's mine.

1. *Whose* refs to _____.
   a. book   b. table

2. *Mine* means _____.
   a. my book   b. my printer

Conversation 2:

JOSE: Maria, is that your translator?

MARIA: No, it's Marco's. Mine is in my backpack. His is over there.

3. *Marco's* means ___a_____.
   a. Here is Marco.   b. Marco's translator

4. *Mine* means _____.
   a. my translator   b. my backpack

5. *His* means _____.
   a. Marco's backpack   b. Marco's translator

Conversation 3:

SUN HI: How is Mi Young related to you?

JUN: She's my father's brother's wife.

6. My *father's brother's wife* is _____.
   a. my uncle   b. my aunt

Conversation 4:

EROL: Where are the workbooks?

AYLA: I put on them on the bookshelves near the door.

7. *Them* refers to _____.
   a. the bookshelves   b. the workbooks

EXERCISE 2: Possessive Nouns

(Grammar Notes 1–2)

A | *Read about the Zhang family. Underline the possessive nouns in the reading.*

This is the Zhang family. The older man is Lao Zhang. Lao's wife is Feng. They have two daughters, Hua and Mei. Hua's husband is Gang. They have a son, Bao. Mei's husband is Jinsong. They have a daughter, Ting.

B | *Complete the sentences. Underline the correct noun or possessive noun form.*

1. Ting's **mothers / mother's** mother is Ting's **grandmother / grandmother's**.

2. Hua's **sister / sister's daughter / daughters** is Hua's niece.

3. Gang's **wife / wife's sister / sister's** is his sister-in-law.

4. Bao's **uncle / uncle's** apartment is in Shanghai.

5. Bao and Ting are **cousins / cousin's**. Their **mothers / mother's** are **sisters / sister's**.

6. Lao Zhang is the **families / family's** oldest member. 成员

EXERCISE 3: Possessive Adjectives

(Grammar Notes 1, 3)

Complete the sentences. Use a possessive adjective.

1. My sister studies in Toronto. _____*Her*_____ school is on Victoria Street.

2. She goes to Edgewood University. She likes _____ classes.

3. Carlos's parents work at the United Nations. _____ jobs are interesting.

   His mother is a translator, and his father is an interpreter.

4. Right now my brother is in Peru, _____ wife is in Belize, and

   _____ children are in the United States.

5. The children have a rabbit. _____ fur is soft.

6. Does your brother like _____ job?

7. Do you use _____ calculator every day in math class?

8. Does your grandmother like _____ new apartment? Is she happy there?

EXERCISE 4: Possessive Pronouns

(Grammar Note 5)

Replace the underlined words with a possessive pronoun.

1. **A:** Is that your notebook?

   B: No, it's not ~~my notebook~~. It's <u>his notebook</u>. <u>My notebook</u> is in my book bag.

      mine

      a.   **b.**   **c.**

2. **A:** Is this their house?

   B: No. <u>Their house</u> is in back of the library.

      a.

   A: Whose house is this?

   B: It's <u>our house</u>.

      b.

3. **A:** Are those your sunglasses?

   B: No, they're <u>her sunglasses</u>. <u>My sunglasses</u> are in my bag.

      a.   **b.**

EXERCISE 5: Possessive Adjectives and Possessive Pronouns

(Grammar Notes 1–2, 5, 7)

Complete the conversations with the words in parentheses. Write the correct form.

1. **A:** I think you have my umbrella.

   B: No. This is _____*my*_____ umbrella. _____ is over there. It's next

      a. (my / mine)   **b. (You / Yours)**

   to _____ translator.

      c. (her / hers)

2. **A:** Whose gloves are these? Yours or Julie's?

   B: _____ are black leather. _____ are wool.

      a. (Her / Hers)   **b. (My / Mine)**

3. **A:** Where is _____ car?

      a. (their / theirs)

   B: _____ car is in the garage.

      b. (Their / Theirs)

   A: Is _____ there too?

      c. (your / yours)

   B: No. _____ is on the street.

      d. (Our / Ours)

EXERCISE 6: Subject and Object Pronouns, Possessives

(Grammar Notes 1, 3–5, 7)

Complete the sentences with the words in parentheses. Write the correct form.

1. It's _____ *mine* _____. Please give it to _____.
   a. (I / my / me / mine)   b. (I / my / me / mine)

   _____ need it.
   c. (I / My / Me / I)

2. I don't think _____ is on the train. I don't see _____.
   a. (he / him / his)   b. (he / him / his)

3. Our family is from Edmonton. _____ family is from Vancouver,
   a. (They / Their / Theirs / Them)

   but _____ live in Edmonton now. We live next door to
   b. (they / their / theirs / them)

   _____.
   c. (they / their / theirs / them)

EXERCISE 7: Possessives: Questions and Verb Agreement

(Grammar Notes 3, 5–6)

Complete the conversations with the words in parentheses. Write the correct form.

1. **A:** _____ *Whose* _____ shoes are these?
   (Who's / Whose)

   B: They're my shoes. His _____ over there.
   (is / are)

2. **A:** _____ key is this? _____ it yours?
   (Who's / Whose)   (Is / Are)

   B: No it isn't.

3. **A:** _____ in room 401?
   (Who's / Whose)

   B: Florian and David.

   A: _____ that their usual classroom?
   (Is / Are)

4. **A:** _____ books are those? _____ they hers?
   (Who's / Whose)   (Is / Are)

   B: No, _____ his.
   (they're / it's)

5. **A:** _____ notes are those?
   (Who's / Whose)

   B: Bob's. His notes are messy. Mine _____ neat.
   (is / are)

6. **A:** _____ that woman?
   (Who's / Whose)

   B: Her name is Wu-Shen. She's an English teacher.

7. **A:** My parents live in Italy. Hers _____ in Argentina.
   (live / lives)

EXERCISE 8: Pronouns and Possessive Adjectives

(Grammar Notes 1–4, 7)

Read and complete the article with the words in parentheses. Write the correct form.

International Language Institute Newsletter
Vol. 22

Get to Know New Students at the ILI

New Student of the Month

Sandra Gomes

My name is Sandra Gomes. ___*I'm*___ from São Paulo,
                1. (I / I'm)

Brazil. _____ happy to be a student at the International
       2. (I / I'm)

Language Institute. _____ great to learn English and meet
                3. (Its / It's)

people from all over the world. _____ parents and brother
                  4. (Me / My)

are in Brazil, but _____ sister is here with _____.
        5. (my / mine)   **6. (I / me)**

_____ share an apartment. _____ nice, but
7. (We / Our)   **8. (It / It's)**

_____ far from school. _____ each have a bedroom.
9. (it's / its)   **10. (We / Us)**

_____ is small, but it has a big closet. _____ is large,
11. (My / Mine)   **12. (Her / Hers)**

but it doesn't have a closet. _____ spend a lot of time
              13. (We / Us)

together in _____ apartment. That's because _____
       14. (us / our)   **15. (we / our)**

have a TV, a computer, and a lot of friends who visit _____.
                  16. (we / us)

EXERCISE 9: Editing

Correct the conversations. There are seven mistakes. The first mistake is already corrected. Find and correct six more.

1. **A:** Is that ~~you~~ *your* dictionary?

   B: No. It's his dictionary.

   A: Who's?

   B: Dans.

2. **A:** Is Maria sister here?

   B: No, she's not.

   A: Is Maria here?

   B: No, but his brother is.

   A: Where is Maria?

   B: I think she's with his sister. Their at the movies.

EXERCISE 10: Pronunciation

🎧 **A** | *Read and listen to the Pronunciation Note.*

Pronunciation Note
When you use a possessive, add the sound of **/ z /**, **/ s /** or **/ ɪz /**.

EXAMPLES:

Lisa	Lisa's	**/ z /**
Jack	Jack's	**/ s /**
Ross	Ross's	**/ ɪz /**

🎧 **B** | *Listen to the sentences. Circle the word you hear.*

1. Maria   (Maria's)   Marias   **4.** partner   partner's   partners

2. Maria   Maria's   Marias   **5.** partner   partner's   partners

3. Maria   Maria's   Marias   **6.** partner   partner's   partners

EXERCISE 11: Listening

🎧 **A** | *Listen to the conversation. What are Boris and Jasmine talking about? Circle the correct letter.*

    a. bikes   **b.** baskets   **c.** sales

🎧 **B** | *Listen again. Write the name of the owner above each bicycle. Use the names from the box.*

Amy	Jasmine	Johnny	Roger and Ted

1. _____   2. _____   3. _____   4. _____

EXERCISE 12: Talking about Family Photos

Bring in photos of family members. Write on the back of the photo how the person is related to you (for example, my sister, my mother, my aunt*). Your teacher collects the photos and gives you a different photo. You and your classmates ask questions about the photos.*

EXAMPLE: **ANYA:** Whose sister is this?
PABLO: I think it's Juan's.
JUAN: You're right. She's my sister.

EXERCISE 13: Game: Find Someone Whose / Who's . . .

A | *Complete the questions. Use* **whose** *or* **who's**.

1. _____Whose_____ birthday is in December? _____

2. _____Who's_____ good in art? _____

3. _____ name means something? _____

4. _____ a good athlete? _____

5. _____ eyes aren't dark brown? _____

6. _____ a good cook? _____

7. _____ first name has more than eight letters? _____

8. _____ birthday is in the summer? _____

9. _____ a good dancer? _____

10. _____ handwriting is beautiful? _____

B | *Look back at Part A. Ask your classmates the questions. Write their names. Report to the class.*

EXAMPLE: **MARIA:** Juan, is your birthday in December?
JUAN: No, it's not. Is yours?
MARIA: Yes, it is. (Juan writes Maria's name on the line.)

EXERCISE 14: Writing

A | *Look at Exercise 8 on page 138. Write about yourself and your family for a school newsletter. Use pronouns and possessive adjectives.*

EXAMPLE: I'm from Recife in Brazil. I live with my parents and my younger brother. My older brother, Jose, is married. He is a pilot, and his wife is a pilot too. My mother worries about them, but she is proud of them. My dream is to become a pilot one day too, but it's my secret for now.

B | *Check your work. Use the Editing Checklist.*

Editing Checklist

Did you . . . ?
- ☐ use possessive adjectives, possessive pronouns, and object pronouns correctly
- ☐ check your spelling

UNIT 12 Review

Check your answers on page UR-3.
Do you need to review anything?

A I *Cross out the underlined words. Replace them with* **His, Her, Its,** *or* **Their.**

1. The Browns' car is big.

2. My brother's best friend is a history teacher.

3. That bird is injured. That bird's wing is broken.

4. The students' tests are on the teacher's desk.

5. Our aunt's store is on Main Street.

B I *Underline the correct words to complete the conversations.*

1. **A:** You need an umbrella. Take **me / mine**.

   B: I don't want to use **your / yours**.

   A: It's OK. I have **you / your** rain hat.

2. **A:** **Who / Whose** dictionary is on the floor?

   B: It's **Ali / Ali's**.

3. **A:** Who's talking?

   B: **My / Mine** children have a parrot. **Its / It's** name is Polly. Polly's talking.

4. **A:** **Her / Hers** composition is here, but where is **your / yours**?

   B: **My / Mine** is at home. Sorry.

C I *Correct the conversation. There are five mistakes.*

A: Who's bag is that on the floor?

B: I think it's Maria.

A: No. Her bag is on her arm.

B: Well, it's not mine bag. Maybe it's Rita.

A: Rita, is that bag your?

Before You Read

GROUPS: Do you have a pet or know someone who has one? What kind? Does it have any unusual talents?

Read

Read the online article about an amazing parrot.

WILD NATURE

Home | Animal Facts | Photos | Quizzes | Wild TV

A Genius Parrot

Everyone knows parrots **can talk**. By "talk" we mean they **can repeat** words. Most parrots **can't** really **express** ideas.

N'kisi is different. N'kisi is an African gray parrot. He **can say** almost 1,000 words. He **can use** basic grammar. He **can talk** about the present, past, and future. When he doesn't know a form, he **can invent** one. For example, he used the word "flied," not "flew," for the past of the verb "fly."

N'kisi lives in New York City with his owner, Aimee Morgana. He **couldn't talk** much at first. At first he **could** only **say** a few words. But Aimee was a great teacher, and N'kisi was a good student. Now N'kisi talks to anyone near him.

Donald Broom, a professor of Veterinary Medicine at the University of Cambridge, is not surprised. He says that parrots **can think** at high levels. In that way, they are like apes and chimpanzees.

Les Rance of the Parrot Society says, "Most African grays are intelligent. They **can learn** to do easy puzzles. They **can say** 'good night' when you turn the lights off at night. They **can say** 'good-bye' when you put a coat on. But N'kisi **can do** many more things. N'kisi is an amazing[1] bird. He's not just smart. He's a genius."

---

[1] *amazing:* surprising in a good way

After You Read

A | Practice *PAIRS: Read the article again aloud. Take turns reading each paragraph.*

B | Vocabulary *Complete the sentences with the words from the box. Use the correct form.*

be surprised	genius	intelligent	invent	professor

1. Monkeys and dolphins are very _____

   animals. They can learn many things.

2. Many people _____ by the abilities of

   African gray parrots.

3. Mozart was a _____.

   He wrote great music at the age of six.

4. Try and take his course. He's a very good

   _____.

5. We need to _____ a way to learn languages while we sleep.

C | Comprehension *Write **T (True)**, **F (False)**, or **? (it doesn't say)** for each statement.*

_____ 1. N'kisi can say more than 1,100 words.

_____ 2. N'kisi can't use basic grammar.

_____ 3. N'kisi can talk about the past and the future.

_____ 4. N'kisi can understand Italian.

_____ 5. Parrots can't think at high levels.

_____ 6. N'kisi could only say a few words at first.

CAN / CAN'T FOR ABILITY AND POSSIBILITY; COULD FOR PAST ABILITY

Affirmative Statements		
Subject	**Can / Could**	**Base Form of Verb**
I You* He We	**can** **could**	**talk**.

You is both singular and plural.

Negative Statements		
Subject	**Can't / Couldn't**	**Base Form of Verb**
She It They	**can't** **couldn't**	**talk**.

Yes / No Questions		
Can / Could	**Subject**	**Base Form of Verb**
Can	you	**understand**?
Could		

Short Answers	
Affirmative	**Negative**
Yes, I can.	No, I can't.
Yes, we could.	No, we couldn't.

GRAMMAR NOTES

1	*Can* expresses **present ability** or **possibility**. It comes before the verb. The verb is always in the **base form**.	• He **can say** 950 words. • We **can teach** your bird to talk.
2	The **negative** of *can* is *can't*. *Cannot* is a form of the negative. It is not common.	• I **can't** understand you. • I **cannot** understand you.
3	Reverse the subject and *can* for *yes / no* questions.	• **He can** speak about the past. • **Can he** speak about the past?
4	*Could* expresses **past ability**. *Could not* is the full negative form. The more common form is the contraction, *couldn't*.	• I **could** run fast in high school. • I **could not** drive five years ago. • I **couldn't** drive five years ago.
5	Reverse the subject and *could* for *yes / no* questions.	• **You could** speak English last year. • **Could you** speak English last year?
6	We usually give short answers to questions with *can, can't, could,* or *couldn't*.	• Can he understand me? **Yes, he can.**

EXERCISE 1: Discover the Grammar

A | *Read the sentences in column A. Underline* **can, can't,** *or* **couldn't** *and the base form verbs. Circle the negative statements.*

A

_e_ **1.** N'kisi can invent new words.

____ **2.** We can't understand our professor.

____ **3.** I'm sorry. I can't help you now.

____ **4.** I can't hear you.

____ **5.** He can lift 110 pounds (50 kilos).

____ **6.** They can't express their love.

____ **7.** The boy couldn't reach the button.

B

a. He's very strong.

b. She speaks too fast.

c. He was too short.

d. They never talk about their feelings.

e. He's a smart bird.

f. I'm busy.

g. It's very noisy here.

B | *Look back at Part A. Match the sentences in column A with the possible reasons in column B.*

EXERCISE 2: *Can* and *Can't*   *(Grammar Notes 1–2)*

Complete the sentences with **can** *or* **can't** *and the verbs in parentheses.*

1. Many parrots _____*can learn*_____ to speak. My parrot _____, "You're a
                              (learn)   **(say)**
   genius."

2. My dog _____, but he _____ me my shoes. I'm trying to
                        (sit)   **(bring)**
   teach him to bring things to me.

3. My cat _____ mice. He's very good at
                    (catch)
   that. Her cat _____ mice. He just sits and
                        (catch)
   watches them.

4. Her dog _____ two languages, Spanish
                    (understand)
   and English. She speaks to her dog in English, and her

   husband speaks to the dog in Spanish.

5. Dolphins _____ people in trouble. They are
                      (help)
   smart and show feelings.

EXERCISE 3: *Can / Can't*: *Yes / No* Questions and Answers

(Grammar Note 3)

Read the real conversation between Aimee Morgana and N'kisi, her parrot. Then write
yes / **no** questions with the words in parentheses. Answer the questions.

> **N'KISI:** Wanna (I want to) go in a car right now.
>
> **AIMEE:** I'm sorry. We can't right now—
>
> maybe we can go later.
>
> **N'KISI:** Why can't I go in a car now?
>
> **AIMEE:** Because we don't have one.
>
> **N'KISI:** Let's get a car.
>
> **AIMEE:** No, N'kisi, we can't get a car now.
>
> **N'KISI:** I want a car.

1. **A:** _____ *Can N'kisi talk?* _____
   (N'kisi / talk)
   B: _____ *Yes, he can.* _____

2. **A:** _____
   (he / ask questions)
   B: _____

3. **A:** _____
   (he / make suggestions)
   B: _____

4. **A:** _____
   (Aimee / buy a car now)
   B: _____

5. **A:** _____
   (N'kisi / ask for things)
   B: _____

6. **A:** _____
   (Aimee and N'kisi / go in a car now)
   B: _____

EXERCISE 4: Past Abilities: *Could / Couldn't*   (Grammar Notes 4–5)

Complete the sentences with **could** *or* **couldn't** *and the verbs in parentheses.*

1. My cat was smart. She _____*could close*_____
   (close)

   the door with her paws. _____

   your cat _____ the door?
                (open)

2. Michael was a smart gorilla. He

   _____ sign language. He
   (use)

   _____ 600 different gestures.
   (make)

3. My dog Charlie was a good watchdog, but

   he _____ any tricks.
          (do)

4. My dog Spot was not a good watchdog, but he _____ me my slippers.
                                                        (bring)

5. My bird _____, but he could sit on my finger.
              (talk)

6. _____ your bird _____ anything? My bird
                                        (say)

   _____, "I love you." That's why everyone smiled at him.
       (say)

EXERCISE 5: Editing

Correct the conversation. There are seven mistakes. The first mistake is already corrected. Find and correct six more. Add **can** *to fix one mistake.*

A: Can you ~~coming~~ to my party? It's next Saturday night. You can to meet my new dog.
        come

B: Yes, I'd love to. How I get to your home?

A: You can to take the train or a taxi.

B: Can you meet me at the train station?

A: I'm sorry. I can't. I no can drive. Maybe Bob can meets you. He has a car, and he can to drive.

EXERCISE 6: Pronunciation

A | *Read and listen to the Pronunciation Note.*

> **Pronunciation Note**
>
> When **can** is followed by a base form verb, we usually pronounce it / **kən** / and stress the base form verb:
>
> **EXAMPLE:** *We can **dance**.*
>
> When **can't** is followed by a base form verb, we usually pronounce it / **kaent** / and stress both *can't* and the base form verb:
>
> **EXAMPLE:** *We **can't dance**.*

B | *Listen and complete the sentences with **can** or **can't** and the verb.*

1. A zebra _____ *can see* _____ the color blue, but it _____ the color orange.

2. You _____ a cow upstairs, but you _____ a cow downstairs.

3. Dolphins _____ with their eyes open, but dolphins _____ on dry land.

4. A pet cat _____ a black bear, but a cat _____ a jaguar.

5. Dogs _____ feelings, but they _____ them.

6. Elephants _____ their trunks to spray water, but they _____.

C | *Listen again and repeat the sentences.*

EXERCISE 7: Listening

A | *Listen to a conversation about dolphins. Circle three things the dolphins in Florida could do.*

catch a ball   paint pictures   play basketball   talk

B | *Listen again to the conversation. Read the questions. Check (✓) the correct answers.*

1. What can all the dolphins at a marine institute in Mississippi do?

   ____ **a.** hold onto a paper and play with it

   ____ **b.** exchange paper for fish

2. Which four things can Kelly do?

   ____ **a.** hide paper under a rock

   ____ **b.** use paper to catch fish

   ____ **c.** tear paper

   ____ **d.** eat paper

   ____ **e.** catch a bird

   ____ **f.** exchange pieces of paper for fish

EXERCISE 8: Game: Find Someone Who . . .

A | *Walk around the classroom. Ask your classmates questions with **can** or **could**. Ask about now and about five years ago. If they answer **yes,** write their names in the chart.*

EXAMPLE: VICTOR: Can you play an instrument?

            CAROLINA: Yes, I can. I can play the guitar.

              VICTOR: Could you play the guitar five years ago?

            CAROLINA: No, I couldn't.

	Now	Five Years Ago
play an instrument	*Carolina*	
teach a bird to talk		
design a Web page		
ride a motorcycle		
train a dog		

B | *Report your answers to your class.*

EXAMPLE: Erna can play the piano and design a Web page. Five years ago she could play the piano, but she couldn't design a Web page.

EXERCISE 9: Game: What Can Your Group Do?

Work in small groups. Read the questions. When your group can do one of the tasks, raise your hand. The first group to do a task wins.

1. Can you think of 12 different animals that start with 12 different letters of the alphabet?

   EXAMPLE: a = ape   b = bear

2. Can you say "I love you" in more than four languages?

3. Can you name the colors of the flags of six countries?

4. Can you name the capitals of eight countries?

EXERCISE 10: Writing

A | *Write about an interesting pet or other animal. Use **can** or **can't**. Answer these questions in your paragraph:*

- What kind of animal is it? What does it look like?
- Where does it live?
- Is it your pet? Does it have a name?
- What can this animal do? What can't it do?

EXAMPLE: I have a beautiful parakeet. His feathers are bright green. His name is Chichi. He is two years old. He lives in a cage in the living room. Sometimes he flies around the room. Chichi can sing very beautifully. Chichi couldn't do anything when he was younger. But now he can sit on my finger and eat from my hand. He can't speak, but I'm happy about that. I tell him all my secrets, and he doesn't tell anyone. That's a wonderful quality. I love my Chichi.

B | *Check your work. Use the Editing Checklist.*

Editing Checklist
Did you . . . ? ☐ use ***can*** and ***can't*** correctly ☐ check your spelling

Review

Check your answers on page UR-3.

Do you need to review anything?

A | Complete the sentences with **can, could, can't,** or **couldn't** and the verbs in parentheses.

1. Last year I _____ much English. Now I _____ a lot more.
   (understand)   (understand)

2. Jill doesn't have time to exercise these days, so she _____ fast. In high
   (run)
   school she was on a team, and she _____ a mile in seven minutes
   (run)

3. I _____ five years ago. Now I have a driver's license, and I
   (drive)
   _____ well.
   (drive)

B | Complete the questions and answers. Use **can, could, can't** or **couldn't.**

1. **A:** _____ you understand your dreams?

   B: Yes, I _____. They're easy to understand.

2. **A:** _____ you write reports last year?

   B: No, I _____, but now I _____.

3. **A:** _____ he fix cars?

   B: Yes, he _____. He's a good mechanic.

C | Correct the conversation. There are seven mistakes.

A: Can you to get online?

B: No, I can't not. I couldn't got online last night either.

A: My brother is good with computers. Maybe he can helps.

B: Great. I can no figure out what's wrong.

A: I no can reach him now, but I can to call him after 6 P.M.

Permission: *Can* or *May*

HEALTH AND DIET

STEP 1 GRAMMAR IN CONTEXT

Before You Read

Foods are mainly made of protein, carbohydrates, and fat. Which category do these foods belong in? Write them below. Then check your answers on page 154.

~~beef~~ ~~bread~~ ~~butter~~ cake chicken fish oil pasta rice

Protein: *beef,* _____

Carbohydrate(s): *bread,* _____

Fat: *butter,* _____

Read

Read the online article about diets. What do you think about them?

www.healthandnutritionmagazine.com/therightdiet

Health & Nutrition

fashion | beauty | health & fitness | shopping

The Right Diet

Marita is a college junior. She was 5 pounds overweight. She gained those 5 pounds in her freshman year. She tried many diets, but they didn't work. Then three months ago she joined Weight Watchers®. Most nutritionists say that exercise and calorie reduction is the best way to lose weight. The Weight Watchers® diet follows both principles. It also uses a point system. You **can eat** any food, but you **may not eat** more than a certain number of points each day. Different foods have different numbers of points. For example, an orange has 1 point. A piece of chocolate cake has 7 points. Dieters **can follow** a weekly class or follow the program online. Marita is happy. She lost the extra weight and feels terrific.

(continued on next page)

Bill Morgan is a businessman. He eats many meals out. He was 25 pounds overweight. Bill doesn't want to count points, so he's following the Atkins™ diet. In this diet you **may eat** foods high in protein and fat, such as red meat and cheese, but you **can't eat** carbohydrates such as bread, cereal, pasta, and rice. The first two weeks are especially strict. You **can't have** fruit, grains, cereals, bread, or most vegetables. You also **can't drink** any milk or juice. But after three weeks Bill weighs 10 pound less. He's thrilled.

Many people, like Marita and Bill, lose weight on diets, but they don't keep it off. So they have to start all over again. Dieters don't always agree on the best diet, but almost every dieter would like to take a pill one day, become slim the next, and never regain the weight.

Comments (115)   Post a comment   Share

After You Read

A | Practice *PAIRS: Now read the article aloud. Take turns reading each paragraph.*

B | Vocabulary *Complete the sentences with the words from the box. Use the correct form.*

特别的　　　　　　　薪待　　　　　　　　　　　　过重的　　　　　磅

especially	gain	lose	overweight	pound

1. These days many people eat more than they need, and they become

   _____. They need to _____ weight.

2. That diet is _____ hard to keep.

3. People often lose weight, but after a while they _____ it back.

4. How many _____ does he want to lose?

C | Comprehension *Write* **T (True)**, **F (False)**, *or* **? (it doesn't say)** *for each statement.*

_____ **1.** You can eat small portions of everything on the Weight Watchers® diet.

_____ **2.** You can't eat meat on the Atkins™ diet.

_____ **3.** You may follow the Weight Watchers® diet online.

_____ **4.** You can't eat cereal in the first two weeks of the Atkins™ diet.

_____ **5.** An overweight person can take a pill and become slim the next day.

_____ **6.** You may not drink coffee on the Atkins™ diet.

Answers to Before You Read, page 153: Protein: beef, chicken, fish; **Carbohydrates:** bread, cake, pasta, rice; **Fat:** butter, oil

CAN OR MAY FOR PERMISSION

Statements			
Subject	Can / Can't May / May Not	Base Form of Verb	
You	can can't	start	today.
He	may may not	eat	nuts.

Yes / No Questions					Answers
Can / May	Subject	Base Form of Verb			
Can May	I	have	the day off?		Yes, you can. Yes, you may. Sure. Of course. I'm sorry. We're too busy.

Wh- Questions				
Wh- Word	Can	Subject	Base Form of Verb	
When	can	I	borrow	the car?
Where		we	park?	

GRAMMAR NOTES

1 Use **can** or **may** to **give permission**. (It's OK to . . .) Can and may are followed by the base form of the verb.
Use **can't** or **may not** to **deny permission**. (Something is not OK.)
There is no contraction for *may not*.

- You **can see** the doctor now.
- You **may eat** fish.

- You **can't drive** a truck on this road.
- You **may not use** my car.
  Not: You ~~mayn't~~ drive a car without a license.

2 Use *can* or *may* to **ask for permission**.
May is more formal than *can*.
We respond with a short affirmative response (*Yes, you may*) or a short apology and a reason. (*Sorry, I . . .*)

A: **May** I see the doctor this afternoon?
B: Yes, you may. OR
   No, I'm sorry. The doctor is out.

3 We use **Can I help you?** or **May I help you?** to offer help to someone.
We thank the speaker or say no thank you and give a reason.

A: **Can I help you?** OR **May I help you?**
B: **Thanks.** I'm looking for a winter jacket.
   OR
   No thanks. I'm just looking.

EXERCISE 1: Discover the Grammar

A | *Read the conversation. Underline* **can, can't, may,** *or* **may not.** *Then complete Part B.*

___A___ **A:** Can I eat meat?

___G___ **B:** Yes, you can, but you can only have boiled, grilled, or baked meat.

___A___ **A:** What about fried chicken? Can I have it? I love fried chicken.

___D___ **B:** Sorry. You may not have any fried food on this diet.

___A___ **A:** Can I eat nuts?

___G___ **B:** Yes, you may, but don't eat too many. And remember, there are many things on

this diet that you can eat. You may eat as many green vegetables as you want,

and you can drink as much green tea as you want.

A: Well, that sounds good.

___G___ **B:** If you have any more questions, you can call me weekdays between 11:00

and 1:00.

B | *Look back at Part A. Write* **A** *for sentences that ask for permission,* **G** *for sentences that give permission, and* **D** *for sentences that deny permission.*

EXERCISE 2: *Can / May*: Affirmative, Negative, *Yes / No* Questions   (Grammar Notes 1–3)

Complete the conversations with **can** or **may** and the verbs from the box.

drive	help	~~return~~
eat	keep	see
have	look	take

1. **(Can)**

   A: You're doing great.

   B: I feel good too, Dr. Lam. When ___can___ I ___return___ to work?

   A: Next week.

   B: And when ___Can___ I ___drive___?

   A: Wait another week. Take the train next week.

   B: OK.

   A: But remember. Watch your diet. Don't eat heavy food and stay away from dessert.

   B: ___Can___ I ___eat___ out?

   A: Sure. Just watch what you order.

2. **(May)**

   A: ___May___ I ___help___ you?

   B: Thanks. I'd like to make an appointment with Ms. Stein.

   A: She's free next Tuesday at 10:00. Here are some booklets about nutrition. You

   ___May___ ___take___ them home and read them.

   B: Thanks. Do you want them back?

   A: No. You ___May___ ___keep___ them.

3. **(Can)**

   A: Your fish comes with a salad.

   B: OK. ___Can___ I ___have___ the dressing on the side?

   A: Of course.

   B: And ___Can___ we ___see___ the dessert menu?

   C: Bob, you're on a diet! You can't have dessert.

   B: But I ___Can___ ___look___ at the desserts and dream about them.

EXERCISE 3: Permission: *May / Can*

(Grammar Notes 1–3)

Complete the conversation. Write questions with **can** or **may** and the information in parentheses.

RECEPTIONIST: (May) _May I help you?_
               1. (Do you need my help?)

NURAY: Yes, thanks. I'm Nuray Attaturk. I have an appointment with Dr. Lee for 2:00.

RECEPTIONIST: Thanks Ms. Attaturk. (May) _May I see your health insurance card?_
               2. (I want to see your health insurance card.)

DR. LEE: OK, Nuray. Here's your diet. Any questions?

NURAY: (Can) _Can I eat snacks_
               3. (Is it OK to eat snacks?)

DR. LEE: Yes, but you can only have light snacks.

NURAY: (Can) _Can I eat ice cream_
               4. (Is it OK to eat ice cream?)

DR. LEE: No, you can't, but you can have low-fat yogurt instead. 代替 I in'sted7

NURAY: (May) _May I call you with questions_
               5. (Is it OK to call you with questions?)

DR. LEE: Certainly. But don't worry. Everything is on these papers. Just read the diet

and follow the directions. You'll feel better in no time.
指示 说明

NURAY: Thanks, Dr. Lee.

point 尖一点. 分数.

part

certainly 必然地.
I 'sə:tənli] 当然.

EXERCISE 4: Editing

Correct the conversations. There are six mistakes. The first mistake is already corrected. Find and correct five more.

1. **A:** Can we ~~paid~~ pay in two installments?

   B: Yes, you can pays half now and half next month.

2. **A:** May I speaks to the doctor?

   B: I'm sorry. He's with a patient now. Give me your number and he'll call you back.
   speaking

3. **A:** Can I to use salt?

   B: Yes, but not a lot.

4. **A:** Can I drink coffee or tea?

   B: You may drink tea, but you mayn't drink coffee.

5. **A:** May I helping you?

   B: Thanks. I'd like to make an appointment for next week.

EXERCISE 5: Listening

A | *Listen to a telephone conversation. A patient calls a doctor. What is the woman's problem?*

    a. her ankle

    b. her elbow

    c. her knee

B | *Listen again and answer the questions.*

    1. What can she do for the swelling and pain? _____

    2. What activities can she do?_____

    3. What activities can't she do?_____

EXERCISE 6: Pronunciation

A | *Read and listen to the Pronunciation Note.*

> **Pronunciation Note**
>
> The vowel / eɪ / as in *lay*, is tense. The vowel / ɛ / , as in *egg*, is lax. The tongue is higher and the lips are more spread for / eɪ / than for / ɛ / .

B | *Listen and repeat the words with the / eɪ / sound.*

    break   day   explain   late   name   plate   play   say   scale

C | *Listen and repeat the words with the / ɛ / sound.*

    egg   get   guess   leg   less   let   mess   met   stress   west

D | *Listen to the sentences. Check (✓) the sound of the underlined word.*

	/ eɪ /	/ ɛ /
1. He drinks <u>eight</u> bottles of water a day.	✓	
2. The doctor can't see you until <u>May.</u>		
3. Can I eat <u>eggs</u> on this diet?		
4. You can have <u>steak</u> on the Atkins™ diet.		
5. They met at a <u>Weight</u> Watchers® session.		
6. <u>May</u> I help you?		
7. The nutritionist's office is on <u>West</u> Street.		

EXERCISE 7: Information Gap

*Work in pairs (**A** and **B**). **Student A,** follow the instructions on this page. **Student B,** look at the Information Gap questions on page 161. Ask Student A the questions.*

1. Read the information for patients of Dr. Green.

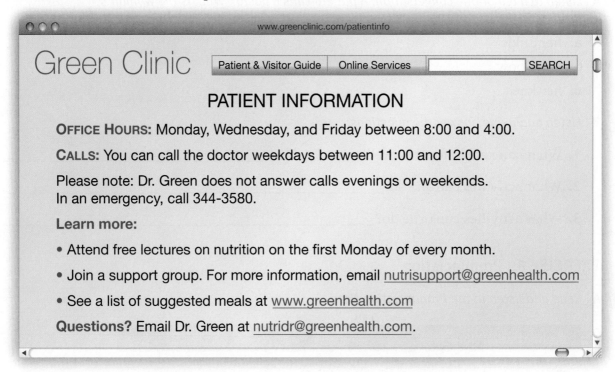

www.greenclinic.com/patientinfo

Green Clinic

Patient & Visitor Guide | Online Services | SEARCH

PATIENT INFORMATION

OFFICE HOURS: Monday, Wednesday, and Friday between 8:00 and 4:00.

CALLS: You can call the doctor weekdays between 11:00 and 12:00.

Please note: Dr. Green does not answer calls evenings or weekends.
In an emergency, call 344-3580.

Learn more:

• Attend free lectures on nutrition on the first Monday of every month.

• Join a support group. For more information, email nutrisupport@greenhealth.com

• See a list of suggested meals at www.greenhealth.com

Questions? Email Dr. Green at nutridr@greenhealth.com.

2. Answer Student B's questions. Use ***can***, ***may***, ***can't***, or ***may not***.

EXERCISE 8: Writing

A | *You and your friend want to lose weight. You found three diets online: The Skinny, 8-Minutes, and The Biggest Loser. Write an email to your friend. Tell your friend the requirements of each diet. Use **can** or **may**.*

Can I . . . ?	The Skinny	8-Minutes	The Biggest Loser
Eat out	Yes, often. The Skinny gives advice for foods in restaurants.	Occasionally.	It's difficult.
Drink coffee	Three times a day.	Not too much.	Yes.
Follow a vegetarian diet	Yes. There are many vegetarian possibilities.	Yes.	No. Many suggestions include meat.

EXAMPLE: On the Skinny diet, we can eat out often.

B | *Check your work. Use the Editing Checklist.*

<table>
<tr><td>

Editing Checklist

Did you . . . ?
- ☐ use **may** and **can** for permission
- ☐ check your spelling

</td></tr>
</table>

INFORMATION GAP FOR STUDENT B

Ask Student A the questions about the Green Clinic.

1. When can I see the doctor?

2. When can I call her?

3. Can I contact her by email?

4. What can I do in an emergency?

5. Are there any free lectures on nutrition?

6. Can I join a support group?

7. How can I get good meal suggestions?

14 Review

Check your answers on page UR-3.

Do you need to review anything?

A | Complete the paragraph with the words in parentheses. Use the correct form of the affirmative or negative.

It's a great diet. You ___may eat___ whatever you like. You just
                        1. (may / eat)

___can't eat___ a lot. For example, for breakfast you ___can have___ a slice of
   2. (can / eat)   3. (can / have)

toast, an egg, and an orange. You can put jelly on the toast, but you ___may not use___
                                                                         4. (may / use)

butter. You ___may drink___ coffee, tea, or milk.
            5. (may / drink)

B | Write John's questions for his doctor. Use **can** and the words in parentheses.

1. ___When can I return to work?___
   (When / I / return to work)

2. ___When can I take a shower?___
   (When / I / take a shower)

3. ___Can I go to the gym?___
   (I / go / to the gym)

4. ___Can I ride my bike?___
   (I / ride / my bike)

C | You are taking a language test. Read the rules. Then write sentences with **may** or **may not**.

NO	OK
food	a bottle of water
pencil	a black or blue pen
phone calls	dictionary 辞典

1. ___You may not eat food.___

2. ___You may not use a pencil.___

3. ___You may not___

4. ___You may drink a bottle of water___

5. ___

6. ___You may use a dicitonary.___

D | Correct the conversation. There are five mistakes.

A: May I sees a menu?   might 的直叙述过去式.

B: Sure, you ~~might~~. Here you go.
                  may

A: And can we ~~to~~ have some water?

B: I'll be right back with the water. . . . Ready?

                                                    have
A: Yes. I want the chicken with mushroom sauce. But may I ~~has~~ the sauce on the side?

B: You may not. We cook the chicken in the sauce.

A: Oh? Well, then I'll have grilled chicken with rice.
                                  烤

From Grammar to Writing

PUNCTUATION I: THE APOSTROPHE, THE COMMA, THE PERIOD, THE QUESTION MARK

1 | *Read this email. Circle all the punctuation marks.*

I'm bored
I'm boring 无聊的
I'm excited 兴奋的
I'm exciting

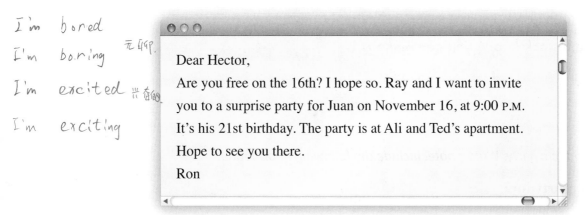

Dear Hector,

Are you free on the 16th? I hope so. Ray and I want to invite you to a surprise party for Juan on November 16, at 9:00 P.M. It's his 21st birthday. The party is at Ali and Ted's apartment. Hope to see you there.

Ron

2 | *Study these rules of punctuation.*

1	**The apostrophe (')** Use an apostrophe to show possession and to write contractions.	• **Carol's** book is here. • We **aren't** late.
2	**The comma (,)** Rules for commas vary. Here are some places where commas are almost always used: **a.** in a list of more than two things **b.** after the name of a person you are writing to **c.** after *yes* or *no* in a sentence **d.** when you use *and* to connect two sentences.	• He is wearing **a shirt, a sweater,** and a **jacket**. • Dear **John,** • **Yes,** I am. OR **No,** I'm not. • His house is huge, **and** his car is expensive.
3	**The period (.)** **a.** Use a period at the end of a statement. **b.** Use a period after abbreviations.	• We are English language **students**. • The party is on **Nov.** 16.
4	**The question mark (?)** Use a question mark at the end of a question.	• Are you planning a **party?** • Where are you **going?**

3 | *Add punctuation marks to this note.*

Dear Uncle John

Bob and I want to invite you to a party for my parents 25th wedding anniversary Its on Sunday Dec 11

The party is at our home at 23 Main St Its at three o'clock I hope you can make it

                    Emily

4 | *Invite a friend to a party. Write a note. Include the following information.*

Who is the party for?

Who is giving the party?

What is the occasion?

When is the party?

Where is the party?

5 | *Exchange papers with a partner. Did your partner follow the directions? Correct any mistakes in grammar and spelling.*

6 | *Talk to your partner. Discuss the mistakes you made. Then rewrite your own paper and make any necessary changes.*

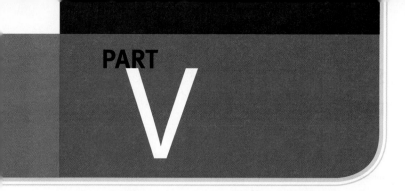

PART V

PRESENT PROGRESSIVE

UNIT 15 Present Progressive: Affirmative and Negative Statements

HIGH SCHOOL

STEP 1 GRAMMAR IN CONTEXT

Before You Read

PAIRS: Answer the questions.

1. How many hours a day do high school students spend in school?
2. Were you very busy during your high school years?
3. Is a very busy schedule good for high school students? Why or why not?

Read

Read the online article about two cousins.

www.nineteen.com/lifestyle

Nineteen

| quizzes & games | fashion | lifestyle | celebrities | guys |

Mi Young and Julie are cousins. Mi Young lives in Seoul, and Julie lives in New York City. Both teens are *juniors*[1] in high school. It's the second week of the semester.

It's 10:00 at night. Mi Young is still in school. She's **working** on some tough math problems. She's tired, but she's **not giving up**. Mi Young goes to public school from 8:00 to 3:00. Then she goes to a private study school from 3:30 to 10:00. Her friends are in the study school with her. Like Mi Young, they're **hoping to** go to a top college. There is a lot of competition and pressure to get into top schools. These private schools—or "cram" schools—are popular with middle class[2] and wealthy families all over East Asia.

12 hours later

It's 10 P.M. in New York City. Julie is in her family's apartment. She's **texting** her friend. They're **making plans** to study together. Julie goes to school from 9:00 to 3:00. She swims on the school swimming team. Then she does her homework. Julie and her friends **are** all **working** hard this year. They're **going** to school. They're **preparing** for the SATs.[3] They're **playing** on teams, and they're **doing** a lot of other extra-curricular activities. They're **not getting** enough sleep. They're **feeling** a lot of pressure.[4] Julie only takes a break[5] once in a while.

Just like Mi Young and her friends, they're **doing** all this work because they want to attend a top-rated college.

But is a "top" school really so important? What are they learning and what are they missing?

---
[1] *juniors:* students in their third year of high school
[2] *middle class:* the group of people in a society who are not rich and not poor
[3] *SAT:* a test students take to get into many colleges
[4] *pressure:* things in your life that make you worry
[5] *take a break:* rest

After You Read

A | Practice *PAIRS: Now read the online article aloud. Take turns reading each paragraph.*

B | Vocabulary *Match the words from the article with their meaning.*

_____ **1. tough** 坚强的
_____ **2. give up**
_____ **3. extracurricular**
_____ **4. top**
_____ **5. competition** 比赛
_____ **6. wealthy** 丰富的

a. in addition to school work
b. people trying to be better than others
c. stop doing something
d. rich
e. best
f. difficult

C | Comprehension *Look back at the online article. Complete the chart. Check (✓) what is true about Mi Young and Julie or both. It's 10 P.M.*

	Mi Young	Julie
1. in school	✓	✓
2. at home	✗	✓
3. working hard	✓	✓
4. hoping to get into a top college	✓	✓
5. texting a friend	✗	✓
6. feeling a lot of pressure 压力	✓	✓
7. doesn't have a lot of free time	✓	✓

STEP 2 GRAMMAR PRESENTATION

PRESENT PROGRESSIVE

Affirmative Statements			Negative Statements			
Subject	**Be**	**Base Form of Verb + -ing**	**Subject**	**Be**	**Not**	**Base Form of Verb + -ing**
I	am		I	am		
He			He			
She	is		She	is		
It		relaxing.	It		not	sleeping.
We			We			
You*	are		You	are		
They			They			

*You can be both singular and plural subjects.

GRAMMAR NOTES

1	Use the **present progressive*** to talk about an **action** that is or is not **happening now**.	• I **am** driving • We **are not** walking.

Now

Past ———————X——————→ Future

	We can use the time expressions *now*, *right now*, and *at the moment* with the present progressive.	• The machine **isn't working now**. • **Right now** she's resting. • **At the moment** he's talking on the phone.
	BE CAREFUL! We don't usually use non-action verbs in the present progressive.	• The textbook costs $80. Nᴏᴛ: ~~The textbook is costing $80.~~

2	Use **contractions** in speaking and informal writing.	• **I'm** not studying. **I'm** resting. • Luis **isn't** playing a game. **He's** reading. • We **aren't** playing a game. **We're** practicing.

3	Do not repeat the verb *be* when the subject is doing two things.	• They**'re singing** and **dancing**. Nᴏᴛ: ~~They're singing and are dancing.~~

4	If a verb ends in a silent *-e*, drop the final *-e* and add *-ing*.	• She's **driving** home. (drive) • I'm **taking** a test. (take)

5	We sometimes use the present progressive for an action that is taking place at this time, but may not be happening at this moment.	• **These days** Julie **is working** hard.

*The present progressive is also called present continuous.

REFERENCE NOTES
See Unit 17, page 188 for a discussion of non-action verbs.
See Appendix 8, page A-8 for more spelling rules for the present progressive.

STEP 3 FOCUSED PRACTICE

EXERCISE 1: Discover the Grammar

A | *Read about Mi Young and Julie. Underline the present progressive.*

1. 6:00 A.M.   Mi Young is getting ready for school. She's putting on her school
   uniform. Julie is still sleeping.

2. 7:00 A.M.   Mi Young and her classmates are taking the bus to school. Julie is
   washing her face and combing her hair.

3. 3:30 P.M.   Mi Young is <u>studying</u> English. Julie is <u>swimming</u> at her high school pool.

4. 7:00 P.M.   Mi Young is <u>having</u> dinner with her classmates. Julie is <u>eating</u> at home.

5. 11:00 P.M.   Mi Young is <u>riding</u> home on the bus. Julie is <u>studying</u> physics.

B | *Write the base form of the words you underlined in Part A.*

1. _____get_____	4. _____take_____	7. _____study_____	10. _____eat_____
2. _____put_____	5. _____wash_____	8. _____swim_____	11. _____ride_____
3. _____sleep_____	6. _____comb_____	9. _____have_____	12. _____study_____

EXERCISE 2: Present Progressive Statements

(Grammar Notes 1–4)

Write about Julie's day with the words in parentheses. Use the present progressive.

1. It's 9:00 A.M. on Saturday morning.

(Julie / get / up) _____Julie is getting up_____. She's late.

(She / not / eat breakfast) _____She is not eating breakfast_____

2. 9:40 A.M.

(Julie / take the bus) _____Julie is taking the bus_____ to her SAT prep class.

3. 1:00 P.M. Julie is at her school for a swimming competition. 比赛 ʃ, kəmpi'ti [ən]

(Julie / compete) _____Julie is competing_____ against 20 swimmers. 游泳者.
比赛   [ə'geinst]
Three swimmers are ahead of Julie.   反对, 紧挨

提利
(Julie / not / give up) _____Julie's not giving_____ up.
放弃: 小缩

4. 4:00 P.M. Julie is home.

(She / study / physics) _____She's studying physics_____
物理学
5. 8:00 P.M.   ʃ'fiziks]

(Julie / hang out) _____Julie's hanging out_____ with
悬挂
some friends.

(They / not / study) _____They are not studying_____

(They / not / compete) _____They ann't compete_____

(They / relax and have fun) _____They'ar relaxing and having fun_____

EXERCISE 3: Present Progressive Statements (Grammar Notes 1–2, 4)

It's 10:00 P.M. at Julie's home. Complete the sentences with the words from the box. Use the present progressive form.

| chat | go / not | sleep / not | study / not | ~~turn~~ |
| | | | take | worry |

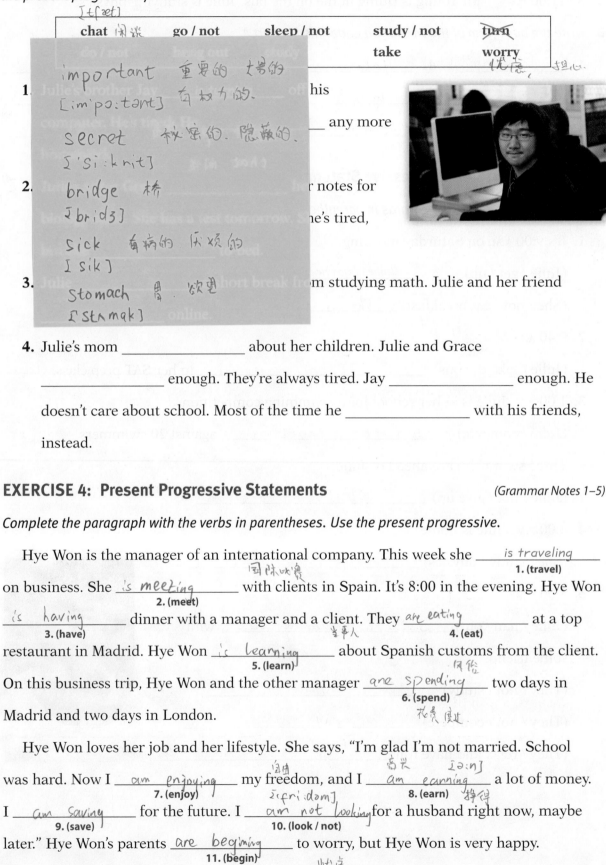

1. Julie's brother Jay _____ his _____ any more

2. _____ her notes for _____ she's tired,

3. _____ from studying math. Julie and her friend

4. Julie's mom _____ about her children. Julie and Grace

_____ enough. They're always tired. Jay _____ enough. He

doesn't care about school. Most of the time he _____ with his friends,

instead.

EXERCISE 4: Present Progressive Statements (Grammar Notes 1–5)

Complete the paragraph with the verbs in parentheses. Use the present progressive.

Hye Won is the manager of an international company. This week she ___is traveling___
1. (travel)
on business. She _is meeting_ with clients in Spain. It's 8:00 in the evening. Hye Won
2. (meet)
is having dinner with a manager and a client. They _are eating_ at a top
3. (have) **4. (eat)**
restaurant in Madrid. Hye Won _is learning_ about Spanish customs from the client.
5. (learn)
On this business trip, Hye Won and the other manager _are spending_ two days in
6. (spend)
Madrid and two days in London.

Hye Won loves her job and her lifestyle. She says, "I'm glad I'm not married. School
was hard. Now I _am enjoying_ my freedom, and I _am earning_ a lot of money.
7. (enjoy) **8. (earn)**
I _am saving_ for the future. I _am not looking_ for a husband right now, maybe
9. (save) **10. (look / not)**
later." Hye Won's parents _are begining_ to worry, but Hye Won is very happy.
11. (begin)

EXERCISE 5: Editing

Correct the journal entry by a high school student. There are eight mistakes. The first mistake is already corrected. Find and correct seven more.

> *sitting*
> I'm ~~sit~~ in the park. It's a beautiful day. The leaves changing color. Today there
>
> are a lot of children in the park. They laughing and are playing. They no are studying.
>
> They're lucky. It's hard to study on a beautiful day.
>
> I trying to memorize vocabulary words for the SATs. I'm wait for my friend
>
> Grace. She's in my Saturday SAT prep class. We planning to study together all
>
> afternoon and evening.

STEP 4 COMMUNICATION PRACTICE

EXERCISE 6: Listening

A | *Listen to a telephone conversation. Where is the mother calling from?*

She's _____.

B | *Listen again and answer the questions.*

1. What's the father doing?

   He's cooking.

2. What's Jay doing?

   _____

3. What's Julie doing?

   _____

4. Where's Grace?

   _____

5. What time will the mother arrive?

   _____

EXERCISE 7: Pronunciation

A | *Read and listen to the Pronunciation Note.*

Pronunciation Note
When we use the present progressive, we do not stress the **-ing** ending. The -ing is unstressed.
EXAMPLES:
She's **wait**ing for Janet.   He's **study**ing for finals.

B | *Read and listen to the sentences. Then listen and repeat.*

1. She's taking a test.
2. He's not giving up.
3. We're trying out for the play.
4. We're studying together.
5. He's driving home.
6. They're watching the news.

EXERCISE 8: Game: Describing a Photo

A | *GROUPS: You have 10 minutes. Look at the photo. Write as many affirmative and negative statements as you can. Use the present progressive.*

B | *Now compare the class in the photo to your own class.*

EXERCISE 9: Writing

A | *Look at people in a school cafeteria, a park, a mall, or on a train or a bus. Write about two people. Answer these questions. Use the present progressive.*

- Where are you? What time is it?
- What are the people doing? What are they wearing?

EXAMPLE: I'm in our school cafeteria. It's 12:30 P.M. Two girls are paying for their food. One girl is very tall. The other is not. The tall girl is wearing black pants and a black T-shirt. The shorter girl is wearing jeans and a red sweater. They're carrying a lot of books. The tall girl isn't smiling. She's carrying a tray with a cup of yogurt and a salad. The shorter girl is carrying a tray with a sandwich, a salad, an apple, and cookies. She's talking a lot. The tall girl is listening. She isn't saying a word. I think they're in the same class. I don't think they're close friends.

B | *Check your work. Use the Editing Checklist.*

Editing Checklist
Did you . . . ?
☐ use the present progressive correctly
☐ check your spelling

UNIT 15 Review

Check your answers on page UR-3.
Do you need to review anything?

A | Circle the correct words to complete the sentences.

1. I'm not getting / no am getting enough sleep.

2. We are prepare / 're preparing for the SATs now.

3. She isn't playing / no is playing tennis now.

4. They doing / 're doing a lot of extracurricular activities.

5. He is feel / 's feeling a lot of pressure.

B | Complete the sentences with the words from the box. Use the present progressive form.

carry	drive	listen to	run	stand and talk

1. A man ___listening to___ music on his iPod.

2. Two women ___standing and talking___ on a street corner.

3. Some children _____ to catch their school bus.

4. A young man _____ a red sports car.

5. An older man _____ a briefcase.

C | Complete the sentences with the verbs in parentheses. Use the affirmative or negative form of the present progressive.

1. John ___is texting___ his friend. He ___isn't calling___ him. John says texting is
      (text)   (call)
   faster.

2. Mary and Lulu ___are working___ on some tough physics problems. The problems
            (work)
   are difficult, but they ___aren't giving up___
            (give up)

3. Julie ___is swimming___ fast. She ___is trying___ to win a race.
      (swim)   (try)

D | Correct the paragraph. There are four mistakes.

    My classmates and I am sitting in a computer lab. One student writing a composition. Two students are check their email. A teacher is helps a student. The other students are surfing the Internet.

Before You Read

A | *Where do you like to watch movies? Check (✓) your favorite place:*

☐ on a flat-screen TV

☐ at the theater

☐ on your computer

☐ on your phone

Movie theater in India

B | *Look at the stamps that show famous movies. Do you like these kinds of movies? Check (✓) the types that you like.*

☐ Fantasy/Adventure ☐ Romance ☐ Action

C | *Look at the list of other kinds of movies. Check (✓) each kind of movie you like.*

☐ animation   ☐ crime / horror   ☐ mystery

☐ comedy   ☐ drama   ☐ science fiction

Read

Abby has a cold. Her co-worker Greg is calling to see how she is. Read their conversation.

ABBY: Hello.

GREG: Hi, Abby. **How are you feeling?** Any better?

ABBY: Uh-huh. I'm coughing less, and the fever is going down.

GREG: Good. **Are you resting?** 静止的

ABBY: Yes, and I'm watching a DVD.

GREG: Oh? **What are you watching?**

ABBY: *The Wizard of Oz.*[1]

GREG: *The Wizard of Oz?*

ABBY: I know its a kid's movie, but I really like it.

GREG: So **what part are you watching? What's happening?**

ABBY: I'm watching the scene where Dorothy meets the Tin Man.

GREG: **Is Dorothy giving the Tin Man oil?**

ABBY: Yes, she's putting oil in his mouth.

GREG: **Is he talking?**

ABBY: No, not yet. Dorothy and the Scarecrow are talking to him, but he can't talk.

GREG: I remember the scene. It's amazing. The film is still popular after so many years.

ABBY: Well, it's a classic. **So what's going on at work?**

GREG: Same old same old.[2] We're working on ten things at once.

ABBY: **Is Mr. Brooks going crazy?**[3]

GREG: Uh-huh. And tomorrow he'll be worse.

ABBY: Why?

GREG: I'll be out. I think I'm catching your cold.

---

[1] ***The Wizard of Oz:*** 1939 film about a Kansas farm girl. Her house goes up in the air during a storm and she lands in a magical place called Oz.

[2] ***same old same old:*** nothing new

[3] ***going crazy:*** feeling very upset because many things are happening all at once

A | Practice *PAIRS: Now read the conversation aloud.*

B | Vocabulary *Complete the sentences with the words from the box.*

艺术家	咳嗽	特别喜欢的	发烧	一场, 一幕

catching a cold	classic	coughing	favorite	fever	scene

古典的, 迷人的

1. In this ___Scene___ Dorothy meets the Tin Man.

2. I don't feel well. I think I'm

   ___catching a cold___

3. Do you feel hot? Do you have a

   ___fever___.

Eddie Murphy

4. Take this medicine. But if you're

   ___coughing___ a lot, maybe you

   should see a doctor.

5. The movie *Casablanca* is a

   ___classic___. It's still popular after more than 60 years.

6. Eddie Murphy is my ___favorite___ actor. I watch every comedy he is in.

C | Comprehension *Correct the false statements to make them true.*

1. Abby is staying home from work because her daughter has a cold and fever.

F 2. Greg is taking care of Abby.

F 3. Greg and Abby are watching *The Wizard of Oz*.

F 4. Dorothy is giving the Tin Man water.

F 5. The Tin Man is talking.

F 6. Greg's boss, Mr. Brooks, isn't going crazy.

PRESENT PROGRESSIVE: *YES / NO* QUESTIONS AND *WH-* QUESTIONS

Yes / No Questions

Be	Subject	Base Form of Verb + *-ing*
Am	I	
Are	you	
Is	he she it	resting? 休息
Are	we you they	

Short Answers

Affirmative			Negative		
Yes,	you	are.	No,	you're	not.
	I	am.		I'm	
	he she it	is.		he's she's it's	
	you we they	are.		you're we're they're	

Wh- Questions

Wh- Word	Be	Subject	Base Form of Verb + *-ing*	
Why		you	staying	home?
What	are		watching?	
Where		they	going?	
Who	is	she	meeting?	

Answers

I'm sick.
The Wizard of Oz.
To the movies. They're going to the movies.
Her teacher. She's meeting her teacher.

Wh- Questions about the Subject

Wh- Word	Be	Base Form of Verb + *-ing*
Who	is	reading?
What		happening?

Answers

My friend (is).
They're singing.

GRAMMAR NOTES

1	Use the **present progressive** to ask about **something that is happening now**. Reverse the subject and *be* when asking a **yes / no** question.	**I'm singing** in the rain. • He is singing. ✗ • Is he singing?
2	Most **wh- questions** in the present progressive use the same word order as *yes / no* questions. Use *whom* only for formal English.	• **Where is** he **working**? • **What are** they **doing**? • **Who are** you **meeting**? • **Whom** is the president meeting?
3	**Who** and **What questions about the subject** use statement word order.	STATEMENT • Dorothy is singing. *WH-* QUESTION • Who is singing? What is happening?

STEP 3 FOCUSED PRACTICE

EXERCISE 1: Discover the Grammar

A | *Read the conversation again on page 175. Write the three other* **yes / no** *questions.*

1. Are you resting?
2. Is Dorothy giving the Tin Man oil?
3. Is she talking?
4. Is Mr. Brooks going crazy?

B | *Look at the conversation again. Write the four other* **wh-** *questions in the charts.*

Wh- word + *be*	Subject	Base Form of Verb + *-ing*
1. How are	you	feeling?
2. What are	you	watching
3. what part are	you	watching

Wh- word + *be*	Base Form of Verb + *-ing*	Verb (动词)
4. what's	happening	
5. whats	going on at work	

EXERCISE 2: Present Progressive: *Yes / No* and *Wh-* Questions   *(Grammar Note 1)*

Write questions with the words in parentheses. Use the present progressive. Then match the questions with the answers below.

___b___ **1.** (you / watch / a movie) _Are you watching a movie?_

___d___ **2.** (what / Johnny Depp / do / now?) _What's Johnny Depp doing now?_

___c___ **3.** (you / watch / it / on your DVD) _Are you watching it on your DVD?_

___a___ **4.** (you / tape / it / for me) _Are you taping it for me?_

     a. No, sorry, but it will be on again.

     b. Yes. I'm watching *Pirate of the Caribbean: Curse of the Black Pearl* with Johnny Depp.

     c. No. It's on TV.

     d. He's standing on the deck of his ship.

EXERCISE 3: Present Progressive: *Yes / No* and *Wh-* Questions   *(Grammar Notes 1–3)*

Abby and Greg are talking on the telephone. Complete their conversation with the words in parentheses. Use the present progressive.

ABBY: Hi, Greg. _____How are you feeling_____? _____Are you feeling any better?_____
                              1. (How / you / feel)   **2. (you / feel / any better)**

GREG: No, I'm not.

ABBY: _____Are you taking the medicine_____
            3. (you / take / the medicine)

GREG: Yes, I am. _____Where are you calling from_____?
                    4. (Where / you / call from)

ABBY: I'm at an Italian restaurant. Greg. Listen to this. Meryl Streep is eating here.

GREG: No kidding! _____Who is she eating with_____?
                  5. (Who / she / eat / with)

ABBY: I think she's with her daughter. I'm not sure.

GREG: _____Are people asking for her_____? autograph
              6. (people / ask for her autograph)

ABBY: No. Nobody's bothering her, but everyone knows she's there.

GREG: Well, when you pass her table, say, "Bon appétit!" That was my favorite line in *Julie and Julia.*

Concentrating

EXERCISE 4: Common Two-Word Verbs *(Grammar Notes 1–2)*

Complete the questions with the words from the box. Use the present progressive.

listen to	look at	look for	~~wait for~~

1. **A:** Is that *Shrek 3*?

   B: No. I _m waiting for_ *Shrek 3* to start. I'm watching a preview of some other film.

2. **A:** _____ you _____ a good

   movie to watch?

   B: Yes, I am. Why? Do you have an idea?

3. **A:** What _____ she _____?

   B: She's looking at some online movie reviews.

4. **A:** What _____ they _____?

   B: The music from *The Wizard of Oz*.

EXERCISE 5: Editing

Correct the conversations. There are six mistakes. The first mistake is already corrected. Find and correct five more.

1. **A:** Excuse me, who^s collecting tickets?

   B: He isn't here now. Wait a minute. He'll be right back.

2. **A:** What you doing?

   B: I'm turning off my cell phone.

3. **A:** Is Dad buy popcorn?

   B: Yes, he is.

4. **A:** What taking him so long?

   B: He's waiting in a long line.

5. **A:** Excuse me, is someone sits here?

   B: No, no one sitting here. Please sit down.

EXERCISE 6: Listening

A | *Listen to the conversation. What is Dan shopping for? Circle the correct letter.*

    a. an HDTV   **b.** a DVD player   **c.** a DVR player

B | *Listen again and answer the questions.*

1. Who is Dan getting a gift for?   *for his dad*

2. What's the occasion?   _____

3. When can he use the gift?   _____

4. What does Dan's friend tell him to buy?   _____

5. What's happening at Goodbuys this week?   _____

EXERCISE 7: Pronunciation

A | *Read and listen to the Pronunciation Note.*

Pronunciation Note

When letters are used in abbreviations, we usually stress the last syllable.

EXAMPLES:

    •
MTV   •
PC

B | *Listen and repeat the abbreviations.*

    CD   DVD   DVR   TV   ISBN   BA

C | *Change the underlined words to abbreviations. Then take turns reading the sentences. Stress the last letter of each abbreviation.*

           DVD
1. We're buying a new <u>digital video disc</u> player.

2. That 50-inch flat screen <u>television</u> is on sale.

3. Do you have an extra <u>compact disc</u>?

4. Give me the <u>international standard book number</u>.

5. We want to get a <u>digital video recorder</u> so we can record shows.

6. He has a <u>bachelor of arts</u> in film.

D | *Listen to the sentences in Part C. Then repeat the sentences.*

EXERCISE 8: Role Play

PAIRS: Write a telephone conversation with your partner. Student A is watching a movie when Student B calls. Student B, ask Student A questions about his or her movie. Use the present progressive. Continue the conversation.

B: Hi, _____? This is _____. Are you busy?

A: Oh, hi, _____. I _____ a movie.

(watch)

B: What _____?

(watch)

A: _____.

B: What's happening?

A: _____.

EXERCISE 9: Describing Pictures

A | *PAIRS: On a separate piece of paper, write questions about the picture. Use the present progressive. Ask another pair your questions.*

B | *Draw a picture. Include four people or more and a basket. Use four of these actions:* **sing, dance, wear, look at, look for, carry.** *Do not show your partner your picture.*

C | *PAIRS: Ask your partner questions about his or her picture. Then try to draw the picture your partner describes. Answer your partner's questions about your picture. Compare pictures.*

> **EXAMPLE:** **A:** Who is singing?
> **B:** Two girls are singing.
> **A:** What are they wearing?

EXERCISE 10: Writing

A | *PAIRS: Interview each other about your favorite movies. Ask some questions with the present progressive:*

- What's the name of the movie? Who's the director? Who's the star? What language is it in?
- What do you like best about the movie?
- What's your favorite in the scene?
- Where is it taking place? When?
- What are the people doing?

B | *Now write about the movie you talked about. Use the present progressive when possible.*

EXAMPLE: The movie is *Avatar*. The director is James Cameron. It's a science fiction fantasy. It takes place in a world called Pandora. The digital art is the best part of the movie. In this scene the hero Jake is an avatar. He's flying on Pandora with his girlfriend. He is helping her people and trying to save Pandora from greedy people from Earth.

C | *Check your work. Use the Editing Checklist.*

Editing Checklist

Did you . . . ?
- ☐ use the present progressive correctly
- ☐ check your spelling

Check your answers on page UR-3.

Do you need to review anything?

A | *Complete the conversations with the verbs in parentheses. Use the present progressive.*

1. **A:** The kids are screaming. ___Are___ they ___watching___ a horror
   (watch)

   show?

   B: Yes, ___they are___.

2. **A:** What ___Are___ you ___doing___?
   (do)

   B: I ___am listening___ to my favorite CD.
   (listen)

3. **A:** What ___is happening___ outside?
   (happen)

   B: Uncle John ___is putting___ up a new fence.
   (put)

B | *Write **yes** / **no** questions with the words in parentheses. Use the present progressive.*

1. ___Are you working?___
   (you / work)

2. ___Is he buying tickets online?___
   (he / buy tickets online)

3. ___Are they watching a mystery?___
   (they / watch a mystery)

4. ___Is she enjoying the movie?___
   (she / enjoy the movie)

C | *Write **wh-** questions in the present progressive with the words in parentheses.*

1. ___Where are they going___
   (Where / they / go)

2. _____
   (What music group / perform)

3. _____
   (Where / they / play)

4. _____
   (Why / Bob stay home)

D | *Correct the conversations. There are four mistakes.*

1. **A:** Is it's raining outside?

   B: Yes. I hope it stops.

2. **A:** Are they playing soccer?

   B: No, they not. They're playing rugby.

3. **A:** You watching a good movie?

   B: It's OK.

4. **A:** What they doing?

   B: They're fixing the cabinets.

Simple Present and Present Progressive; Non-Action Verbs

SMARTPHONES

Before You Read

Do you have a cell phone? How many ways do you use it?

Read

Read the online article about today's phones.

ARTS	SCIENCE	POLITICS	TECHNOLOGY	SEARCH:

Cell Phone Mania | Technology Today

More than 4¹/₂ million people **have** them. People under 30[1] **don't know** a world without them. They **come** in all colors and shapes. Some **are** waterproof and shockproof.[2] What **are** they? Cell phones.

Today's cell phones **have** many different features. Take Xavier. He**'s** at a picnic in a park. He **needs** a ride to a party that evening. He**'s texting** a friend. The couple in the car were in a minor accident. The man **is taking** a photo with his phone. And John **is checking** email from his phone.

It**'s** easy to understand the popularity of these phones. People **want** to connect with others, and at the same time, they **want** to be *mobile*.[3] Cell phones **make** it possible to do both. Cell phones **are** big business, and the technology **is** constantly **improving**. What about the future? What will it bring? Nobody **knows**, but here **are** the wishes of two people.

Emily, age 15, **says**, "I often **forget** to charge my phone. I **want** a phone with endless power."

Robert, a college freshman **says**, "I **want** a phone that can teach me a foreign language while I **sleep**."

Well, Emily may get her wish a lot sooner than Robert. But of course, with the speed at which things **are changing**, you never **know** what the future will bring.

---

[1] *under 30:* less than 30 years old
[2] *shockproof:* doesn't break when it falls
[3] *mobile:* able to move around

After You Read

A | Practice *PAIRS: Now read the article aloud. Take turns reading each paragraph.*

B | Vocabulary *Circle the best meaning for the words in blue.*

1. We **connect** through Facebook®.

   a. join [dʒɔin] 连接   **b.** make contact

2. That watch is **waterproof**. You can swim with it on.

   a. not hurt by water   **b.** dry
   佐建

3. That new computer comes with a lot of **features**.

   a. parts that make it better   **b.** memory 记忆力
   部防

4. He calls her **constantly**. Is he in love?

   a. all the time   **b.** from time to time 时不时的

5. Your work is **improving**. 改良

   a. getting better   **b.** changing.

6. There's a **minor** problem with my computer.

   a. serious   **b.** small

C | Comprehension *Complete the sentences. Circle the correct letter.*

1. More than _____*b*_____ people have cell phones today.
   a. 450,000   **b.** 4,500,000   **c.** 4,500,000,000

2. The man in the car accident is using the phone as a ____*b*____.
   a. radio   **b.** camera   **c.** computer

3. Telephone technology is _____*C*_____.
   a. making phones harder to use   **b.** using video   **c.** improving all the time

4. Emily wants her phone to ____*a*____.
   a. have power all the time   **b.** have a beeper   **c.** teach her a language

SIMPLE PRESENT AND PRESENT PROGRESSIVE

The Simple Present	The Present Progressive
I **eat** at eight o'clock.	I**'m eating** now.
He **eats** at 8:00 too.	He**'s eating** now.
She **doesn't eat** with me.	She **isn't eating** with him.
They **don't eat** with us.	They **aren't eating** with us.
Does he **eat** meat?	**Is** he **eating** chicken?
Do you **eat** in the cafeteria?	**Are** you **eating** chicken?

NON-ACTION (STATIVE) VERBS

State of Being	Emotion	Sense / Appearance	Need / Preference	Mental Action	Possession	Measurement
be	love	hear	want	agree	have	cost
	hate	see	need	disagree	own	weigh
	like	feel	prefer	guess	belong	owe
	dislike	taste		understand		
		smell		know		
		sound		remember		
		look		believe		
				think		
				mean		
				worry		

GRAMMAR NOTES

1	Use the **simple present** to tell or ask about **habits**, **customs**, **routines**, or **facts**. **Now** Past —X—X—┼—X—X—→ Future *She shops every Saturday.*	• I **check** Facebook® every morning. • **Do** you **check** Facebook® in the morning?
2	Use the **present progressive** to tell or ask about an action happening **right now** or **these days**. Past ——————X————→ Future **Now**	• He**'s checking** email now. • **Is** Enrique **checking** email? • Jon **is teaching** computer science this year.
3	Some verbs do not describe actions. These verbs are called **non-action** or **stative verbs**.	• I **have** a great idea. • This **belongs** to me. • They **love** that phone.
4	**Non-action verbs** do the following: **a.** express emotion **b.** describe sense or appearance **c.** express a need or preference **d.** describe a thought **e.** show possession **f.** give a measurement **g.** *Be* expresses a state of being.	• We **like** that computer. • The music **sounds** relaxing. • I **prefer** email. • Jennifer **knows** you. • It **belongs** to me. • It **costs** a lot of money. • I **am** tired now.
5	We usually do not use non-action verbs in the present progressive (*-ing*) form.	• I **own** a smartphone • It **costs** a lot. NOT: I'm owning a smartphone. It's costing a lot.

EXERCISE 1: Discover the Grammar

Underline the simple present. Circle the present progressive. Underline twice all non-action verbs.

Raisa has a new phone with a lot of great features. She likes her phone a lot. Her phone keeps her in touch with her friends wherever she is. Right now Raisa is texting friends. They are making plans for the evening. She and her friends often text. They don't talk much on the phone. They also connect through Facebook®. Raisa often adds new friends to her site. Sometimes she doesn't know them very well. Raisa's mother, Olga, worries about that. Olga doesn't use social networks. She prefers to talk on the phone or connect through email.

EXERCISE 2: Simple Present; Non-Action Verbs; Present Progressive *(Grammar Notes 1–5)*

Complete the conversation with the words in parentheses. Use the simple present or present progressive. Use contractions when possible.

A: What _____ *are* _____ you _____ *doing* _____?
    1.   **2. (do)**

B: I _____ my messages. Look. That's my friend from high school.
        3. (check)

   She _____ three kids now. They _____ happy birthday to
        4. (have)   **5. (sing)**

   their father.

A: Oh. That's nice.

B: _____ you _____ social networking sites?
        6.   **7. (use)**

A: No, I _____. I _____ to email my friends. I _____
            8.   **9. (prefer)**   **10. (think)**

   it's more personal. Also, I _____ there are privacy features in social
                                  11. (know)

   networking sites, but I _____ about my privacy.
                              12. (worry)

EXERCISE 3: Simple Present; Non-Action Verbs; Present Progressive (Grammar Notes 1–5)

Complete the conversation with the words in parentheses. Use the simple present or present progressive. Use contractions when possible.

A: I'm worried about Tim. This term he _____*is*_____ always online or

_____ friends. He _____ well in school. I _____
    2. (text)   **3. (do / not)**   **4. (think)**

he _____ Spanish.
   5. (fail)

B: Oh. What _____ he _____?
             6.   **7. (say)**

A: Nothing. Right now he _____ some new game. He _____
              8. (play)   **9. (love)**

computer games. I _____ he _____ a computer addict.
          10. (think)   **11. (become)**

EXERCISE 4: Simple Present; Non-Action Verbs; Present Progressive (Grammar Notes 1–5)

Complete the paragraph with the verbs from the box. Use the correct form. Use contractions.

answer	ask	be	talk	think	want	~~work~~

Phuong is a fisherman. He _____*is working*_____ on a boat. His old phone is broken. Phuong
                     1.

_____ a new phone. He _____ about getting a waterproof smart
   2.   **3.**

phone with a lot of features. Right now he _____ to a saleswoman in a wireless
                  4.

phone store. He _____ a lot of questions. The saleswoman _____
        5.   **6.**

his questions. She _____ very helpful.
       7.

EXERCISE 5: Editing

Correct the paragraph. There are six mistakes. The first one has been corrected for you. Find and correct five more.

      hate
I ~~hates~~ cell phones. My boss is thinking he can call me anytime, even on weekends.

I'm dislike email for the same reason. People in my company work all the time.

There's no "off" time. Look at John over there. It's his lunchtime, but he answering

calls and is checking email. This wasn't possible in my parents' day. I don't think

it's right. Technology great in some ways, but it's awful in other ways.

STEP 4 COMMUNICATION PRACTICE

EXERCISE 6: Listening

A | *Listen to the phone messages. Which calls are from co-workers? Which calls are from family? Check (✓) **co-worker** or **family** next to the call.*

Phone Message	Co-worker	Family	Message
1.			Please send me a copy of the Smith report.
2.			She's _____.
3.			She needs to _____.
4.			She's looking for _____.

B | *Look back at Part A. Listen again. Complete the messages.*

EXERCISE 7: Pronunciation

A | *Read and listen to the Pronunciation Note.*

> **Pronunciation Note**
>
> We can use intonation to express emotions such as surprise or anger.
>
> **EXAMPLES:** I'm surprised at you! (surprised)   I'm surprised at you! (angry)

B | *Listen to this conversation. How does the woman sound? Circle the correct letter.*

    a. surprised   **b.** angry

C | *Listen to this conversation. How does the woman sound? Circle the correct letter.*

    a. surprised   **b.** angry

D | *PAIRS: Practice the conversation. Take turns reading each part. Practice showing surprise. Then practice showing anger.*

    A: I have a call coming in. It's my boss.

    B: But it's 2:00 A.M.! Why is he calling now?

EXERCISE 8: Conversation

PAIRS: Read about these people. Guess why they're doing something different today.

  1. Paul and Ana usually shop at Electronics Plus for their electronics. Today they're shopping at Goodbuys.

    EXAMPLE: Paul and Ana are shopping at Goodbuys today because there is a big sale.

  2. Maria usually texts friends. Today she's calling and speaking to them.

  3. Joaquin usually wears jeans and a T-shirt in class. Today he's wearing a suit.

  4. Ali usually brings his lunch to work. Today he's eating out.

EXERCISE 9: Survey

A | *GROUPS: Match the pictures and sentences. Write the correct letter.*

1. __d__

2. _____

3. _____

a. She's checking her messages.

b. He's texting a friend

c. They're reading e-books.

d. He's using a landline.

e. He's using a desktop computer.

4. _____

5. _____

B | *Complete the survey for yourself. Write your preference and a reason why.*

Which do you prefer?	I prefer_____.
using email or Facebook®	*Facebook®. I think it's more fun. It's easy to connect with everyone at once.*
texting or talking on the phone	
ebooks or printed books	
cell phones or landlines	
laptops or desktop computers	

C | GROUPS: One student asks the others for their preferences and takes notes. Another student reports the results to the class.

> EXAMPLE: **Juan:** Marta, do you prefer social network sites or email?
>
> **Marta:** I prefer email.
>
> **Juan:** Emiko, what about you? Do you prefer . . .
>
> **Paul:** In our group four people prefer social networking sites, and two prefer email.

EXERCISE 10: Writing

A | Look at the pictures. Write about the people. They are doing many things at once. What are they doing? Use the present progressive.

> EXAMPLE: The man is drinking a cup of tea . . .

B | Now write about times when you do many things at once. Use the simple present.

> EXAMPLE: I'm always busy in the morning. I usually walk to school. Sometimes I look at the other people and I wonder about their lives.

C | Check your work. Use the Editing Checklist.

Editing Checklist
Did you . . . ? ☐ use simple present, present progressive and non-action verbs correctly ☐ check your spelling

A | Complete the sentences with the words in parentheses. Use the affirmative or negative form of the simple present.

1. They _____ a car.
   (own / not)
2. He _____ to drive.
   (like / not)
3. She _____ a new bike.
   (have)
4. She _____ a lock for it.
   (need)
5. They _____ to buy bikes too.
   (want)

B | Complete the paragraph with the verbs in parentheses. Use the simple present or present progressive.

John _____ his new computer now. He _____ the
        1. (use)   2. (surf)
Internet. He _____ information about events in his area. His computer
              3. (get)
_____ a lot of great features. John _____ to learn how to use
     4. (have)   5. (want)
all of them.

C | Complete the conversation with the words in parentheses. Use the simple present or present progressive.

A: What _____ Tom _____?
                              1. (do)
B: He _____ to fix his printer again.
          2. (try)
A: What _____ the problem now?
             3. (be)
B: I _____.
        4. (know / not)
A: _____ he _____ a new printer? This one is pretty old!
                        5. (need)

D | Correct the conversations. There are five mistakes.

1. **A:** Where you calling from?

   B: Downtown. I walk along Second Street.

2. **A:** Is she play tennis at West Park?

   B: No, she's not. She no like those courts.

3. **A:** Does he understands Greek?

   B: Yes, he does. He was in Greece for a year.

From Grammar to Writing

SUBJECTS AND VERBS

1 | What's wrong with these sentences?

1. He a handsome man.
2. She a red skirt.
3. I from Argentina.

4. Am wearing blue pants.
5. Are tired?
6. Is a cool day.

Sentences 1–3 are missing a verb. Sentences 4–6 are missing a subject.

2 | Study the information about subjects and verbs.

Every sentence needs a subject and verb.	**SUBJECT VERB** My **mother works**.
The **subject** is a noun or pronoun. It tells who or what the sentence is about.	• **John** is running. • **They** are watching TV.
The **verb** tells the action or links the subject with the rest of the sentence.	• It **is raining**. • He **is** a doctor.

3 | Correct this paragraph. Then underline the subject and circle the verb in each sentence.

I in Central Park. It a sunny day in September. Is crowded. Some children soccer.

They're laughing and shouting. Some people are running. Three older women on a bench.

Are watching the runners and soccer players. A young man and woman are holding

hands. Are smiling. Are in love. Central Park a wonderful place to be on a beautiful day.

4 | Imagine you are in one of these places. Write a paragraph about the people you see.

an airport   a busy street   a park   a train station

5 | Exchange papers with a partner. Did your partner follow the directions? Correct any mistakes in grammar and spelling.

6 | Talk to your partner. Discuss the mistakes you made. Then rewrite your own paper and make any necessary changes.

APPENDICES

1 Map of the World

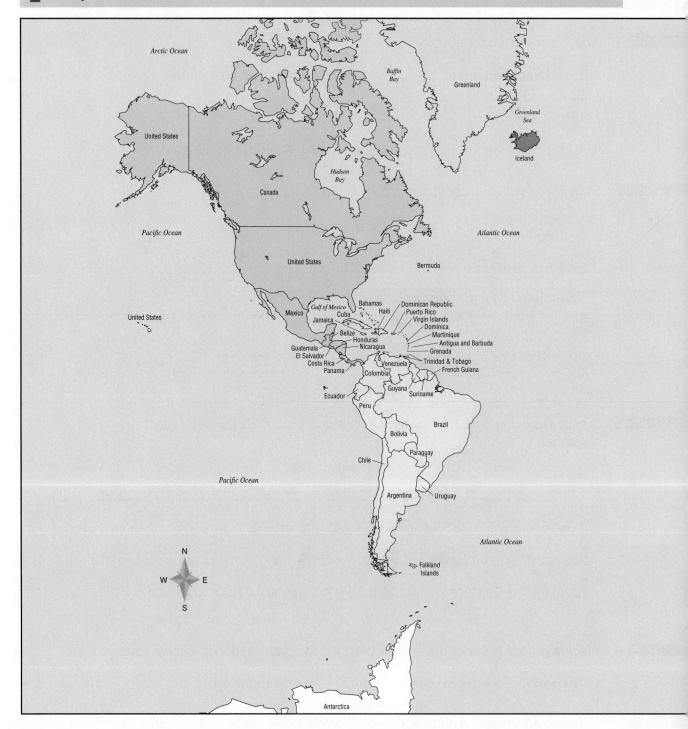

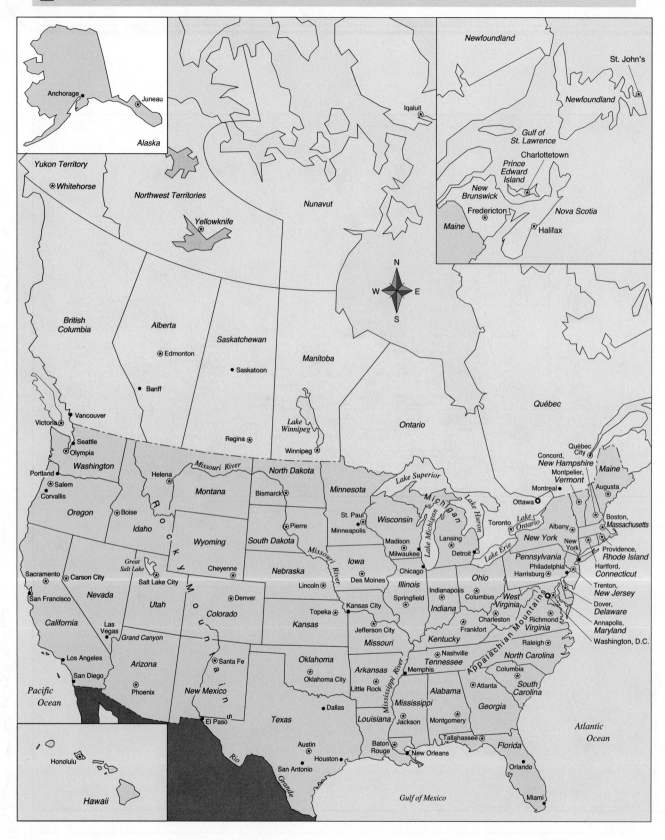

CARDINAL NUMBERS

1 = one	11 = eleven	21 = twenty-one
2 = two	12 = twelve	30 = thirty
3 = three	13 = thirteen	40 = forty
4 = four	14 = fourteen	50 = fifty
5 = five	15 = fifteen	60 = sixty
6 = six	16 = sixteen	70 = seventy
7 = seven	17 = seventeen	80 = eighty
8 = eight	18 = eighteen	90 = ninety
9 = nine	19 = nineteen	100 = one hundred
10 = ten	20 = twenty	101 = one hundred and one
		200 = two hundred
		1,000 = one thousand
		1,000,000 = one million
		10,000,000 = ten million

EXAMPLES

That building has **seventy-seven** pages.
There are **thirty** days in April.
There are **six** rows in the room.
She is **twelve** years old.
He has **four** children.

ORDINAL NUMBERS

1st = first	11th = eleventh	21st = twenty-first
2nd = second	12th = twelfth	30th = thirtieth
3rd = third	13th = thirteenth	40th = fortieth
4th = fourth	14th = fourteenth	50th = fiftieth
5th = fifth	15th = fifteenth	60th = sixtieth
6th = sixth	16th = sixteenth	70th = seventieth
7th = seventh	17th = seventeenth	80th = eightieth
8th = eighth	18th = eighteenth	90th = ninetieth
9th = ninth	19th = nineteenth	100th = one hundredth
10th = tenth	20th = twentieth	101st = one hundred and first
		200th = two hundredth
		1,000th = one thousandth
		1,000,000th = one millionth
		10,000,000th = ten millionth

EXAMPLES

He works on the **seventy-seventh** floor.
It's April **thirtieth**.
He's in the **sixth** row.
It's her **twelfth** birthday.
Bob is his **first** child. Mary is his **second**. John is his **third**, and Sue is his **fourth**.

TEMPERATURE

We measure the temperature in degrees (°).

Changing from degrees Fahrenheit to degrees Celsius:

$$(°F - 32) \times 5/9 = °C$$

Changing from degrees Celsius to degrees Fahrenheit:

$$(9/5 \times °C) + 32 = °F$$

DAYS OF THE WEEK

Weekdays	Weekend
Monday	Saturday
Tuesday	Sunday
Wednesday	
Thursday	
Friday	

MONTHS OF THE YEAR

MONTH	ABBREVIATION	NUMBER OF DAYS
January	Jan.	31
February	Feb.	28*
March	Mar.	31
April	Apr.	30
May	May	31
June	Jun.	30
July	Jul.	31
August	Aug.	31
September	Sept.	30
October	Oct.	31
November	Nov.	30
December	Dec.	31

*February has 29 days in a leap year, every four years.

(continued on next page)

THE SEASONS

NORTHERN HEMISPHERE

Spring: March 21–June 20

Summer: June 21–September 20

Autumn or Fall: September 21–December 20

Winter: December 21–March 20

SOUTHERN HEMISPHERE

Spring: September 21–December 20

Summer: December 21–March 20

Autumn or Fall: March 21–June 20

Winter: June 21–September 20

TITLES

Mr. (Mister)	/ mɪstər /	unmarried or married man
Ms.	/ mɪz /	unmarried or married woman
Miss	/ mɪs /	unmarried woman
Mrs.	/ mɪsɪz /	married woman
Dr. (Doctor)	/ dɑktər /	doctor (medical doctor or Ph.D.)

4 Time

It's one o'clock.
(It's 1:00.)

It's five after one.
(It's 1:05.)

It's one-ten.
It's ten after one.
(It's 1:10.)

It's one-fifteen.
It's a quarter after one.
(It's 1:15.)

It's one twenty-five.
It's twenty-five after one.
(It's 1:25.)

It's one-thirty.
It's half past one.
(It's 1:30.)

It's one forty-five.
It's a quarter to two.
(It's 1:45.)

It's one-fifty.
It's ten to two.
(It's 1:50.)

TALKING ABOUT TIME

1	You can talk about time this way:	**A: What time is it?** **B:** It's one o'clock.
2	**A.M.** means before noon (the hours between midnight and noon). **P.M.** means after noon (the hours between noon and midnight). **BE CAREFUL!** When people say 12:00 A.M., they mean midnight. When people say 12:00 P.M., they mean noon.	It's 10:00 A.M. It's 10:00 P.M.
3	We often write time with numbers.	It's one o'clock. = It's **1:00**. It's two-twenty. = It's **2:20**.

PLURAL NOUNS: SPELLING RULES

1	Add **-s** to form the plural of most nouns.	student chief picture	students chiefs pictures
2	Add **-es** to form the plural of nouns that end in **ss**, **ch**, **sh**, and **x**. (This ending adds another syllable.)	class watch dish box	classes watches dishes boxes
3	Add **-es** to form the plural of nouns that end in **o** preceded by a consonant. **EXCEPTION:** Add **-s** to plural nouns ending in **o** that refer to music.	potato piano soprano	potatoes pianos sopranos
4	Add **-s** to form the plural of nouns that end in **o** preceded by a vowel.	radio	radios
5	To form the plural of words that end in a consonant + **y**, change the **y** to **i** and add **-es**.	dictionary fly	dictionaries flies
6	To form the plural of words that end in a vowel + **y**, add **-s**.	boy day	boys days
7	To form the plural of certain nouns that end in **f** or **fe**, change the **f** to **v** and add **-es**.	half loaf knife wife	halves loaves knives wives
8	Some plural nouns are **irregular**.	woman child person mother-in-law man foot tooth	women children people mothers-in-law men feet teeth
9	Some nouns **do not have a singular form**.	(eye) glasses clothes pants scissors	
10	Some plural nouns are the same as the singular noun.	Chinese fish sheep	Chinese fish sheep

PLURAL NOUNS: PRONUNCIATION RULES

1	The **final sounds** for regular plural nouns are / s /, / z /, and / ɪz /.	boots	boys	horses
2	The plural is pronounced / s / **after** the **voiceless sounds** / p /, / t /, / k /, / f /, and / θ /.	cups hats works	cuffs myths	
3	The plural is pronounced / z / **after** the **voiced sounds** / b /, / d /, / g /, / v /, / m /, / n /, / ŋ /, / l /, / r /, and / ð /.	crabs cards rugs	doves drums fans	rings girls stores
4	The plural *s* is pronounced / z / **after** all **vowel sounds**.	day toe	days toes	
5	The plural *s* is pronounced / ɪz / **after the sounds** / s /, / z /, / ʃ /, / tʃ /, and / dʒ /. (This adds another syllable to the word.)	races causes dishes	churches judges	

6   The Simple Present: Spelling and Pronunciation Rules

THE THIRD-PERSON SINGULAR AFFIRMATIVE: SPELLING RULES

1	Add **-s** to form the third-person singular of most verbs. Add **-es** to words that end in *ch*, *s*, *sh*, *x*, or *z*.	Pete works. I work too. Doug wears sweatshirts. I wear shirts. Norma teaches Spanish. I teach English. Lulu washes her clothes on Tuesday. Elenore and Pete wash their clothes on Sunday.
2	When a base-form verb ends in a **consonant** + *y*, change the *y* to *i* and add **-es**. Do not change the *y* when the base form ends in a **vowel** + *y*. Add **-s**.	I study at home. Carol studies at the library. Dan plays tennis. I play tennis too.
3	*Have*, *do*, and *go* have **irregular forms** for the third-person singular.	I have. He **has**. I do. She **does**. I go. It **goes**.

🎧 THE THIRD-PERSON SINGULAR AFFIRMATIVE: PRONUNCIATION RULES

1	The **final sound** for the third-person singular form of the simple present is pronounced / **s** /, / **z** /, or / **ɪz** /. The final sounds of the third-person singular are the same as the final sounds of plural nouns. See Appendix 9 on pages A-8 and A-9.	/ s / talk**s**	/ z / love**s**	/ ɪz / danc**es**
2	**Do** and **say** have a change in vowel sound.	I say. / seɪ / I do. / du /	He say**s**. / sɛz / He do**es**. / dʌz /	

7 Possessive Nouns

1	Add **'s** to form the possessive of singular nouns.	Lulu**'s** last name is Winston.
2	To form the possessive of plural nouns ending in **s**, add only an **apostrophe (')**.	The girl**s'** gym is on this floor. The boy**s'** locker room is across the hall.
3	In hyphenated words (*mother-in-law*, *father-in-law*, etc.) and in phrases showing joint possession, only the last word is possessive in form.	My sister-in-law**'s** apartment is big. Elenore and Pete**'s** apartment is comfortable.
4	To form the possessive of plural nouns that do not end in **s**, add **'s**.	The men**'s** room is next to the water fountain.
5	To form the possessive of one-syllable singular nouns that end in **s**, add **'s**. To form the possessive of words of more than one syllable that end in **s**, add an **'** or an **'s**.	**James's** apartment is beautiful. **McCullers'** novels are interesting. OR **McCullers's** novels are interesting.
6	**BE CAREFUL!** Don't confuse possessive nouns with the contraction of the verb **be**.	**Carol's** a student. = **Carol** *is* a student. **Carol's** book is open. = **Her** book is open.

8 The Present Progressive: Spelling Rules

1	Add *-ing* to the base form of the verb.	drink see eat	drink**ing** see**ing** eat**ing**
2	If a verb ends in a silent *e*, drop the final *e* and add *-ing*.	smil**e**	smil**ing**
3	If a one-syllable verb ends in a consonant, a vowel, and a consonant (**CVC**), double the last consonant before adding *-ing*. However, do not double the last consonant if it is a *w*, *x*, or *y*.	**CVC** sit run sew mix play	si**tt**ing ru**nn**ing se**w**ing mi**x**ing pla**y**ing
4	In words with two or more syllables that end in a consonant, a vowel, and a consonant (**CVC**), double the last consonant only if the last syllable is stressed.	admit whisper	admi**tt**ing *(stressed)* whispe**r**ing *(not stressed)*

9 Direct and Indirect Objects

Group One									
Subject	Verb	Direct Object	*To*	Indirect Object	Subject	Verb	Indirect Object	Direct Object	
She	sent	a gift it	to	us.	She	sent	us	a gift.	

Group Two									
Subject	Verb	Direct Object	*For*	Indirect Object	Subject	Verb	Indirect Object	Direct Object	
They	found	a towel it	for	him.	They	found	him	a towel.	

Group Three						Group Four				
Subject	Verb	Direct Object	*To*	Indirect Object		Subject	Verb	Direct Object	*For*	Indirect Object
He	repeated	the question	to	the class.		He	fixed	the shelves	for	me.

Group One Verbs (*to*)		Group Two Verbs (*for*)	Group Three Verbs (*to*)	Group Four Verbs (*for*)
email	sell	build	explain	cash
give	send	buy	prove	close
hand	show	find	repeat	fix
lend	teach	get	say	pronounce
owe	tell	make	whisper	translate
pass	throw			
read	write			

RULES FOR DIRECT AND INDIRECT OBJECTS

1 With **Group One** and **Group Two verbs**, there are **two** possible **sentence patterns** if the **direct object** is a **noun**.

	DIRECT OBJECT	TO/FOR	INDIRECT OBJECT	
I gave the	**money**	to	**him**.	=

	INDIRECT OBJECT	DIRECT OBJECT
I gave	**him**	**the money**.

	DIRECT OBJECT	TO/FOR	INDIRECT OBJECT	
We bought	**the book**	for	**him**.	=

	INDIRECT OBJECT	DIRECT OBJECT
We bought	**him**	**the book**.

If the **direct object** is a **pronoun**, it always comes **before the indirect object**.

	DIRECT OBJECT	TO/FOR	INDIRECT OBJECT
I gave	**it**	to	**him**.
Please get	**them**	for	**me**.

Nᴏᴛ: I gave ~~him it~~.
Nᴏᴛ: Please get ~~me them~~.

2 With **Group Three** and **Group Four verbs**, the **direct object** always comes **before the indirect object**.

	DIRECT OBJECT	TO/FOR	INDIRECT OBJECT
Explain	**the sentence**	to	**John**.
She translated	**the letter**	for	**us**.

Nᴏᴛ: Explain ~~John the sentence~~.
Nᴏᴛ: She translated ~~us the letter~~.

THE SIMPLE PAST: SPELLING RULES

1	If the verb **ends in an e**, add **-d**.	arrive like	arrive**d** like**d**
2	If the verb **ends in a consonant**, add **-ed**.	rain help	rain**ed** help**ed**
3	If a **one-syllable verb** ends in a consonant, a vowel, and a consonant **(CVC)**, double the last consonant and add **-ed**. However, do not double the last consonant if it is a **w**, **x**, or **y**.	**CVC** hug rub bow mix play	hu**gged** ru**bbed** bow**ed** mi**x**ed pla**y**ed
4	If a **two-syllable verb** ends in a consonant, a vowel, and a consonant **(CVC)**, double the last consonant only if the last syllable is stressed.	re•fer •enter	refe**rred** *(stressed)* enter**ed** *(not stressed)*
5	If the verb ends in a **consonant + y**, change the **y** to **i** and add **-ed**.	worry carry	worr**ied** carr**ied**
6	If the verb ends in a **vowel + y**, do not change the **y** to **i**. Add **-ed**. There are **exceptions** to this rule.	play annoy pay lay say	play**ed** annoy**ed** **paid** **laid** **said**

THE SIMPLE PAST: PRONUNCIATION RULES

1	The **final sounds** for regular verbs in the simple past are / **t** /, / **d** /, and / **ɪd** /.	walk**ed**	plann**ed**	wait**ed**
2	The final sound is pronounced / **t** / **after** the **voiceless sounds** / **f** /, / **k** /, / **p** /, / **s** /, / **tʃ** /, and / **ʃ** /.	laugh**ed** lick**ed**	si**pped** mi**ssed**	wat**ched** wi**shed**
3	The final sound is pronounced / **d** / **after** the **voiced sounds** / **b** /, / **g** /, / **dʒ** /, / **l** /, / **m** /, / **n** /, / **r** /, / **ŋ** /, / **ð** /, / **ʒ** /, / **v** /, and / **z** /.	ru**bbed** hu**gged** ju**dged** pu**lled**	hu**mmed** ba**nned** occu**rred** ba**nged**	ba**thed** massa**ged** liv**ed** surpri**sed**
4	The final sound is pronounced / **d** / **after vowel sounds**.	play**ed** ski**ed**	ti**ed** sn**owed**	arg**ued**
5	The final sound is pronounced / **ɪd** / after / **t** / and / **d** /. / **ɪd** / adds a syllable.	want instruct rest attend	wan**ted** instruc**ted** res**ted** atten**ded**	

11   Base Forms and Past Forms of Common Irregular Verbs

Base Form	Past Form	Base Form	Past Form	Base Form	Past Form
become	became	give	gave	say	said
begin	began	go	went	see	saw
bite	bit	grow	grew	send	sent
blow	blew	hang	hung	shake	shook
break	broke	have	had	shoot	shot
bring	brought	hear	heard	shut	shut
build	built	hide	hid	sing	sang
buy	bought	hit	hit	sit	sat
catch	caught	hold	held	sleep	slept
choose	chose	hurt	hurt	speak	spoke
come	came	keep	kept	spend	spent
cost	cost	know	knew	stand	stood
do	did	lead	led	steal	stole
draw	drew	leave	left	swim	swam
drink	drank	lend	lent	take	took
drive	drove	lose	lost	teach	taught
eat	ate	make	made	tear	tore
fall	fell	meet	met	tell	told
feed	fed	pay	paid	think	thought
feel	felt	put	put	throw	threw
fight	fought	quit	quit	understand	understood
find	found	read*	read*	wake	woke
fly	flew	ride	rode	wear	wore
forget	forgot	ring	rang	win	won
get	got	run	ran	write	wrote

*Pronounce the base form / rid /. Pronounce the past form / rɛd /

COMMON NON-COUNT NOUNS*

Liquids

milk	soda
coffee	water
oil	beer
juice	

Food

bread	ketchup
cheese	jam
lettuce	jelly
broccoli	fish
ice cream	meat
butter	sour cream
mayonnaise	soup

Too Small to Count

sugar	baking powder
salt	cereal
pepper	spaghetti
cinnamon	wheat
rice	corn
sand	

School Subjects

math	biology
history	chemistry
geography	music

City Problems

traffic
pollution
crime

Weather

snow
rain
ice
fog

Gases

oxygen
carbon dioxide
nitrogen
air

Abstract Ideas

love	advice
beauty	help
happiness	noise
luck	time

Others

money	jewelry
mail	garbage
furniture	toothpaste
homework	paper
information	

*Some nouns can be either count or non-count nouns.

I'd like some **chicken**. (non-count) Did you eat any **cake**? (non-count)
There were three **chickens** in the yard. (count) I bought a **cake** at the bakery. (count)

QUANTIFIERS: CONTAINERS, MEASURE WORDS, AND PORTIONS

a bottle of (milk, soda, ketchup)
a bowl of (cereal, soup, rice)
a can of (soda, beans, tuna fish)
a cup of (hot chocolate, coffee, tea)
a foot of (snow, water)
a gallon of (juice, gas, paint)
a head of (lettuce)
an inch of (snow, rain)
a loaf of (bread)

a pair of (pants, skis, gloves)
a piece of (paper, cake, pie)
a pint of (ice cream, cream)
a quart of (milk)
a roll of (film, toilet paper, paper towels)
a slice of (toast, cheese, meat)
a tablespoon of (flour, sugar, baking soda)
a teaspoon of (sugar, salt, pepper)
a tube of (toothpaste, glue)

METRIC CONVERSION

1 liter	=	.26 gallons or 1.8 pints
1 gallon	=	3.8 liters

1 mile	=	1.6 kilometers
1 kilometer	=	.62 mile
1 foot	=	.30 meter or 30 centimeters
1 meter	=	3.3 feet
1 inch	=	2.54 centimeters

1 ounce	=	28 grams
1 gram	=	.04 ounce
1 pound	=	.45 kilogram
1 kilogram	=	2.2 pounds

These are the pronunciation symbols used in this text. Listen to the pronunciation of the key words.

VOWELS		CONSONANTS			
Symbol	**Key Word**	**Symbol**	**Key Word**	**Symbol**	**Key Word**
i	beat, feed	p	pack, happy	ʃ	ship, machine, station, special, discussion
ɪ	bit, did	b	back, rubber		
eɪ	date, paid	t	tie	ʒ	measure, vision
ɛ	bet, bed	d	die	h	hot, who
æ	bat, bad	k	came, key, quick	m	men
ɑ	box, odd, father	g	game, guest	n	sun, know, pneumonia
ɔ	bought, dog	tʃ	church, nature, watch	ŋ	sung, ringing
oʊ	boat, road	dʒ	judge, general, major	w	wet, white
ʊ	book, good	f	fan, photograph	l	light, long
u	boot, food, student	v	van	r	right, wrong
ʌ	but, mud, mother	θ	thing, breath	y	yes, use, music
ə	banana, among	ð	then, breathe	t̬	butter, bottle
ɚ	shirt, murder	s	sip, city, psychology		
aɪ	bite, cry, buy, eye	z	zip, please, goes		
aʊ	about, how				
ɔɪ	voice, boy				
ɪr	ear, beer				
ɛr	bare				
ɑr	bar				
ɔr	door				
ʊr	tour				

GLOSSARY OF GRAMMAR TERMS

action verb   A verb that describes an action. It can be used in the progressive.
- *Sachiko **is planning** a big party.*

adjective   A word that describes (or modifies) a noun or pronoun.
- *That's a **great** idea.*

adverb   A word that describes (or modifies) an action verb, an adverb, an adjective, or a sentence.
- *She drives **slowly**.*

adverb of frequency   A word that tells the frequency of something.
- *We **usually** eat lunch at noon.*

adverb of manner   A word that describes a verb. It usually answers the question *how*.
- *She speaks **clearly**.*

affirmative statement   A sentence that does not use a negative verb form (*not*).
- ***I have a car**.*

apostrophe   A punctuation mark used to show possession and to write a short form (contraction).
- *He's in my father's car.*

base form   The simple form of the verb without any ending such as -*ing*, -*ed*, or -*s*. It is the same as the infinitive without *to*.
- *Arnold will **come** at 8:00. We should **eat** then.*

***be going to* future**   A verb form used to make predictions, express general facts in the future, or talk about definite plans that were made before now.
- *Mei-Ling says it**'s going to be** cold, so she**'s going to take** a coat.*

capital letter   The big form of a letter of the alphabet. Sentences start with a capital letter.
- ***A**, **B**, **C**, etc.*

comma   Punctuation used to separate single things in a list or parts of a sentence.
- *We went to a restaurant**,** and we ate chicken**,** potatoes**,** and broccoli.*

common noun   A noun for a person, place, or thing. It is not capitalized.
- *The **man** got a **book** at the **library**.*

comparative form   An adjective or adverb ending in -*er* or following *more*. It is used in comparing two things.
- *My sister is **older** and **more intelligent** than my brother.*
- *But he studies **harder** and **more carefully**.*

consonant   The letters *b, c, d, f, g, h, j, k, l, m, n, p, q, r, s, t, v, w, x, y, z*.

contraction   A short form of two words. An apostrophe (') replaces the missing letter.
- ***It is** late and **I am** tired. I **should not** stay up so late.*
- ***It's** late and **I'm** tired. I **shouldn't** stay up so late.*

count noun   A noun you can count. It usually has a singular and a plural form.
- *In the **park**, there was a **man** with two **children** and a **dog**.*

definite article   *The*; It makes a noun specific.
- *We saw a movie. **The** movie starred Sean Penn.*

demonstrative adjective   An adjective used to identify the noun that follows.
- ***This** man is resting, but **those** men are busy.*

demonstrative pronoun   A pronoun used in place of a demonstrative adjective and the noun that follows.
- ***This** is our classroom, and **these** are my students.*

direct object   A noun or pronoun used to receive the action of a verb.
- *She sold a **car**. He bought **it**.*

exclamation point   A punctuation mark (!) used at the end of a statement. It shows strong emotion.
- *Help**!** Call the police**!***

formal language   Language we usually use in business settings, academic settings, and with people we don't know.
- ***Good morning, ladies** and **gentlemen. May** we begin?*

gerund   The -ing form of a verb. It is used as a noun.
- **Skiing** is fun, but we also enjoy **swimming**.

imperative   A sentence used to give an instruction, a direction, a command, or a suggestion. It uses the base form of the verb. The subject (you) is not a part of the sentence.
- **Turn** right at the corner. **Drive** to the end of the street. **Stop!**

indefinite article   A and an; used before singular, nonspecific non-count nouns.
- Jaime brought **a** sandwich and **an** apple for lunch.

infinitive   To + the base form of a verb.
- **To travel** is my dream. I want **to see** the world.

informal language   The language we usually use with family and friends, in email messages, and in other informal settings.
- **Hey, Doug, what's up?**

inseparable phrasal verb   A phrasal verb that cannot have an object between the verb and the particle.
- She **ran into** John.

irregular verb   A verb that does not form the simple past by adding -d or -ed.
- They **ate** a fancy meal last night. The boss **came** to dinner.

modal   A word that comes before the main verb. Modals can express ability, possibility, obligation, and necessity.
- You **can** come early, but you **mustn't** be late, and you **should** wear a tie.

negative statement   A statement with a negative verb form.
- He **didn't study**. He **wasn't** ready for the test.

non-action verb   A verb that does not describe an action. It can describe an emotion, a state, a sense, or a mental thought. We usually don't use non-action verbs in the progressive.
- I **like** that actor. He **is** very famous, and I **believe** he won an Oscar.

non-count noun   A noun we usually do not count. We don't put a, an, or a number before a non-count noun.
- All you'll need is **rice, water, salt,** and **butter**.

noun   A word that refers to a person, animal, place, thing, or idea.
- **Paula** has a **friend** at the **library**. She gave me a **book** about **birds**.

noun phrase   A phrase formed by a noun and words that describe (modify) it.
- It was **a dark brown leather jacket**.

object   A noun or pronoun following an action verb. It receives the action of the verb.
- I sent **a letter**. He read **it**.

object pronoun   A pronoun following a verb or a preposition.
- We asked **him** to show the photos to **them**.

period   A punctuation mark (.) used at the end of a statement.
- I'd like you to call on Saturday**.** We need to talk**.**

phrasal verb   A two-part (or three-part) verb that combines a verb and a particle. The meaning of the parts together is often different from the meaning of the verb alone.
- We **put on** our gloves and **picked up** our umbrellas.

phrase   A group of words that can form a grammatical unit.
- She lost **a red hat**. He found it **under the table**.

plural   The form that means more than one.
- **We** sat in **our chairs** reading **our books**.

possessive   An adjective, noun, or pronoun that shows possession.
- **Her** book is in **John's** car. **Mine** is at the office.

preposition   A small word that goes before a noun or pronoun object. A preposition often shows time or place.
- Maria saw it **on** the table **at** two o'clock.

prepositional phrase   A phrase that consists of a preposition followed by a noun or a noun phrase.
- Chong-Dae saw it **under the black wooden table**.

present progressive   A verb form that shows an action happening now or planned for the future.
- I**'m working** hard now, but I**'m taking** a vacation soon.

pronoun A word that replaces a noun or a noun phrase. There are subject pronouns, object pronouns, possessive pronouns, and demonstrative pronouns.

- *He is a friend—I know him well. This is his coat; mine is black.*

proper noun The actual name of a person, place, or thing. A proper noun begins with a capital letter.

- *Tom is living in New York. He is studying Russian at Columbia University.*

quantifier A word or phrase that comes before a noun and expresses an amount of that noun.

- *Jeannette used a little sugar, some flour, four eggs, and a liter of milk.*

question mark A punctuation mark (?) used at the end of a question.

- *Where are you going? When will you be back?*

quotation marks Punctuation marks (" . . . ") used before and after the actual words a person says.

- *I said, "Where are you going?" and "When will you be back?"*

regular verb A verb that forms the simple past by adding -d or -ed.

- *We lived in France. My mother visited us there.*

sentence A group of words with a subject and a verb.

- *We opened the window.*
- *Did they paint the house?*

separable phrasal verb A phrasal verb that can have an object between the verb and the particle.

- *She put on her coat. She put it on before he put his coat on.*

simple past A verb form used to show a completed action or idea in the past.

- *The plane landed at 9:00. We caught a bus to the hotel.*

simple present A verb form used to show habitual actions or states, general facts, or conditions that are true now.

- *Kemal loves to ski, and it snows a lot in his area, so he's very happy.*

singular The form that means only one.

- *I put on my hat and coat and closed the door.*

small letter The small form of a letter of the alphabet. We use small letters for most words except for proper nouns and the word that starts a sentence.

- *a, b, c, etc.*

subject The person, place, or thing that a sentence is about.

- *The children ate at the mall.*

subject pronoun A pronoun used to replace a subject noun.

- *Irene works hard. She loves her work.*

superlative form An adjective or adverb ending in -est or following most. It is used in comparing three or more things.

- *We climbed the highest mountain by the most dangerous route.*
- *She drives the fastest and the most carelessly of all the drivers.*

syllable A group of letters with one vowel sound. Words are made up of one or more syllables.

- *One syllable—win*
- *Two syllables—ta ble*
- *Three syllables—im por tant*

verb A word used to describe an action, a fact, or a state.

- *He drives to work now. He has a new car, and he is a careful driver.*

vowel The letters a, e, i, o, or u, and sometimes y.

wh- question A question that asks for information. It begins with what, when, where, why, which, who, whose, or how.

- *What's your name?*
- *Where are you from?*
- *How do you feel?*

will future A verb form used to make predictions, to talk about facts in the future, to make promises, to offer something, or to state a decision to do something at the time of speaking.

- *It will probably rain, so I'll take an umbrella. I'll give you my extra one.*

yes/no question A question that has a yes or a no answer.

- *Did you arrive on time? Yes, I did.*
- *Are you from Uruguay? No, I'm not.*
- *Can you swim well? Yes, I can.*

UNIT REVIEW ANSWER KEY

Note: In this answer key, where a short or contracted form is given, the full or long form is also correct (unless the purpose of the exercise is to practice the short or contracted forms).

UNIT 1

A 1. are 3. am 5. are
2. is 4. is

B 1. 'm 3. 're 5. 're
2. 's 4. 's

C 1. He isn't (He's not) 3. We aren't (We're not)
2. They're 4. She's

D My father and mother are from India, but they're in Canada now. My parents are doctors.

My father *is* a sports doctor and my mother ~~she~~ is a foot doctor. My parents and I love sports. My

father ~~are~~ *is* a soccer fan, and my mother *is* a baseball

fan. I'm a soccer fan. My father and I ~~am~~ *are* fans of

Lionel Messi and Nuno Gomes. My sister ~~no is~~ *isn't*

good at sports. She's not a sports fan. She loves movies.

UNIT 2

A 1. Where's 3. What's 5. Is
2. How's 4. Are

B 1. I am
2. it isn't (it's not)
3. they aren't (they're not)
4. we are
5. you aren't (you're not)

C 1. What's today's date?
2. Where's the men's room?
3. Why is he absent? (Why's he absent?)
4. When's your first class?
5. Who's your teacher?

D 1. ~~She~~ *Is she* your teacher?
2. What *is* your name?
3. Where *is* your class?
4. ~~Is~~ *Are* Bob and Molly good friends?
5. Why *are* you late?

UNIT 3

A 1. was 3. Were 5. Was
2. was 4. were

B 1. c 3. d
2. b 4. a

C 1. was 5. were
2. was 6. wasn't
3. Were 7. was
4. was

D John ~~is~~ *was* at a job interview yesterday. It ~~were~~ *was* for a

job at a bank. The questions ~~no were~~ *weren't* easy, but

John's answers were good. He was happy. It *was* a good day for John.

UNIT 4

A 1. a 3. Ø 5. Ø
2. an 4. Ø

B 1. cities 3. clothes 5. people
2. watches 4. fish or fishes

C lin = Lin london = London
ali = Ali thanksgiving = Thanksgiving

D Melanie Einzig is *an* artist and ~~an~~ *a* photographer.
She was born in Minnesota, but lives in

New ~~york~~ *York*. Einzig captures moments in time.

Her ~~photograph~~ *photographs* are striking. They are in ~~museum~~ *museums*

in San ~~francisco~~ *Francisco*, Chicago, and Princeton.

UNIT 5

A 1. a 3. Ø 5. Ø
2. Ø 4. an

B 1. c 3. b 5. b
2. a 4. c

C 1. I'm at the new museum.
2. It is full of interesting things to see.
3. It has unusual bowls from long ago.
4. It has beautiful carpets too.
5. The museum is a great place to visit.

D The Grand Canyon National Park in Arizona is ~~a~~ *an* awesome place to visit. Almost five million people

visit this ~~park unusual~~ *unusual park* each year. The weather

is good in the late spring and summer, but it *is* crowded during those months. There are seven

~~differents~~ *different* places to stay in the park. I like El Tovar.

It is ~~a~~ *an* old hotel with a great view.

UNIT 6

A 1. on   3. behind   5. in front of
    2. under   4. next to

B 1. at   3. at, on the
    2. at

C

Box containing circle with X, triangle with Y, and square with Z.

D A: Is Jon at ~~the~~ school?

    B: No. He's ~~in~~ *at* home.

    A: Where does he live?

    B: He lives ~~at~~ *on* Oak Street, between First and

      Second Avenue ~~at~~ *in* Lakeville.

    A: Does he live in an apartment?

    B: Yes. He lives ~~in~~ *on* the third floor.

UNIT 7

A 1. Let's get   4. Let's not meet
    2. Why don't we invite   5. Don't touch
    3. Don't buy

B 1. Wear   4. Don't bring
    2. Don't wear   5. pay
    3. Bring

C 1. Let's go to the gym.
    2. Let's watch a movie this afternoon.
    3. Why don't we take a trip together?
    4. Why don't we hang out with Pietro this weekend?

D 1. Why ~~you~~ *you* don't ask Andrij for help?
    2. You look really tired. ~~Why don't you~~ You take a short nap ?
    3. Let's ~~to~~ walk to work. Let's not drive.
    4. Don't ask Boris to fix the car. ~~Asks~~ *Ask* Mickey.
    5. I'm on a diet, so buy yogurt at the store. Don't ~~to~~ buy sour cream.

UNIT 8

A 1. shops   3. don't like   5. has
    2. likes   4. go

B 1. don't need   3. play
    2. need   4. doesn't like

C 1. is   3. wears   5. are
    2. works   4. don't wear

D 1. My son doesn't ~~has~~ *have* a suit.
    2. He always ~~wear~~ *wears* jeans, T-shirts, and hoodies.
    3. He ~~need~~ *needs* a suit for my brother's wedding.

4. Suits ~~is~~ *are* expensive and my son ~~don't~~ *doesn't* like to wear them.

5. We ~~wants~~ *want* to rent or borrow a suit for him.

UNIT 9

A 1. Do   3. Does   5. Am
    2. Is   4. Are

B 1. Do / have   3. Does / watch   5. Are
    2. Does / speak   4. Is

C 1. Are the neighbors noisy?
    2. Does the apartment building have an elevator?
    3. Is the apartment near trains or buses?
    4. Does the bedroom have two closets?
    5. Is the bedroom big?

D 1. A: Does he have a big TV in his room?
      B: Yes, he ~~has~~ *does.*
    2. A: Does she ~~needs~~ *need* help?
      B: No, she ~~don't~~ *doesn't.*
    3. A: ~~Do you are~~ *Are you* friends?
      B: Yes, we ~~aren't~~ *are.* (OR No, we aren't.)

UNIT 10

A 1. Why   3. Who   5. Where
    2. When   4. How

B 1. Who snores in your family?
    2. What do you dream about?
    3. What time does your mother get up?
    4. What time do you go to bed?
    5. Where does your brother sleep?

C 1. Who meets his uncle at the diner (on Saturdays)?
    2. Who does John meet at the diner (on Saturdays)?
    3. Where does John meet his uncle (on Saturdays)?
    4. When does John meet his uncle at the diner?

D 1. Where *do* you live and who *do* you live with?
    2. Why *does* he daydream in class?
    3. When does she ~~gets~~ *get* up?
    4. How *do* they feel about sleeping pills?
    5. Who ~~does~~ *do* you dream about?

UNIT 11

A 1. A: Are there   B: there are
    2. A: Are there   B: there aren't
    3. A: Is she   B: she is

4. A: Are they   **B:** they aren't
5. A: Is there   **B:** there isn't

B 1. There's / It's
2. There are / They're
3. There's / She's

C Visit the new Shopper's Mall on Route 290.

There are
~~There's~~ over 100 stores. ~~There~~ *There's* a movie theater,

there
and ~~they~~ are ten great places to eat. Come early.

there's
Every morning at 10:30 ~~there are~~ a free show for children. The mall is three miles from the Tappan Bridge on Route 290.

UNIT 12

A 1. Their   3. Its   5. Her
2. His   4. Their

B 1. **A:** mine   **B:** yours   **A:** your
2. **A:** Whose   **B:** Ali's
3. My / Its
4. **A:** Her / yours   **B:** Mine

C **A:** *Whose* ~~Who's~~ bag is that on the floor?

Maria's
B: I think it's ~~Maria~~.

A: No. Her bag is on her arm.

mine (OR my bag)   *Rita's*
B: Well, it's not ~~mine bag~~. Maybe it's ~~Rita~~.

yours (OR your bag)
A: Rita, is that ~~bag your~~?

UNIT 13

A 1. couldn't understand / can understand
2. can't run / could run
3. couldn't drive / can drive

B 1. **A:** Can   **B:** can
2. **A:** Could   **B:** couldn't / can
3. **A:** Can   **B:** can

C **A:** Can you ~~to~~ get online?

get
B: No, I can't ~~not~~. I couldn't ~~got~~ online last night either.

A: My brother is good with computers. Maybe he

help
can ~~helps~~.

can't
B: Great. I ~~can no~~ figure out what's wrong.

can't
A: I ~~no can~~ reach him now, but I can ~~to~~ call him after 6 P.M.

UNIT 14

A 1. may eat   4. may not use
2. can't eat   5. may drink
3. can have

B 1. When can I return to work?
2. When can I take a shower?

---

3. Can I go to the gym?
4. Can I ride my bike?

C 1. You may not eat. (You may not bring food.)
2. You may not use a pencil.
3. You may not make phone calls.
4. You may bring a bottle of water.
5. You may use a black or blue pen.
6. You may use a dictionary.

D **A:** May I ~~sees~~ *see* a menu?

Sure.
B: ~~Sure, you might~~. Here you go.

A: And can we ~~to~~ have some water?

B: I'll be right back with the water. . . . Ready?

A: Yes. I want the chicken with mushroom sauce.

have
But may I ~~has~~ the sauce on the side?

I'm sorry.
B: ~~You may not~~. We cook the chicken in the sauce.

A: Oh? Well, then I'll have grilled chicken with rice.

UNIT 15

A 1. 'm not getting   4. 're doing
2. 're preparing   5. 's feeling
3. isn't playing

B 1. is listening to
2. are standing and talking
3. are running
4. is driving
5. is carrying

C 1. is texting / isn't ('s not) calling
2. are working / aren't giving up
3. is swimming / 's trying

D My classmates and I ~~am~~ *are* sitting in a computer lab.

is
One student ^ writing a composition. Two students

checking   *helping*
are ~~check~~ their email. A teacher is ~~helps~~ a student. The other students are surfing the Internet.

UNIT 16

A 1. **A:** Are / watching   **B:** they are
2. **A:** are / doing   **B:** 'm listening
3. **A:** 's happening   **B:** is putting

B 1. Are you working?
2. Is he buying tickets online?
3. Are they watching a mystery?
4. Is she enjoying the movie?

C 1. Where are they going?
2. What music group is performing?
3. Where are they playing?
4. Why is Bob staying home?

it
D 1. **A:** Is ~~it's~~ raining outside?

B: Yes. I hope it stops.

2. A: Are they playing soccer?

B: No, they ~~not~~. They're playing rugby. [*'re* above *they*]

3. A: ~~You~~ watching a good movie? [*Are you* above]

B: It's OK.

4. A: What they doing? [*are* inserted]

B: They're fixing the cabinets.

UNIT 17

A 1. don't own   4. needs
2. doesn't like   5. want
3. has

B 1. is using   3. 's getting   5. wants
2. is surfing   4. has

C 1. is / doing   4. don't know
2. 's trying   5. Does / need
3. 's

D 1. **A:** Where you calling from? [*are* inserted]

B: Downtown. ~~I walk~~ along Second Street. [*I'm walking* above]

2. **A:** Is she ~~play~~ tennis at West Park? [*playing* above]

B: No, she's not. She ~~no~~ like those courts. [*doesn't* above]

3. **A:** Does he ~~understands~~ Greek? [*understand* above]

B: Yes, he does. He was in Greece for a year.

UNIT 18

A 1. watched   4. Last night
2. visited   5. didn't land
3. an hour ago

B 1. helped   4. didn't ask
2. stayed   5. didn't want
3. didn't snow

C 1. canceled   4. played
2. didn't stay   5. didn't enjoy
3. didn't rain

D Hello from London. Our friends ~~did~~ invited us here for a week. We're having a great time.

Yesterday we ~~visit~~ Big Ben, and we ~~tour~~ the Royal [*visited*, *toured* above]

Palace. This morning we ~~watch~~ the Changing of [*watched* above] the Guard. We wanted to shop this afternoon, but we didn't. The prices were high, but we ~~are~~ enjoyed looking at the store windows.

UNIT 19

A 1. saw   3. tried
2. was / wanted   4. got / didn't want

B A lucky man **found** a pot of gold. He **kept** the pot of gold in a hole in the ground of his garden. A jealous worker **stole** the gold from the man.

The man **became** upset. But a neighbor laughed because the man **didn't use** the gold. He just enjoyed counting it.

C 1. didn't stay   3. ran   5. took
2. lost   4. didn't see

D 1. William Sidney Porter born in North Carolina in 1862. [*was* above]

2. He was a famous American short story writer. He wrote under different names, but he ~~did~~ became best known as O. Henry.

3. His stories ~~were~~ had surprise endings.

4. O. Henry had many talents, but he ~~did get~~ into trouble and spent time in prison. [*got* above]

UNIT 20

A 1. Did they go to the theater?
2. Did she get there by bus?
3. Did you have good seats?
4. Did he understand everything?
5. Did we miss the beginning?
6. Did it have a happy ending?

B 1. What play did you see?
2. Where did you see it?
3. How long was the show?
4. Did you enjoy the performance?
5. Who were the stars?
6. Did you go out after the show?
7. Where did you go?
8. What did you order?

C 1. Where ~~he did~~ go last night? [*did he* above]
2. What ~~saw he~~? [*did he see* above]
3. Did he ~~enjoyed~~ it? [*enjoy* above]
4. Who he met? [*did meet* above]
5. When they go? [*did* above]
6. Who ~~did pay~~ for it? [*paid* above]

UNIT 21

A 1. was born   5. started
2. grew up   6. became
3. attended   7. expanded
4. went

B 1. When did she go to college?
2. Who did they meet?
3. Where did he study?
4. How long did they live in Canada?

C 1. Were   3. Was   5. Did
2. Did   4. Did

D Steve Paul Jobs ~~did start~~ *started* college in 1970, but he ~~no did~~ *didn't* finish it. In 1976 Jobs and his friend ~~begin~~ *began* to make their own computers. They worked in the Jobs' garage. That was the beginning of Apple® Computers. Their company ~~become~~ *became* a big success. Apple® changed the field of computers, and by the age of 30, Jobs was a multimillionaire.

UNIT 22

A
1. starting
2. to sell
3. to return
4. to become
5. flying / seeing
6. to help

B
1. to work
2. to change
3. quitting / going
4. to study
5. doing

C Carol volunteers at a hospital. She enjoys ~~to take~~ *taking* care of patients. Some patients refuse ~~do~~ *to* exercise, but Carol keeps ~~to push~~ *pushing* them. Carol intends ~~study~~ *to* study physical therapy in college. She needs ~~taking~~ *to take* a lot of science courses. She expects to ~~went~~ *go* to college next fall. She hopes ~~get~~ *to* get a degree in physical therapy in five years. She prefers ~~to~~ working with teenagers, but she will work with adults too.

UNIT 23

A
1. is taking
2. make
3. made
4. likes

B
1. invented
2. didn't work
3. wanted
4. became
5. started
6. use
7. are sewing

C
1. Where did you go last weekend?
2. How did you get there?
3. What did you see at the museum?
4. How was the museum?
5. Do you go there often?

D
1. Last night I ~~did watch~~ *watched* a movie about fish.
2. I thought the fish were beautiful, and I ~~enjoy~~ *enjoyed* the movie.
3. My brother is watching the movie now, but he ~~don't~~ *doesn't* like it.
4. He ~~is only liking~~ *only likes* action films.

UNIT 24

A
1. is going to build
2. 's going to cost
3. 's going to have
4. are going to be
5. isn't going to begin

B
1. are not going to increase
2. aren't going to play
3. 're going to visit
4. 's going to retire
5. 'm not going to do

C
1. **Q:** When is she going to the dentist? **A:** On Monday at 5:30.
2. **Q:** Where is she meeting Yu Chen? **A:** At Pappa Pizza.
3. **Q:** Is she meeting Yu Chen on Monday? **A:** No, she isn't.

D This city ~~going~~ *is* going to change under our new mayor. ~~People's~~ *People are* going to ride bikes and they're ~~gonna~~ *going to* use public transportation. They're ~~no~~ *not* going to drive big cars. There are probably going to be higher tolls on bridges and more bike paths on the roads.

UNIT 25

A
1. Where will people travel in twenty years?
2. Will people fly to the moon?
3. How will they get around?
4. Will the climate change?
5. Will people look different?

B
1. won't
2. won't
3. will
4. will
5. won't

C
1. Will / be hot
2. Will / have a test
3. Will / be a storm
4. Will / rain
5. Will / work late

D I usually bring my lunch to work, but tomorrow I ~~no will~~ *won't* bring it because it's my birthday. My co-workers will ~~takes~~ *take* me out to a restaurant. We'll ~~to~~ order a few different dishes, and we'll share them. They'll ~~singing~~ *sing* "Happy Birthday," and they'll give me a small gift. I'm sure it will ~~is~~ *be* a lot of fun.

UNIT 26

A
1. go
2. buy
3. might not
4. may
5. Will

B
1. may (might) snow
2. may (might) not get
3. may (might) need
4. may (might) not see
5. may (might) stay

C 1. There may (OR There might) be a restroom in the library.
2. He may (OR might) be the director.
3. The plane might (OR may) be late.
4. They may (OR might) be cousins.
5. It might (OR may) be his coat.

D 1. He might ~~goes~~ *go* on vacation next week.
2. He may ~~works~~ *work* late tomorrow.
3. They might ~~to~~ visit him tomorrow. Are you free?
4. I might not help him. I might ~~to~~ help her instead.
5. She ~~maybe~~ *may* take a yoga class.

UNIT 27

A 1. a few 3. an
2. the 4. any

B 1. many 3. a little
2. much 4. a few

C 1. a 4. the
2. a 5. a
3. the 6. a

D 1. **A:** What are you looking for?
B: I need a ~~little~~ *few* stamps. I wrote ~~any~~ *some* postcards, and I want to mail them.
2. **A:** There isn't ~~some~~ *much* yogurt in the refrigerator. There's only half a container.
B: There ~~isn't much~~ *aren't many* eggs either. We need to go shopping, but we don't have ~~many~~ *much* time.

UNIT 28

A 1. How many 4. How much
2. How much 5. How many
3. How many

B 1. How often do you go to the movies?
2. How many close friends do you have?
3. How much time do you spend online?
4. How many people live in your home?
5. How often do you check email?

C 1. I usually bake a few times a week.
2. They never have enough food in the house.
3. Every weekend we play soccer in the park.
4. He spilled a glass of grape juice.
5. She added a little salt to the soup.

D 1. ~~Never~~ I *never* eat breakfast at home.
2. ~~She once in a while~~ *Once in a while she* bakes.
3. Do you have ~~milk enough~~ *enough milk*?
4. How ~~much~~ *many* tomatoes did they buy?
5. I rarely ~~don't~~ cook.

UNIT 29

A 1. too long
2. too much homework
3. too much milk
4. too many trucks
5. too much time

B 1. too / too little
2. too few
3. too much
4. too many

C 1. There's too little rain.
2. There are too few subways.
3. There's too little sunlight.
4. There are too few traffic lights.
5. There is too little water.

D The climate here is terrible. It gets too ~~much~~ hot in the summer and too cold in the winter. There's too ~~many~~ *much* snow and ice. Winters are ~~to~~ *too* long. There are too ~~little~~ *few* comfortable days with mild temperatures and blue skies. Also, there's too ~~many~~ *much* air pollution from all the traffic on the streets. I want to move.

UNIT 30

A 1. should 4. ought to
2. had better 5. better not
3. shouldn't

B 1. had better not 3. had better not
2. had better 4. had better

C 1. should 3. should
2. shouldn't 4. shouldn't

D 1. Where should we ~~meets~~ *meet* after work?
2. We *'d* better take an umbrella tonight. It's going to rain.
3. Should I ~~to~~ make a reservation now for my flight? I think I ~~outta~~ *ought to* buy it soon.
4. What ~~I should~~ *should I* see during my business trip to Uruguay?
5. Should we ~~leaves~~ *leave* Brazil tonight or tomorrow?
6. You ought *to* bring flowers to your hostess to thank her for dinner.

UNIT 31

A 1. Would you like 4. We'd like
2. Could you pass 5. Can you
3. I'd like

B 1. Of course. 4. Sorry, I need it.
2. Sure. 5. I'd be glad to.
3. Thanks.

C 1. Could you please
   2. I'd like
   3. Could you please
   4. Would you like
   5. I'd like

D 1. A: Could ~~please~~ you *please* move my car at 11:00?
    B: ~~No, I wouldn't.~~ *Sorry.* I'll be at work then.
   2. A: ~~I like~~ *I'd like* to see you this weekend. Would you like to go to the park?
    B: ~~I could.~~ *Yes, I would.*
   3. A: Would you like *to* have some more ice cream?
    B: No, thanks. I'm full.

UNIT 32

A 1. don't have to   4. doesn't have to
   2. have to   5. have to
   3. must not

B 1. mustn't   3. don't have to
   2. has / has to   4. has to

C 1. had to work
   2. have to read / answer
   3. had to give OR have to give
   4. didn't have to bring

D The test starts at 8:10. You must ~~to~~ be in the room at 8:00. You mustn't ~~came~~ *come* late. You have to ~~has~~ *have* two number two pencils and an eraser. You ~~musts~~ *must* ~~brings~~ *bring* proper identification, such as a photo ID or a passport. You must leave your cell phone in the front of the room.

UNIT 33

A 1. much   5. higher
   2. than   6. better
   3. more popular   7. brother's
   4. worse

B 1. A bus ride is more expensive in Sun City than in New City.
   2. A cup of coffee is cheaper in New City than in Sun City.
   3. The average home is less expensive in New City than in Sun City.
   4. The average income is higher in Sun City than in New City.

C We moved to the countryside, and we're much ~~more~~ happier. Our home is ~~more~~ larger, and the air is cleaner and polluted *less* ~~less~~. It less *is*

expensive than the city too. Fruits and vegetables are ~~more cheap~~ *cheaper*. The people are ~~friendlier~~ *friendlier*. Of course our commute is ~~more bad~~ *worse*; it's much ~~more long~~ *longer*, but we listen to Spanish tapes, and our Spanish is ~~more good~~ *better*.

UNIT 34

A 1. quickly   3. well   5. clearly
   2. fluently   4. slowly

B 1. good   3. nervous   5. quickly
   2. carefully   4. badly

C 1. good   3. clearly (briefly)   5. honestly
   2. briefly (clearly)   4. fast

D A: I think my speech went ~~good~~ *well*.
    B: Did they appreciate your jokes?
    A: They laughed ~~polite~~ *politely*, but I'm not sure they laughed ~~sincere~~ *sincerely*.
    B: It's hard to be funny.
    A: I ~~hard worked~~ *worked hard*, and I prepared carefully, but I was ~~nervously~~ *nervous*.

UNIT 35

A 1. big enough   3. too   5. from
   2. as   4. as

B 1. warm enough   4. too short
   2. very late   5. enough time
   3. too busy   6. very good

C I didn't like the prom this year as much ~~than~~ *as* last year. I usually like parties, but the music at the prom was much ~~very~~ *too* loud. Also, my dress was the same as ~~Julia~~ *Julia's*! That was a ~~too~~ *very* big shock. Also, the dinner portions weren't ~~enough large~~ *large enough* and the servers this year were very rude. Then we tried to dance, but there was ~~no~~ *not* enough room and the room was ~~too much~~ *much too* hot. The music was also not *as* good as last year. We had a ~~more~~ better time last year.

A **1.** the funniest
   2. the biggest
   3. the best
   4. The largest / the most dangerous

B **1.** the hottest day
   2. the oldest woman
   3. the busiest shopping day
   4. the most interesting show
   5. the most popular animals

C **1.** one of the most intelligent animals
   2. one of the best zoos
   3. one of the worst seats
   4. one of the longest days
   5. one of the most expensive trips

D **1. A:** What is the ~~most good~~ *best* way to get to the park?

   B: The shortest route is also the *most* ⌃complicated. I'll give you the most direct way.

   2. A: What's the ~~most~~ hardest part of your job here at the zoo?

   B: Well, the ~~nicer~~ *nicest* part is taking care of the animals. The ~~most~~ worst part is telling people not to feed the animals or bother them.

CREDITS

PHOTO CREDITS:

All photos are used under license from Shutterstock.com except for the following:

Page 1 (right) Stephane Reix/For Picture/Corbis; **p. 2** (left) Jeff Kravitz/Getty Images, (right) AP Images/Peter Kramer; **p. 6** (bottom) AF archive/Alamy; **p. 9** (bottom right) Stephane Reix/For Picture/Corbis; **p. 13** iStockphoto.com; **p. 40** (left) Reuters/Corbis, (right) Henri Cartier-Bresson/Magnum Photos; **p. 41** Henri Cartier-Bresson/Magnum Photos; **p. 43** Ron Chapple/Getty Images; **p. 44** Henri Cartier-Bresson/Magnum Photos; **p. 46** Henri Cartier-Bresson/Magnum Photos; **p. 54** www.Gamirasu.com; **p. 55** (bottom) Dreamstime.com; **p. 60** (bottom left) Bigstock.com; **p. 71** (left) Anthony Redpath/Corbis; **p. 72** Photolibrary.com; **p. 81** Anthony Redpath/Corbis; **p. 84** Ocean/Corbis; **p. 113** (right) Jeffrey Mayer/Getty Images; **p. 116** James Marshall/Corbis; **p. 143** Bigstock.com; **p. 165** (right) MGM/Photofest; **p. 166** (left) Henrik Sorensen/Getty Images, (right) Photos.com; **p. 169** Photos.com; **p. 170** Hill Street Studios/Getty Images; **p. 172** Gary Conner/PhotoEdit; **p. 174** (bottom middle) Bigstock.com; **p. 175** MGM/Photofest; **p. 179** AF archive/Alamy

ILLUSTRATION CREDITS:

Steve Attoe: p. 193; **ElectraGraphics, Inc.:** pp. 25, 26, 29, 69, 99 (keys, iPhone, iPad), 105, 182; **Paul McCusker:** p. 99 (lipstick, comb, watch, sunglasses, driver's license, photo); **Suzanne Mogensen:** p. 63; **Dusan Petricic:** pp. 10, 126 ; **Dave Sullivan:** p. 93; **Gary Torrisi:** pp. 18, 64, 65, 76, 102, 131, 185, 192

INDEX

This index is for the full and split editions. All entries are in the full book. Entries for Volume A of the split edition are in black. Entries for Volume B are in red.